Students with Mild Disabilities in the Secondary School

Students with Mild Disabilities in the Secondary School

Paul Retish
University of Iowa

William Hitchings
*United Township
High School District*

Michael Horvath
Bradley University

Bonnie Schmalle
*North Fayette
Community Schools*

Longman
New York & London

Students with Mild Disabilities in the Secondary School

Longman, 95 Church Street, White Plains, N.Y. 10601

Associated companies:
Longman Group Ltd., London
Longman Cheshire Pty., Melbourne
Longman Paul Pty., Auckland
Copp Clark Pitman, Toronto

Senior editor: Naomi Silverman
Development editor: Elsa Van Bergen
Production editor: Camilla T. K. Palmer
Cover design: Lee Goldstein
Text art: K & S Graphics

Library of Congress Cataloging in Publication Data

Students with Mild Disabilities in the Secondary School / Paul Retish . . .
   [et al.].
      p.   cm.
   Includes bibliographical references.
   ISBN 0-8013-0166-1
   1. Handicapped children—Education (Secondary)—United States.
   2. Mainstreaming in education—United States. I. Retish, Paul.
LC4031.M55 1990
371.9'0473—dc20   90–31600
                                                                  CIP

ABCDEFGHIJ–HA–99 98 97 96 95 94 93 92 91 90

The authors would like to thank their spouses, Esther, Julie, Stephanie, and Verdell, and their families. Their support has been our strength.

Contents

Students with Mild Disabilities in the Secondary School

Introduction

In 1978 Leone and Retish published an article entitled "A handicapped kid in my class?" That article and the questions it raised are at the core of this book, which focuses on ways that secondary schools prepare students with mild handicaps for later life. We do try to set the price of mainstreaming at the lowest level possible but aim above all to keep the quality of the education delivered to students with special needs at the highest level.

The questions that arose as we planned this text concerned the needs of the students and teachers. What do these two groups need to make their lives in the high school as productive as possible? After identifying these needs, we decided what we could do to offer solutions or directions to both of these groups.

Secondary schools have been studied and criticized and have received suggestions for major changes (Boyer, 1983). Lack of appropriate teaching and finances, teachers who are content oriented rather than student centered, lack of family support, poorly maintained schools, and lack of practical applications of the subject matter are just some of the concerns raised by Boyer. We agree with these concerns, but education must continue despite of and because of obvious restrictions and weaknesses.

The purpose of this text is to give readers skills to recognize the strengths and to compensate for the limitations of the ongoing system, a starting point for educating secondary-age students who have special learning needs. Furthermore, this text will be of practical use to teachers who have mainstreamed students in their classes, to parents who want to know what might occur with their children in schools, and especially to special education teachers who are teaching in secondary schools but are not always sure what directions to take.

We intend to give readers some ancillary assistance in developing quality curricula and delivering instruction in academic, career, and life skills. We know that teachers want to assist their students in every manner possible so that they will be successful once they leave school. This text will identify strategies and also cite resources (people and agencies) that can make the job much easier.

Although we cannot plan all interventions for all adolescents for all times, we can give you, professionals or interested individuals, a starting point from which to go

1

on to use the given resources, to expand your knowledge, and to tailor it to your learners' needs and your own. Specifically interested in the needs of adolescents who are special needs learners, we will approach all that we suggest from the perspective of the functional use of the material for the learner. Students, by the time that they reach this age (adolescence) and this level of school (junior and senior high school), need to be prepared to be as independent as possible. Therefore, the material presented and the suggestions given will be based on the precepts of their functional use and the generalizability of a classroom setting.

The format of this text moves from theory to practical applications in teaching. In Chapter 1 we discuss types of delivery systems, characteristics of students in special education, and curricula to prepare students for a fully functional role in the community. Chapter 2 provides an overview of developmental stages and career and social skills and how these dimensions constitute one of five keys to success in preparing competent adults. Chapter 3 outlines methods of assessing student needs in terms of overall diagnosis and present stage of progress.

Chapters 4, 5, and 6 present in detail models and methods to design and deliver instruction. Chapter 4 focuses on the diagnostic-prescriptive teaching model, which works with curriculum-based assessment to offer a systematic individualized approach to answering special needs. Chapter 5 shares many strategies for implementation, taking you through the whole process: identifying problems, increasing motivation, using instructional modifications, and building specific skills. Chapter 6 brings us to teachers currently serving students with special needs for a number of case studies of implementation in action and looks at what special education teachers do day to day.

Chapter 7 examines the various issues raised about the place of academics in special education: how this component should be delivered and what modifications are possible. Chapter 8 gives a complete look at the important area of vocational education, from analysis of the basic stages of vocational development to assessment, instruction design and implementation, ideas on using the classroom as a worksite, and how to coordinate work experience.

Chapter 9 is a valuable start at compiling, in an ongoing way, resources that are ready and able to assist you as you work with learners who have special needs; these resources are categorized and described and include books, organizations, software, and much more.

With Chapter 10 we attempt to bring together the basic themes of the book, concluding with a framework for addressing the total needs of students with mild handicaps as they enter the world after school.

We are aware of the unique status and the relationship of adolescents within the system of which they are a part. The transitional aspects of adolescence will always be a consideration as we present suggestions for curriculum and implementation. We concern ourselves, furthermore, with the history of failure that many students with special needs have experienced. This impacts on how the materials are framed, to what degree the students have input and can understand and use the information, and the evaluation schemes presented.

We also cannot ignore the research cited in the Mithaug and associates (1985), Hasazi and associates (1985), and Hitchings and Retish (1985) studies, which question the validity of the curriculum, goals, and results of contemporary classrooms in terms of the lack of success of graduates of special education classes. Regardless of the level of need of the individual, the chances for full-time employment with full benefits seems to be dependent upon contacts with relatives or friends who will hire graduates. This fact brings into question not only curriculum and goals but methods and placement of learners with special needs in classrooms in contemporary schools. The authors of this text use the results of recent research to suggest some alternative methods for approaching learners with special needs.

The four authors of this text work in very different settings and bring this diversity to the text, thereby strengthening the content and scope of the suggestions. We range from a secondary work-study teacher in a rural area to a supervisor of secondary programs in an urban setting to a department chair in a private university to a professor in a large research-oriented university. This diversity should help to make what we write more applicable to the diverse audience we are attempting to reach.

The common thread that the authors have, besides knowing each other, is that we all have taught or are teaching learners with special needs in secondary schools. Our experiences are diverse in terms of the size of the schools, the location of the schools, and the cooperativeness of the faculties with whom we worked. Again, this broad base of experience should be an asset in what we write. What we all know is that we do agree that there is no single best way to teach, counsel, and assist these learners in being successful. Each of us has our favorite ways of teaching, introducing lessons, and delivering what we think are the keys we can give to others. We hope that this diversity of opinion comes through in this text so that the reader realizes that there are many ways to reach the same end. The matter of which one to choose or how to put so many different ideas together is a task for the reader to accomplish. Our job is to give you enough information to start to make these choices.

It would be helpful to you to remember that some of the resources we suggest will become antiquated or go out of business. Get into the habit of maintaining a list of up-to-date resources, keeping informed on what new products companies are producing, what new ideas are being suggested, and what innovations are currently in the field. This text is meant to start you off and to give you resources to continue your study and planning.

REFERENCES

Boyer, E. (1983). *High School*. New York: Harper & Row.

Hasazi, S., Gordon, L., & Roe, C. (1985). Factors associated with the employment status of handicapped youth exiting from high school from 1979 to 1983. *Exceptional Children, 51*(6), 455–469.

Hitchings, W., & Retish, P. (1985). Successful transition requires planned community entry. *Techniques: A Journal for Remedial Education and Counselling, 1*(6), 455–462.

Leone, P., & Retish, P. (1978). A handicapped kid in my class? *The Social Studies, 69*(1), 1–20.

Mithaug, D., Horiuchi, C., & Fanning, P. (1985). A report on the Colorado statewide follow-up survey of special education students. *Exceptional Children, 51*, 397–404.

CHAPTER 1

Special Education in Secondary Schools: Ways It Fulfills Its Charge

Failure to develop successful students and competent adults, disagreement over ways to promote academic achievement, questions about where special education students should be taught, have all led to heated debate across the United States. The issues are not only educational but political, economic, legal, and ethical. This book builds toward and concludes with reflection on the present state of transition—how today's educators are trying to reverse past patterns of answering special needs inadequately. It begins, in this chapter, with the fact that to understand what the goals of special education are and how they may be reached, one should first have an understanding of the different types of organizations within schools.

This chapter explores the nature of special needs, various ways special education is offered, and guidelines that can be used when considering placement. Underlying the whole of special education today is the mandate to prepare the individual for successful transition into the community, the school, and the adult world. How this impacts on special education organization is considered here; subsequent chapters are the building blocks toward planning and implementing a curriculum that will foster success in later life.

SPECIAL NEEDS LEARNERS

If asked why we have schools, teachers-in-training usually answer that schools have a number of purposes, including literacy, assimilation, acculturation, and preparation for life. We agree with most of these answers and try to push on to why we have invited special needs students into schools, especially secondary schools. We usually get answers similar to those cited from special education student teachers, but when one asks regular classroom teachers, the answers often differ. The responses may be couched in terms of both legal and ethical responsibility, babysitting, or "the law makes us." Therefore, judgment on the place of special education in secondary schools depends on whom you ask and what the reasons are for asking.

Likewise, schools today do not fit into a particular profile. It is difficult to generalize about "the" schools. Rather, one tends to meet at some satisfactory middle ground and indicate as often as possible the spectrum that can be found. Schools do not all look the same, they are not governed the same, there are wide differences in the variety of services provided, and the students are different depending on geographical, economic, and changing population patterns. Secondary schools range from tranquil places where learning may or may not be going on to armed camps where learning may or may not be going on. For many teachers, the school is an exciting, enriching atmosphere; for others, schools are despicable places, and they work there because they need the money. For the purpose of this book, we will try to speak to those schools and teachers falling into the middle range of those groups.

This aim is complicated by the fact that the spectrum includes *good* secondary schools that do not want to meet the needs of secondary-aged students with special needs. Invariably, students suffer the consequences of inadequate facilities, teachers, and support systems. Some schools try and attempts are being made by regular classroom teachers to provide quality education for students with special needs. Yet regardless of the admirable intention, the results, as measured against criteria such as employment, self-care, and independent living, indicate that students with special needs are not successful after leaving school, and therefore the schools have been less than successful (Hasazi, 1986; Hitchings & Retish, 1985; Mithaug et al., 1985). These findings and what can be done to improve the picture are threads woven together throughout this book.

By definition, students with mild handicaps or special needs are entitled and need to receive special things from schools. For them to learn efficiently, these students should be addressed in a special manner, through a specially knowledgeable teacher or special classroom or facility and through curricula and individualized plans and special strategies. Special needs students include those with learning problems, sight and hearing problems, emotional and physical problems. (When a student has a disability not significantly represented in a school's population, this causes additional problems, which are discussed on page 42.) It should always be the degree of the problem and how it affects students' abilities to learn that is the determining factor in the type of educational placement decided upon, rather than politics, prejudice, or convenience. As we look at the situation today, changes are in order, not only for the schools but for the community and support agencies. But first, let us look at where we are now.

TYPES OF LEARNING PROGRAMS

Special education in secondary schools takes many forms. We start by examining the most restrictive of the in-school programs. Traditionally, the *self-contained class* that meets the needs of special education students of various learning levels has been most prominent. In this model, students spend all day in the same classroom regardless of the level of need. The classroom teacher is responsible for delivering all of the needed information to students in the realms of academics or socialization. Although the law discourages this environment, it still prevails in many districts as the easiest way to deliver schooling to those students identified as special needs pupils.

A slightly different concept that is prevalent in secondary schools is similar to a segregated class but includes some mainstreaming. Unfortunately, the integration with students not requiring special education is limited and usually occurs in lunch, music, industrial arts, and home economics. Within many secondary schools, this organizational method is considered mainstreaming. These *special classes with integration* (SCI) are not meeting the intent of the law (the Education for All Handicapped Children Act of 1975, PL 94-142) passed to assist students in becoming full members of the school community. The intent of the law is that a student be educated in the least restrictive educational environment that provides an appropriate instructional program. It aims to minimize the cases in which a student would need to be out of the regular classroom for a special class. Due to budget and attitudinal problems of families, teachers, and students themselves, great numbers of students in secondary schools are in isolated classrooms despite the law (Salvia & Ysseldyke, 1981).

From these two organizational approaches we proceed to less segregated classes. The most common approach today is that of a *resource room*. In this case, the students spend from one to three or four periods a day in a classroom designed to help them cope with being mainstreamed into classes or because they have not been pulled into a special education classroom. These classes, with a low teacher-to-pupil ratio, are designed to give teachers and students opportunities to work on classroom skills and other skills that students will need for work in and out of school. Usually, students in this type of classroom are mildly disabled and show potential for much independent work. Many times, students in this room represent quite a range of disabilities, and teachers must be certified to address a variety of needs.

Work-study programs are more a description of class content rather than a type of organization. Students who may be in self-contained, integrated, or resource rooms can be involved in a work-study program that allows them to go to school part of the day and work for the rest of the day. They may receive not only pay for this experience but also high school credits counting toward graduation. Work-study programs involve many forms of scheduling, and much of the in-school time is related to jobs and to increasing necessary skills. In some programs, work-study students come into other special education classrooms and describe what they have learned and teach these other students job skills. Sometimes teachers not only must teach in the school but also must find jobs, place students, and supervise students on the job. More often, the responsibility of job finding and supervision is handled by a coordinator or supervisor.

The *home-bound program*, which uses itinerant teachers, is the only organizational model that can be used to teach certain students. These pupils are taught by teachers who visit their homes in person or by television, telephone, or radio. These models are not used very frequently: In accordance with the provisions of the law, local schools must show due cause why students are not in school, and parents or guardians, in most cases, must agree to this process. In high school, students themselves, when they are capable of understanding, must agree to all placements.

Other placements for secondary special needs students involve *sites outside regular high schools*: institutions, sheltered workshops, and activity centers. All of these sites are specifically designed for students who cannot learn in a regular school setting, for whom it is deemed profitable to be taught in a specialized setting. It is up to schools to make the case why students do not belong in regular schools, and students and parents or guardians must agree to this alternative placement. A very small percentage of those students who are labeled as having a learning disability need this type of placement, and the system must be very careful that outside placement is not used to dump students as a convenience to schools and to avoid addressing the educational needs of the student.

A final accommodation strategy for secondary-level students is *institutionalization* in a residential facility. The least used and most restrictive of any system, this strategy can be used in those extreme cases in which students cannot benefit from placement in regular schools or special classrooms. Such students may be severely disturbed, severely retarded, or incarcerated due to court order, which then changes the legal ramifications. Again, the onus is on the schools to justify this radical departure from education in regular classrooms. While in institutions, students must have education programs that are appropriate for their needs and that represent the best that can be done to assist individuals in being independent. For a comprehensive discussion of the rights and obligations of students, parents, and schools, see the publication by the Council for Exceptional Children, no. 94-142. This publication explains the provisions of the new acts related to the special needs students in the schools.

ISSUES IN PLACEMENT DECISION MAKING

Students with special needs at the age of 12 to 13, the approximate time when most enter junior high schools, can be placed in a number of situations that are deemed appropriate to continue their education. It should always be remembered that what is appropriate must be determined through agreement between parents, students (if able), and responsible educators. If the placement decided upon is other than a regular class placement or in a regular school, it is mandated by PL 94-142 that the school justify this unique placement. This intervention, its plans, and its goals are covered by the Individualized Educational Plan (IEP) and must be agreed upon by both the parent and, when possible, the student.

Therefore, the most common placement is in the regular junior high school or high school, with some time devoted to special education. This is usually accomplished through the use of a resource room—a location within the school that is staffed by a trained special education teacher and whose goal it is to assist the student in being successful in the regular classroom and, also, to teach generalizable skills so that students can use them outside the school. This placement is commonly used with the most mildly handicapped students and those who have little to no behavioral problems. According to Hammill and Bartel (1978), most resource rooms are a tutorial for the students' regular classroom; students do not get any training for generalized knowledge that is useful outside school. It has been said that many teachers of resource rooms feel as if they are going through school as they once did when they were at that level. This feeling occurs because the teacher of a resource room is constantly helping a student to do homework assignments in all of the classes. The teacher and student are basically going through the classes and trying to make it day by day.

The second most popular placement in schools is in special education classrooms. These classrooms can take many forms and are dependent on the level of abilities in the classroom. The key factor in use of these classrooms is the amount of integration the students are given with the rest of the school. The more able the students, the more time spent outside the classroom and with mainstreamed students. For some students, mainstreaming limited to the lunch room, physical education, and some of the trade courses and home economics is sufficient, but for those who can do or need more, a higher level of mainstreaming is needed and sometimes is hard to come by. A salient variable is the political climate of the schools that would or would not allow these students to be integrated into regular classrooms. Mainstreaming at the secondary level is complicated, only partly because of the large numbers of students and teachers who are affected by such a move. Therefore, all placement can be judged by the amount of integration the student has (from total special education [SC] to some levels of integration [SCI]).

The difficulty of mainstreaming can be affixed to some important points about secondary schools and teachers who are the faculty. For one thing, as the Holmes Report (1986) pointed out, secondary teachers are subject oriented and not as student oriented as elementary teachers. Although this is not a criticism, it does directly affect the special needs students in classes when they are expected to keep up with the material with the least amount of assistance that can be afforded by teachers who have many students and who are subject oriented.

Mainstreaming at the secondary level has become a political tool, and serious questions must be raised about the merit of the movement and whose needs this movement is satisfying (Retish, 1982). In a system that judges the teachers only by how fast the students move in grades, special education students are liable to be returned to schooling as it was before the 1960s. Teachers who are concerned by how the students perform on standardized tests cannot wish to have low-performing students. Competency, so defined, will exclude low-performing students from those teachers who want to be judged as highly competent. We are still wrestling with competencies for students who have learning problems and for the teachers who teach them (see Florida Department of Public Instruction, 1987; Texas Department of Public Instruction, 1987). Unless judgment is based on other criteria besides grades, college attendance, and ACT or SAT scores, students with special needs will have difficulties in schools.

Another important aspect of the instructional environment is the impact of special education funds on the schools. For some, it is the only reason that services are provided for special needs students: The interest from these funds is used for other aspects of education. Purchases of equipment, teacher time, secretarial time, and even lights for the baseball diamond are derivatives of some special education funding. Other funding sources for education programming and personnel are available through agencies that cooperate in providing services for students with special needs. Vocational rehabilitation, social services, and private funds are available for some educational services for these students. All of these assets affect the judgment of school districts in the provision of services for special needs students.

A further variable is the attitude of all educators regarding their role with those students who have a special need. If expectations are such that teachers are asked to teach students who have learning difficulty without support, training, and assistance, all participants in the effort will suffer and especially the students. Mainstreaming—regardless of the name it goes by, whether through the use of a resource room, integration from a special class, or tutorial—will be effective only if the necessary training and support are available (Skrtic, 1978). Others have suggested that the price paid by students, teachers, and the school is so great that more use of self-contained classes should be reexamined for use at the secondary school level (Retish, 1982).

Organizational structures (such as businesses) use budget considerations and chain of command as rationales for programming and delivery of services. In budget development, attention needs to be paid to distribution of funds and availability of funds for materials, field trips, and support for work experience. As local schools receive money specifically for the education of learners with special needs, careful attention to the distribution of these funds and their appropriate use must be taken.

Another consideration in the secondary school is the organization of special education. That is, to whom does each of the staff members report, and what real decision-making ability does the teacher or special education administrator have in that school? Too many decision makers causes a lack of decision making with the result of splitting who will be responsible for the organization of special education.

Various organizational differences occur between elementary and secondary schools and in the delivery of special education services. In many secondary schools, special education has followed the model of departmentalizing the educational services for students. That is, whether the student is in a class that is self-contained or self-contained with integration or is in a resource room, the educational material is presented by teachers who teach English, social studies, and so on, rather than special education teachers who teach all subject areas to their students. Little research is available to justify one approach over another, except that in mainstreaming programs there is a high incidence of incompletes, failures, or reduced information for those students who have learning problems (Rose, 1987).

Many of these organizational changes occur because of the monetary policies of states, schools, and local communities. Monetary-driven decisions in an educational system are not necessarily conducive to the development of quality educational programs. Yet within the educational spectrum of delivery systems, secondary programs for students with learning problems must be provided. The basic principle must be one of evaluation and change in the instructional program as needed.

All of these political, economic, and educational decisions affect the possibility of a quality educational program for students with special learning needs. It is arguable whether it is better to begin an educational program without these necessary commitments or whether it is worth it to start and then cope and work for change in a positive direction. If we have learned anything from the history of education, it is that although development and strategies must occur within a system, education is slow to change. Therefore we suggest you do start—and with the very best strategies you can and move upwards (Blatt, 1970, 1981).

Specific Placement Considerations

To crystallize the thinking about where a student should be placed in school and what the ramifications of each decision are, the following two cases are presented with some questions for discussion.

CASE STUDY 1

Mary is 14 years old and has just entered school. The school is from 8th to 12th grade and has 1,600 pupils in it. Classes are heavily academic, and at least 60 percent of the students indicate that they want to continue with their education. Mary has not been successful in school; her reading level is three years behind her grade level, and her social skills are inadequate. There is no evidence of any writing samples in her folder, and she has never been seen by the school psychologist. Her guidance counselor finds her introverted and cannot seem to pull any feelings from her as to what she wants from high school or what she is thinking about doing after leaving high school. Her parents, when called, express concern, but both are working to survive and have not had time to contact the schools about Mary. The counselor contacted her 6th-grade teacher and found that generally, with a great deal of individual help, Mary barely managed to get through the system. After two weeks in 8th grade, Mary is behind in all of her classes and seems lost to the teachers and to other students. There is also no evidence that she has any friends, nor has anyone seen her at a dance or in any extracurricular activities.

Questions: Should she be referred for counseling with a school psychologist or at a family clinic or just left alone to see what develops?

If identified as having a learning problem, is it too late to place, or is placement still a possibility?

What types of classes would you hope would be available to her?

CASE STUDY 2

John is in a special education class for mildly disabled individuals. He has been in this type of class since he was 7 years old. He reads at the 3rd-grade level and is 14 years old. He has many friends and is on the Junior Varsity football team. John is quite verbal and loves to attend as many high school dances and extracurricular activities as possible. He has a girlfriend from 7th grade, and they are seen frequently in the hallways together (sometimes very together). John has gone to his special education teacher and his counselor and has indicated that he wants to get out of special education and go into 7th grade. He feels ashamed of being in special education and does not think he is learning what he will need to get a good job. He also indicates that the people he wants to be friends with make fun of him, and he thinks transferring classes might help this situation. John's parents tend to agree with him and are indicating that they would support placement back into the mainstream and would not sign an IEP keeping him in special education classes.

Questions: What are the school's options for John?

Should he return to regular class without any special education?

Do the parents have the right to pull him out of special education class? Can he take himself out of class?

These case studies focus on the problems in high school faced by teachers, administrators, students, and parents. There are no perfect answers for dealing with the problems presented by these students, but rather the cases present an opportunity to see how creative individuals and systems can be when they are faced with the problems of the individuals represented.

Low-Incidence Disabilities

It is easy to continue to discuss those special needs individuals who belong to groups that have a large representation in school populations. Yet we cannot forget those individuals who are part of low-incidence groups such as those who are hearing impaired or vision impaired or have specific physical problems that interfere with schools delivering their message in a traditional manner.

A case in point is that of five children in North Dakota a number of years ago who comprised the total population of hearing-impaired children in the state. After much consideration, a teacher was hired and classes were set up close to where most of the students lived. This meant that two of the students came for five days and then traveled home for the weekends. When the school year began, three of the students had moved to another state, and the remaining two, who were to travel and reside in the community, refused to do this. The state had hired a teacher, but there were no students to be served. Because of her location, she could not move in an itinerant fashion and ended up being a consultant to the local schools for those teachers who had special needs youngsters in their classes.

There are no easy answers to these problems, either, except to state that the goal of making special needs students as independent as possible cannot be compromised. It is the school's responsibility to provide services that will enhance the possibilities that they will be independent; it is not true that since there are so few individuals, the schools cannot be expected to provide assistance.

The strategies and procedures that we propose in this book are applicable to all students with a special need. It is the schools' and teachers' responsibilities to adapt ideas and strategies for these students who happen to have low-incidence special needs. To transfer the onus to students or families is not in the spirit of what is required of schools and a society that believes in equal access to education.

THE NEED FOR A COMPREHENSIVE CURRICULUM

One can safely state that regardless of the level of disability of the student, the primary role of educational programs is to prepare students to be as self-sufficient and independent as possible. Therefore, curricula in *all* of the facilities need to be judged by how much independence they teach and how many of their graduates are now living at the highest level of independence they can achieve.

Our perspective is the functional use of material taught. Later chapters explore in detail the ways of enhancing preparation for life after high school. Here we offer an overview of instructional and curricular considerations that need to be addressed regardless of the organizing mode of special education.

The literature is replete with the conclusion that one thing that all of the existing systems have in common is their lack of success in preparing students to be competent adults (Hasazi, 1985; Leone & Retish, 1977; Meers, 1987; Mithaug, 1985). For too many special needs learners, schools teach dependence. Contributing to this problem is the attitude of most employers and the general public that special needs people should be "somewhere else," not in the public domain. Retish and associates (1987) reported that parents of special needs students expect little and would rather have their children in sheltered situations than at competitive sites.

Concern has increased during the past decade, however, due to the increasing numbers of students leaving or graduating from secondary special education programs and to a shift in the economy from industry to service. Recent surveys (Rusch et al., 1989) have shown that about two-thirds of the adults with handicapping conditions are not working. Of the one-third who do work, about three-quarters or so are employed part time. From Sitlington's (1986) review of the literature, the author concluded that employment problems among the mildly handicapped persist for three reasons: (1) lack of interpersonal skills, (2) lack of job-related academic skills, and (3) lack of specific vocational skills. Chapters 2, 3, and 6, in particular, study the skills needed in the workplace and the instructional means of developing them.

Delivery Systems

Although generalized data are not supportive of what systems are usually doing, there are various programs and projects that seem to have clearly assisted the special needs people in being successful (Schmalle, 1988; Stodden, 1989). Brolin's (1978) basic competencies, Clark's (1979) early career education, and Retish's (1979) life-skills curriculum are all strategies that will move us from traditional programming to inventive programs based on the needs of the students rather than the schools' and teachers' needs.

Materials already developed by Brolin (1973), Project Discovery (1978), and Singer (1978), to name only a few, are available to educators as frameworks for a functional curriculum—instruction to prepare special needs learners for life after school. These materials are designed to give students a realistic look at an occupation and to determine what further training is needed. Although some are expensive, exposure to these ideas can give teachers a framework of what would be appropriate for each of their situations. Therefore, the hope that this strategy of independence can be achieved is based not just on faith and good hope but also on established programs that are working.

Basic questions of education delivery are raised by recent follow-up studies. What skills are needed by both teachers and students to assist in being successful once out of school? Is the system flexible enough to allow for these new skills to be taught in the schools? Any program must first set up goals that indicate to all who enroll, teach, and administer it why the program exists. The curriculum must reflect the need to foster independence in whatever programming is *delivered*—and in how the program is *evaluated*. Ongoing research by Retish and Brown (1988) and the studies by Hasazi and associates (1985) and Mithaug and associates (1985) indicate a wide gap between what is hoped will occur with the students once they leave school and what is in fact occurring. Living at home, part-time jobs, and common dependence on adults or society seem to be the most frequent long-term prospects for students with special needs.

Real World Needs

It becomes obvious that the standard practices of education need to be revised for students with learning problems. When working with such students, each educator must have a working and teaching knowledge of the attributes and skills necessary for the student to be successful once out of school. Consider these case studies.

CASE STUDY 3

Bill is 20 years old and a graduate of the special education program in the local schools. He had a successful work-study program and did well in all of his special education classes. He is now in the job market and hopes to get a position with a local fast-food restaurant. He has worked in the school kitchen and two other restaurants. He would like to work full time, make as much money as possible, and start today. He does not have a car, although he does have a license. His rural community has no bus system, so he would have to carpool. In the area he is looking at, the farm economy has dropped off severely, and there is high unemployment. There is a tourist and recreation area nearby, so there are many fast-food restaurants.

CASE STUDY 4

Mary is a 19-year-old whose schooling was spent between regular classes and a resource room. She has graduated and is looking for a job. Her transcript indicates that she has passed a regular high school program, but in reality she has trouble reading anything over a 5th-grade level and has some difficulty with her math skills. She is personable and has good verbal skills. Her past work history has been nothing more formal than babysitting.

She would like to work in a small store, preferably a clothing store, but she would be satisfied in any small store. Her area of residence has a good bus system and economically is a developing sector.

Both of these cases show what students who have learning problems face once they leave school. Their basic goals are independence, security, enjoyment, and a future: In these ways, they are no different from most other students leaving school. Differences emerge, however, in their skills, lack of skills, resources, and preparation. By analyzing cases like these two, by looking at the full extent of a person's life, a comprehensive curriculum for secondary special education classes can be developed. Leisure activities, interpersonal needs, sexual needs, work needs, are just some of the needs to be covered in a curriculum for students who have learning problems (maybe for all students).

High school programs are considered to be comprehensive when they provide educational opportunities that will prepare students for their transition to the community. The programs of schools reflect what society values. The goals adopted by the North Fayette Community School District, which is a school of approximately 1,500 students in a rural community of 4,000 people, exemplify typical community values; they also reflect goals stated by special educators as desirable for students in special programs. (See Figure 1.1; a more extensive Mental Disabilities Curriculum Framework is reproduced in the concluding chapter to this book.)

By having knowledge of the follow-up research previously cited (Hasazi et al., 1985; Mithaug et al. 1985), available curriculum materials (Brolin, 1973, social skills,

Figure 1.1. Policy Title: NORTH FAYETTE COMMUNITY SCHOOL DISTRICT GOALS
Code # _____100.2_____

The following goals were first determined as a result of the 1975–76 Needs Assessment Project, by the Needs Assessment Steering Committee and the Board of Education. These goals were reevaluated, and subsequently revised, by the local steering committee for the North Central Association evaluation. On December 17, 1984, these goals were presented to the NFCS Board of Education for their approval.

Students will be expected to reach these goals to the best of their ability in order to gain a general education.

These goals are ranked in order of priority.

----

1. Develop skills in reading, writing, speaking, computation, and listening.
2. Develop pride in work and the feeling of self-worth.
3. Learn to respect and get along with people with whom we work and live.
4. Develop a desire for learning now and in the future.
5. Learn how to be a good manager of time, money, property, and resources.
6. Understand and practice the skills of family living.
7. Learn how to gather, analyze, and use information.
8. Develop good character, courtesy, and respect for one's own rights and the rights of others.
9. Learn how to be a good citizen, by understanding and practicing representative democracy and its ideals.
10. Learn about and try to understand the changes that take place in the world.
11. Learn to understand and respect people whom we perceive as different from ourselves.
12. Gather information and develop skills needed to make job selections and enter a specific field of work.
13. Appreciate beauty and culture in the world.
14. Understand and practice the ideas of health and safety.

Adopted:

December 17, 1984

Source: Courtesy of the North Fayette Community School District.

sex education and so on), and competency expectations of the schools and the states, a comprehensive curriculum can be evaluated and changed. It is inappropriate to continue to use what has been done if there has not been an attempt to evaluate past procedures or there has not been an attempt to keep up to date on new materials and methods.

Then, as teachers work with these students, a team approach that meets two levels of needs should be organized: the information needed by all students and the tailoring of information to the specific needs of the students involved. All of this should be delivered taking into account the strengths and weakness of the students in the class. Regardless of where the student is placed (regular or special class) an individualized, tailored program is necessary.

Support services (social workers, vocational rehabilitation, tutors, mentors) are identified, contacted, and integrated into the curriculum. Experiential aspects (bank trips, industry visits, looks at insurance agencies) are identified, developed, and organized for the students and integrated into the curriculum. Support for regular classroom teachers is identified, assigned, and guaranteed so that the teacher feels comfortable having these students in class. Appropriate communication with the student and guardians is done so that all are informed and agreement is reached as to process and goals.

Once the policies have been put together, the actual implementation can begin. It is important, whenever possible, to have these procedures in place before the beginning of the program. The procedures and the agreements will enable a more smoothly running organization that makes problems that will inevitably arise easier to handle.

Implementation

Implementing a functional curriculum on an individual or partial class framework often proves difficult for any one teacher at the secondary level. This book provides a range of techniques. In any setting, the use of aides, grouping, volunteers, tutorials, support from special education teachers, and any other resource is recommended. Use of the community adds to the curriculum, and especially with limited resources and personnel there is a need to identify people qualified to assist in developing and implementing a functional curriculum. One obvious source is retired people who would like to volunteer their time to the schools for the following:

- Teacher-aide positions
- Curriculum development
- Specific teaching of a skill they possess
- Development of resources for teachers and students
- Grandparent programs to act as surrogate family

These resources must be included more and more in the schools. Groups rich with experience, time, and desire would be a welcome addition to any program and especially special education classes. Furthermore, the backgrounds of these people, which are practical in many instances, can give to the teacher and school the resources not normally available. In addition, these delivery systems alleviate the high pupil-to-staff ratio in the secondary schools.

Without these support systems, it is questionable what benefit the students with learning problems will receive and what attitudes will develop among the teaching staff. Parent input, consisting of advocacy and watchdog status, is sometimes needed to insure ongoing quality programming. These parent groups must also be informed of their obligations as well as rights—that is, the necessity of working with the schools rather than harassment of the schools.

Functional curriculum is developed as a result both of the assessments done of the ongoing curriculum in the school and of what is occurring in the community (Brown, 1987; Hitchings & Retish, 1985; Schmalle & Retish, 1989). Skills that assist the student once out of school must be packaged, in the school, so that they can be readily translated to the particular community (Schmalle & Retish, 1989). Too often curriculum and activities are done for the school within the context of what is allowable in a school. Very often this does not generalize to a community setting. Therefore, it is imperative that the educator assist in this transition process. Furthermore, these skills need to be presented in a manner appropriate for the learning style of learners with special needs. Therefore, every effort should be made to teach concretely and every opportunity taken to check that the student has acquired the skills.

In Mr. Thomas's class the junior high school students were once again studying money. The students were each given Monopoly money and cardboard coins to practice purchasing and giving change. As these pieces were given out, the students could be heard saying, "Not again." After the lesson, Mr. Thomas met with each student to determine what was learned and where to go next. He found that most students were still not aware of the necessary skills and were bored. Was it because the activity failed to teach concretely? Why could this have happened? What would or could you do?

Kirk (1962) followed up a study of reward systems and determined that it was not only important to give rewards; the rewards should also be rewarding to each student. Therefore, there is a need to investigate what rewards a student desires; not all objects are perceived as something individuals want to work for. It then reverts to an initial assertion that materials used must not only be concrete to the learner but must also be followed up with concrete rewards that are deemed rewards by the students.

This same design can be further enhanced by development of a program that allows the students time to work outside of schools to apply what they have learned and also to earn money that is rewarding for their work. The ongoing problems of teaching work behavior and rewarding the work with a salary has been addressed by many writers (Brown & Retish, 1987). The principle of rewarding quality work must be continued during this work program. A further need is to be sure the students are not taught that all work and behavior are acceptable. Poor workmanship or poor work habits should not be tolerated, and the student should be rewarded appropriately for this type of behavior. Students need to be prepared for the real world.

A WIDENING CIRCLE OF NEED

Just as there are changes in the educational structures, the face and the language of the future student is changing. This in turn will present the educational system and the society it represents with the possible need for an entirely new system to educate the students of the near future. Statistics provided by the U.S. Bureau of the Census (1987) show the beginning of a new population entering into our schools. The future learner may have more in common with the learners in special education classes than with those commonly thought of as traditional learners. In 1987 the Los Angeles school system student body had more than 50 percent non-English speakers. What are the ramifications of this for teachers, schools, and curricula?

"Unskilled minorities are a growing fraction of the work force and unless their abilities are upgraded, the nation's overall skill level will not be sufficient for tomorrow's economy" Iowa AFL-CIO (1988, C2) Therefore, the information that this book provides may be not just for the special needs learners but rather for a large group of learners who are just beginning to enter the schools—the high school students of tomorrow.

SUMMARY

The schools of today should be understood for what they are and for what they are not. We should be careful not to assume school or teacher roles, but to assist the special needs learners in entering this system, we who are professionals must learn how to open the doors and then learn how to cause the system to change to reflect new populations that have new needs.

We, as educators, must understand the realities of what special needs individuals face each day of their lives. This becomes the heart of what we teach and is applicable to the goals we set for each of these students.

The selection of the correct placement, the options available for the student with a special need, and an in-depth knowledge of what realistically can be accomplished, both in and out of the school, has been discussed in this chapter.

The wide variety of options for students and the variety in the skills and the commitment and resources of local schools has also been discussed. The discrepancy between the stated goals of the schools for each student and what has occurred when students leave schools make many wonder about the value of the education provided.

It is suggested that stronger use be made of what is known pedagogically and also what is known regarding the society in which individuals with special needs live. These sources of information must be combined and be put to use in the classroom. The body of knowledge about learning and developmental theory is discussed in the following chapter, to prepare us for translating it for use in a variety of classrooms.

STUDY QUESTIONS

1. What do the most recent studies of postschool adjustment of people with special needs say about independent living once they are out of school?
2. In deciding on placement, what options are available at the secondary level? How could and should decisions be made about the most beneficial placement?
3. When planning an IEP, who should be included in the planning and delivery of the proposed educational program?
4. List agencies you could contact to assist people who have special needs.
5. Discuss how you could determine whether or not your curriculum has been successful for each student.

REFERENCES

Blatt, B. (1970). *Exodus from Pandemonium, human abuse, and a reformation of public policy.* Boston: Allyn & Bacon.

————. (1981). *In and out of mental retardation.* Baltimore: University Park Press.

Boyer, E. (1983). *High school.* New York: Harper & Row.

Brolin, D. (1973). Career education needs of secondary educable students. *Exceptional Children, 39,* 619–624.

Brolin, D. (Ed.). (1978). *Life-centered career education: A competency-based approach.* Reston, VA: The Council for Exceptional Children.

Brown, J., & Birkell, D. (1988). *Transition from school to work for persons with disabilities.* New York: Longman.

Brown, J., & Retish, P. (1987). Post secondary opportunities for special needs students. In G. Meers (Ed.). *Handbook of special vocational needs education* (2nd ed.), Rockville, MD: Aspen.

Clark, G. M. (1979). *Career education for the handicapped child in the elementary school.* Denver: Love Publishing.

Florida Department of Public Instruction. (1987). *Florida Department of Public Instruction Rules and Regulations.* Tallahassee, FL.

Hammill, D. D., & Bartel, N. R. (Eds.). (1978). *Teaching children with learning disabilities and behavior disorders.* Boston: Allyn & Bacon.

Hasazi, S. B., Gordon, L. R., & Roe, C. A. (1985). Factors associated with the employment status of handicapped youth exiting school between 1979 to 1983. *Exceptional Children, 51,* 455–469.

Hitchings, W., & Retish, P. M. (1985). Successful transition requires planned community entry. *Techniques: A Journal for Remedial Educational Counseling, 1*(6), 455–462.

Holmes Group, Inc. (1986). *Tomorrow's teachers.* East Lansing: Michigan State University.

Kirk, S. (1962). *The diagnosis and remediation of psycholinguistic disabilities.* Urbana: University of Illinois Press.

Leone, P., & Retish, P. (1977). Affective differences among undergraduate students. *Mental Retardation, 15*(2), 13–15.

Leone, P., & Retish, P. M. (1978). A handicapped kid in my class? *The Social Studies, 69*(1), 1–20.

Meers, G. D. (1987). *Handbook of vocational special needs.* Rockville, MD: Aspen.

Mithaug, D. E., Horiuchi, L., & Fanning, P. (1985). A report on the Colorado statewide follow-up survey of special education students. *Exceptional Children, 51,* 397–404.

Project Discovery. (1978). *Project Discovery.* Red Oak, IA.

Retish, P. M. (1976). Work-study: A life-space curriculum. *Education and Training of the Mentally Retarded, 12*(1), 21–23.

———. (1979). Individual education programs in secondary schools for mainstreamed students. *Education and Training of the Mentally Retarded, 14*(3), 235–236.

———. (1982). Mainstreaming in the secondary schools. *The Journal for Special Educators, 18*(2), 46–48.

Retish, P., & Brown, J. (1988). Proceedings of Conference on Empowerment of Disabled, St. Paul, MN: University of Minnesota.

Retish, P., Hitchings, W., & Hitchings, S. (1987). Parent perspectives of vocational services for moderately retarded individuals. *Journal of Career Development, 13*(4), 28–32.

Rose, M. (1987). Personal communication. West High School, Iowa City, IA.

Rusch, J., Rusch, F., & Phelps, A. (1989). Analysis and synthesis of transition issues in transition from school to work for persons with disabilities. In D. Birkell & J. Brown (Eds.) *Transition from school to work for persons with disabilities.* New York: Longman.

Salvia, J., & Ysseldyke, J. E. (1981). *Assessment in special education* (2nd ed). Boston: Houghton Mifflin.

Schmalle, B. (1988). *Interim report.* Fayette, IA: Fayette School District.

Schmalle, B., & Retish, P. M. (1989). Job-task reporting system. *Teaching Exceptional Children, 21*(2), 15–18.

Singer Education Division. (1978). *Singer vocational evaluation.* Rochester, NY.

Sitlington, P. (1986). Support services related to generalizable skills instruction. *The Journal for Vocational Special Needs, 9*(1), 16–19.

Skrtic, T. (1978). "The influence of in-service on the attitudes and behaviors of regular elementary classroom teachers toward mainstreamed learning disabled students." Ph.D. dissertation, University of Iowa, Iowa City.

Stodden, R. (1989). *Assisting in the transition from school to work.* University Affiliated Facility Publication. Honolulu: University of Hawaii.

Texas Department of Public Instruction. (1987). *Curriculum standards.* Austin.

U.S. Bureau of the Census. (1987). *Census Report.* Washington, DC: U.S. Government Printing Office.

U.S. Department of Education. (1980). *Progress toward a free appropriate public education: A report to Congress on the implementation of Public Law 94–142: The education for all handicapped children act.* Washington, DC.

CHAPTER 2

Foundations for Educational Programming

A major concern of all educators can be expressed by the question, "How do I know that what I am doing now will meet the future needs of my students?" That is the thrust of this book, and the purpose of this chapter is to provide guidance in answering the question by laying the foundation for educational programming at the secondary level. There is no universally applicable answer. Each teacher must develop instruction based on his or her philosophy of education. But there is a body of theory that drives instruction and provides guidance in day-to-day planning.

This chapter surveys what is known about learning domains and developmental stages so that we can apply this in formulating curriculum and classroom strategies for special needs students. The developmental patterns and needs that children bring to school are called *dimensions*. Dimensions, the focus of this chapter, constitute the first key to meeting the future needs of students. The other four keys described here are *aims*, or the purpose of schooling; *curriculum*, or the specifics of what is to be taught in schools; *career education*, or helping students determine what they want to accomplish in life; and *climate*, the glue that holds the whole enterprise of school together. After a look at how we can assess individual needs, in Chapter 3, we provide various approaches to improving outcomes.

HOW TEACHERS MEET STUDENTS' NEEDS

To meet the short-term needs of students, teachers rely on district-prescribed subject-matter curricula. Each teacher, however, enjoys a great deal of leeway in resolving the question of how to meet the future needs of students. Some teachers modify the curriculum to accommodate needs perceived in assessment or in the classroom. Some ignore the question and cover the assigned material. Some pick an arbitrary age, such as 25, and program to anticipate the perceived needs of young adults. Some infuse career education into the curriculum. Some decide to follow a linear model and often become heavily involved in remediating basic skills or tutoring to meet immediate academic needs. Some prepare themselves to teach the "whole child," whereas others feel that every activity must have as its ultimate end the enhancement of basic or content-area skills. Some favor affective, social, and other nonacademic skills. Some look to the future and program for information management or base their teaching on the coming "global" environment. Others teach what they were taught. The most fortunate teachers work in an environment in which a K–12 and beyond comprehensive career-education program is in place. No matter what conditions exist, all teachers ultimately settle into their individual styles, based on their philosophical orientations.

Many aspiring teachers have been taught in their foundation courses or placement-office workshops to write a philosophy-of-teaching statement for the interview process. In actuality, it takes five years or so to develop, internalize, and articulate an operationally workable philosophy that is grounded in the aims of teaching. This philosophy statement orients the teacher and serves as a guide to help the teacher know what to do next. It is the combination of training and experience that provides the teacher with an overriding sense of purpose, the capacity to develop goals to achieve that purpose, and the ability to construct the units of instruction and the daily lesson plans to achieve the goals. In short, seasoned teachers have a vision of what students need and know-how to help their students achieve success in their adult lives.

To meet future needs, the teacher must periodically ask, "What is important for adults and how should a teacher look at the long term?" If educators could completely meet the developmental needs of their students, there would be no need for concern about transition programs from preschool to school, from kindergarten to first grade, from elementary school to middle school, from junior high to high school, and from high school to postschool life. There is strong evidence to support the contention that humans progress through developmental stages, each of which may be qualitatively and quantitatively different from the others. Formal education alone, however, cannot meet the developmental needs of students. No matter how good individual teachers are, schooling does not exist in a vacuum. Many variables are outside the control of school personnel. What educators can and must do is find the best possible match between the curricular demands and the developmental needs of their students.

The most useful curricula meet the developmental needs of students in each of the six areas: cognitive, psychomotor, affective, social, moral, and psychological. Systematic instruction in each is possible. All of these dimensions have been structured into classification systems called *taxonomies*. In combination with developmental stages, the taxonomies form the bases for curriculum development. The rest of this chapter looks at long-term programming from this perspective.

Overwhelming amounts of material have been written about these dimensions. Comprehensive coverage of each dimension would result in several books of this size. Although it is not possible to present exhaustive discussions in this text, important issues for consideration in structuring curriculum for secondary schools need to be reviewed. The reader will be referred to additional resources for further consideration.

THE COGNITIVE DIMEMSION

In the development of cognitive skills, two of the most valuable sources are the work of Piaget (Furth, 1969; Ginsburg & Opper, 1969; Inhelder & Piaget, 1958; Muus, 1968; and Phillips, 1975) and the taxonomy constructed by Bloom and associates (1956).

Piaget's Stages

From the study of his children, Jaqueline, Laurent, and Lucienne, Piaget determined that intellectual (cognitive) growth takes place in four distinctly different but overlapping hierarchical stages as the individual actively interacts with the environment. Development of cognition (also called thinking or rational processing) occurs in the four stages as the two cognitive functions of (1) organization and (2) adaptation work in conjunction with physical maturation (time). Thinking as a process in each of the four stages is qualitatively different to the point that the individual can be said to go through four intellectual systems. These differences can be demonstrated through exercises in number, shape, quantity, and space.

In general, as children grow older, they become less stimulus bound and more analytical in processing perceptual information. Instead of attending to the stimulus that has the most visual or auditory impact, children are able to attend to several meaningful stimuli simultaneously to cope better with their environments. Older children, then, are less distractible and better able to stay on task than younger children. As children mature, changes in organization and adaptation lead to better strategies and development of greater cognitive competencies.

Organization.   In Piagetian terms, *organization* is the tendency to mobilize structures into ways of thinking. *Structure* may be thought of as how the brain is organized or as what goes on inside one's head. It is the capacity to behave or function in a certain way and is revealed in integrated schemata (the plural of schema), that is, organized patterns of behavior or what one actually does. Organization evolves as children develop capacities (structures) that are increasingly integrated with behaviors (schemata). This process results in better coping skills. By adolescence, schema and structure seem to have merged so schemata are the outward or behavioral equivalents of the internal capacities or structures. At this point, the individual is able to operate, that is, to solve problems logically.

An important point to remember is that children behave differently at different times as they grow toward adulthood. This is because their cognitive abilities are different. Developmentalists are fond of saying that it is necessary to "meet them where they are" and take them from there. Sensitive teachers rapidly learn through experience to meet their students' needs by adjusting lessons to match the cognitive levels.

Adaptation.   Piaget explained *adaptation* as the interaction between assimilation and accommodation. *Assimilation* is the ability of the individual to deal with new challenges with existing schemata. *Accommodation* is the ability of the individual to alter existing schemata to meet new challenges. Adaptation occurs because the environment is always presenting new stimuli to which adjustments must be made. When the individual is able to handle adaptation, a state of equilibrium exists. At certain times, the structures become overwhelmed by the effects that equilibrium cannot be maintained. It is at these points that structures become changed by equilibration, that is, compensation for external disturbance. When the organization of structures is radically altered by equilibration, a new stage is entered. Each stage is dependent on previous stages, and each is qualitatively different from the others.

Stages.   Although Piaget established approximate age ranges for each stage, it must be noted that not all children pass through each stage at the same rate and that some individuals may never advance to the higher stages. Defining the stages outlined in Figure 2.1 is difficult because there is a tremendous amount of overlap as children gradually move on to higher stages. Foreshadowing of advanced stages is in evidence. The continual organization and reorganization that occurs through a person's active interaction with the environment is reflected in the journey through the four stages. Through the process of growth, the individual moves through thought processes characterized as intuitive, then concrete, and then logical.

Some experts conceptualize students who are mildy handicapped as being frozen in stages below their chronological ages. The temptation to assume incorrectly that areas of development other than cognition would also be arrested is not always successfully resisted. It is much more accurate to characterize individuals who exhibit mild handicaps as exhibiting differential rates of growth across the various dimensions.

1. *Sensorimotor stage.* The first Piagetian stage is called *Sensorimotor*; it nor-

Figure 2.1. Piaget's Stages of Cognitive Development

  I. Sensorimotor (birth to age 2)
    A. Reflexes (birth to 1 month)
    B. Primary circular reactions (1–4 months)
    C. Secondary circular reactions (4–8 months)
    D. Coordination of secondary schemata (8–12 months)
    E. Tertiary circular reactions (12–18 months)
    F. Internationalization of sensorimotor schemata (18–24 months)
  II. Preoperational (ages 2–7)
    A. Extracting concepts from experience (ages 2–4)
    B. Intuitive thought (ages 4–7)
  III. Concrete Operations (ages 7–11)
  IV. Formal Operations (ages 11–adult)
    A. Early period (ages 11–15)
    B. Late period (ages 15–Adult)

Source: Benjamin S. Bloom et al. *Taxonomy of Educational Objectives Handbook I: Cognitive Domain.* Copyright © 1956 by Longman. Reprinted by permission.

mally occurs from birth to the appearance of language at approximately 2 years of age and is characterized by (1) coordination of sensory and motor activity and (2) achievement of object permanence. The infant begins by exploring the environment and manipulating objects in it. Visual pursuit begins to be noted at about 6 months. Eye-hand coordination develops as the infant profits from experience. Object constancy or object permanence occurs between 1 and 2 years when the infant realizes that an object stays the same no matter what the spatial perspective, shading, distance, or side from which the object is viewed, touched, or tasted. Because the child is able to hold an image of a missing object in mind, he or she can find an object when it is placed out of sight but within easy reach.

In this stage, thoughts and ideas (i.e., cognitive activity) depend on immediate sensory experience and motor experience. Responses are almost complete determined by the situation. No language structure exists with which to label, symbolize, and remember events and ideas. The infant's learning is bound to immediate experiences. Perception, recognition, and means-end coordination are developed as opportunities for sensory and motor experiences are presented. In this stage, there is no such thing as deferred gratification.

The Sensorimotor stage is divided into six substages:

a.   Reflexive (0–1 month). Characteristic behavior includes simple reflex activity, such as kicking.
b.   Primary Circular Reactions (1–4 months). Reflexive behavior becomes elaborated and coordinated; for example, eye follows hand movements.
c.   Secondary Circular Reactions (4–8 months). Repeats chance actions to reproduce an interesting change of effect; for example, kicks crib, doll shakes, so kicks crib again.
d.   Coordination of Secondary Scheme (8–12 months). Acts become clearly intentional; for example, reaches behind cushion for ball.
e.   Tertiary Circular Reactions (12–18 months). Discovers new ways to obtain desired goal, such as pulling pillow nearer to get toy resting on it.
f.   Invention of New Means through Mental Combinations (18–24 months). Invents new ways and means; for example, uses stick to reach desired object.

2. *Preoperational stage.* The second stage is *Preoperational*; it normally occurs from ages 2 to 7, approximately, and is characterized by (1) use of language and symbolic representation and (2) an egocentric view of the world. A transition or shift occurs in this stage from the action-oriented schemata of the Sensorimotor stage to the early forms of social behavior, sociocentric speech, and conceptual thought. Language and other forms of symbolic representation are developed to replace concrete experience. A child in the Preoperational stage can treat objects as symbolic of things other than themselves; for example, a stick can be a candle; a block of wood, a truck. The capacity to store images (including words and grammar structure) increases dramatically. Development of language allows the individual to free-associate and fantasize.

Learning is fast. An average 2 year old has a vocabulary of 200 to 300 words, but the 5-year-old knows about 2,000 words. The child is able to go from a present-centered world to one that encompasses past and future. Reasoning, however, is intuitive, and intelligence remains prelogical. The child imitates and tries out different words. Language usage is spontaneous, and children seem to teach themselves. They retain egocentric perspectives, not realizing that reality may look different to someone else. Facts seem to be irrelevant to the preoperational child, who needs to engage in imaginative play, especially when he or she can act out various roles. Exposure to language and other children is vital for optimum development. In this stage, children are dreamers who can share their cognitions socially and create fantasy worlds in which to play.

The Preoperational stage is divided into two substages:

a. Preconceptual (2–4 years). Capable of verbal expression, but speech is repetitious, for example, frequent egocentric monologues.
b. Intuitive (4–7 years). Speech becomes socialized and reasoning is egocentric; for example, "to the right" has one meaning—to his right.

3. *Concrete Operations stage.* The third stage is Concrete Operations; it normally occurs from about ages 7 to 11 and is characterized by the ability to classify and serialize concrete objects or actions; for example, a child can trace his or her route to school on a map. For the first time, children are able to use logical relationships. Language becomes sociometric instead of egocentric, and the child can understand other points of view. Conservation is mastered to the point that the child knows that weight, area, or mass of an object or volume of a liquid does not change when packaged or viewed differently. The concrete operational child can hold several pieces of information in mind and reverse his or her thinking, that is, go back to the starting point. Relational terms such as *bigger, larger*, or *darker* are understood. This child needs to work with classes, relations, and numbers. Arithmetic signs such as *plus, minus, equal to, greater than*, and *less than* should be mastered during this time. In addition, simple set theory operations such as *AND, OR*, and *NOT* should be introduced if not done so previously. Evidence exists that the child must have entered this stage for optimum progress in reading to occur (Briggs & Elkind, 1973). Later in this stage, students often enjoy communication in Morse Code. They may or may not be able to cope with simple syllogistic reasoning but should be exposed to problems such as the following:

Mary, Frank, and Joe are walking in the woods.
Joe is ahead of Mary.
Mary is ahead of Frank.
Is Frank ahead of Joe?

Analogies may also be studied in this stage. Examples are:

1. *Bird* is to *nest* as *bee* is to *hive.*
2. *Bird* is to *bee* as *nest* is to *hive.*

In the Concrete Operations stage, operations are still tied to actions. The child is rule bound and literal minded. New information will not often be sufficient to change a child's point of view. The ability to do abstract reasoning is limited. Facts and hypotheses may not be differentiated. Possibility and probability are often seen as interchangeable. Schools should emphasize skill development and concrete activities such as counting, sorting, building, manipulating, field trips, and kitchen physics.

4. *Formal Operations stage.* The fourth stage is Formal Operations; it normally occurs from about the ages of 11 through the adult years and is characterized by propositional, combinatorial, and hypothetical thinking. The youth has developed a generalized orientation toward problem solving. In the early years of this stage, the youth follows a cumbersome pattern in which discoveries are made in a less than systematic and rigorous fashion. Later, the youth solves problems in an elegant way by formulating generalizations, hypothesizing, and examining all possibilities systematically before coming to closure. The adolescent can go outside his or her experiences and enter the world of ideas, instead of proceeding only from what is real, and reverse directions at will.

Adolescents develop the ability to think about their own thinking (*metacognition*) and the thoughts of others. They are able to engage in error monitoring, self-correction, and internal dialogue. New insights can come from thought instead of the concrete manipulation of objects. They come to understand that different people have different perspectives and accept the idea that there is no one correct point of view. Adolescents can understand symbolism, metaphors, and similes in literature. They can gain deeper meaning from stories, including understanding of a moral if a story has one.

In this stage, the youth needs to work with geometry, proportionality, propositions, and probabilistic reasoning. Teachers should propose problems to solve, engage in discussions of ethical and moral issues, and provide opportunities for personal decision making. Active involvement helps adolescent development. They need to write poems, make films, and take part in drama. Ideas for instruction may be found in several sources, including Piaget (1950) and Flavell (1963).

Ginsburg and Opper (1969) reported that Piaget posed a physics program in which students were to determine which factor or combination of factors would cause a pendulum to swing faster—length, weight, height, or force. Students would experiment and come to the conclusion that length is the determining factor in how fast a pendulum swings. The shorter the pendulum, the faster it swings. Systematic experimentation leads to the conclusion but only if the student is ready to deal with each factor in isolation and in combination with others. It is an experiment that the student in the stage of Formal Operations can perform.

Another problem that demonstrates the qualitative differences between those in this stage and earlier stages has to do with combinations of liquids. What combination of five colorless liquids will produce a colored liquid? The adolescent can test hypotheses and will attack a problem systematically, trying out combinations until they find one that works. The younger child is confused by all the possibilities.

Knowledge.   According to Piaget, there are three kinds of knowledge: physical, logico-mathematical, and social. *Physical knowledge* is discovered through manipulation of objects in the physical world. This may be loosely thought of as things. *Logico-mathematical knowledge* is gained by thinking about relationships and includes the concepts of conservation and classification. This may be loosely thought of as data. *Social knowledge* is transmitted and includes social conventions. This may be thought of as people. O'Brien (1989) illustrated awareness of social knowledge by asking the following questions about George Washington:.

> Did George Washington speak with a British accent? What sort of money did he use? What schooling did youngsters in Colonial America have? Did young George revere the king? What games would be familiar to young George if he came to your town today? What would he find amusing? Surprising? Offensive? (p. 362)

Teachers need to provide learning experiences in each of the three areas. Think of instruction in things, data, and people. This is consistent with career-education approaches in which an objective is to find the best matches possible between clients' interests and aptitudes in these areas (data, people, things) and demands of job types or clusters.

Bloom's Cognitive Hierarchy

Benjamin Bloom proposed a cognitive-domain hierarchy of educational objectives composed of six levels. The model is depicted in Figure 2.2. It is often difficult in secondary school programs to provide the necessary experiences that will allow students with mild handicaps to progress beyond the lower levels of the taxonomy. Much of the instruction delivered to handicapped populations is typically confined to the Knowledge (lowest) or Understanding (next lowest) levels of the taxonomy. To function most effectively in the adult world, however, individuals with handicaps need to acquire at least some higher order skills. Secondary programs for the handicapped

Figure 2.2. The Bloom Taxonomy—Cognitive Domain

I. Knowledge
    A. Specifics
        1. Terminology
        2. Facts
    B. Dealing with specifics
        1. Conventions
        2. Trends and sequences
        3. Classifications and categories
        4. Criteria
        5. Methodologies
    C. Universals and abstractions
        1. Principles
        2. Generations
        3. Theories
        4. Structures

II. Comprehension
    A. Translation
    B. Interpretation
    C. Extrapolation
III. Application
IV. Analysis
    A. Elements
    B. Relationships
    C. Organizational principles
V. Synthesis
    A. Unique communication
    B. Plan for operation
    C. Set of abstract relations
VI. Evaluation
    A. Internal evidence (logical consistency)
    B. External evidence (consistency with external facts)

Source: Benjamin S. Bloom et al. (1956). *Taxonomy of educational objectives, Handbook I: Cognitive domain.* New York: Longman.

cannot meet the needs of students if they are extensions of elementary basic skills instruction. Instead, the focus of the secondary teacher should be on cognitive skills needed in the adult world, even though the mildly handicapped student may not yet have mastered basic skills. The curriculum-based-assessment approach discussed in Chapter 3, and the strategies-intervention approach discussed in Chapter 4 provide guidance in this area.

Applying Bloom. Teachers who want to meet the needs of their secondary mildly handicapped students often infuse career-education units of instruction into the social skills and mathematics courses. As an example, it might be feasible to have a unit on making major purchases in an area such as electronics, transportation, or housing. In transportation, the student could be placed in a hypothetical employment situation. At the knowledge level, he or she would have to know the route to work. At the comprehension level, he or she would have to interpret a bus schedule or determine some other way of getting to work. At the application level, he or she could list the advantages and disadvantages of owning a car. At the analysis level, the student could decide which features are desirable in a car. At the synthesis level, the student would make the decision of whether or not to buy a car. If the decision was to make the purchase, evaluation-level skills are needed to determine which car is the best purchase after shopping is completed.

It can be argued that the cognitive dimension is the most important. The focus in school involves cognitive activities such as reading and mathematics. In the attempt to educate the whole child, other dimensions must be taken into account. Remember that the job of teachers is to teach children first and teach subjects second. The rest of this chapter should provide insight as to why.

THE PSYCHOMOTOR DIMENSION

Minimal levels of physical activity are necessary in the performance of almost any task. With this in mind, a look at a taxonomy for the psychomotor domain is in order. Figure 2.3 depicts a taxonomy developed by Harlow (1972). No matter what the level of cognitive competency, a task that an individual is not physically capable of performing is a task that will not be completed. It is just as important to train for physical competence as it is for mental competence.

To provide the optimum satisfaction that will motivate students to maintain cardiovascular fitness throughout life, physical education or adaptive physical education teachers must be future oriented. At the secondary level, school programs should concentrate on the upper levels of the taxonomy: physical abilities, skilled movements, and nondiscursive communication. The activities must be enjoyable, and everybody must get a chance to discover and pursue activities at which they are successful and likely to continue as adults. Teachers must structure programs so that the needs of all students are met. A wellness program meshed with an expressive-arts program can meet the psychomotor demands of adolescents and provide a foundation for health and well being that will carry over into the adult years. One of the crucial factors in health and well being is a positive attitude. This is a function of affect, discussed next.

Figure 2.3. Taxonomy of the Psychomotor Domain

I. Reflex Movements
    A. Segmental reflexes (i.e., one spinal segment)
    B. Intersegmental reflexes
II. Fundamental Movements
    A. Walking
    B. Running
    C. Jumping
    D. Pushing
    E. Pulling
    F. Manipulating
III. Perceptual Abilities
    A. Kinesthetic
    B. Visual
    C. Auditory
    D. Tactile
    E. Coordination

IV. Physical Abilities
    A. Endurance
    B. Strength
    C. Flexibility
    D. Agility
    E. Reaction-response time
    F. Dexterity
V. Skilled Movements
    A. Games
    B. Sports
    C. Dances
    D. The Arts
VI. Nondiscursive communication
    A. Posture
    B. Gestures
    C. Facial expressions
    D. Creative movements

Source: Anita J. Harrow. *Taxonomy of the psychomotor domain: A guide for developing behavioral objectives.* Copyright © 1972 by Longman. Reprinted by permission.

THE AFFECTIVE DIMENSION

High levels of performance and positive attitudes go hand in hand. Mildly handicapped students do not necessarily come to school with the belief that education is something to be valued. A lack of interest may lead to discipline problems. Corresponding resentment, then, contributes to even poorer attitudes. Students may give up completely. When children develop the feeling that school is an institution designed to punish and humiliate them, a vicious downward spiral results. As the link between affect and achievement becomes more clearly established, educators are becoming increasingly convinced that the curriculum must include components on interests, attitudes, and feelings. Krathwohl, Bloom, and Masia (1964) developed a taxonomy composed of five hierarchical levels. It is reproduced in Figure 2.4. As with the Bloom taxonomy in the cognitive domain, no age levels are proposed. The authors of the taxonomy believe that individuals develop at different rates. The job of educators is to meet each student at his or her level of development and progress from there.

Experts agree that students should embrace and take responsibility for their learning. To accomplish this, they need to have a sense of ownership and participation. Adelman and Taylor (1983) have demonstrated the value of programming based on instrinsic motivation (also called tertiary reinforcement). As students take increasing responsibility, they are better able to understand how to deal with other institutions and life in general. Ultimately, each student develops a philosophy of life based on the sum of his or her experiences and how those experiences are colored by his or her outlook.

Fagan, Long, and Stevens (1975) developed their Self-Control Curriculum to help students better deal with their life experiences. The taxonomy on which the curricu-

Figure 2.4. Taxonomy of Objectives for the Affective Domain.

 I. Receiving
   A. Awareness
   B. Willingness to receive
   C. Controlled or selected attention
 II. Responding
   A. Acquiescence in responding
   B. Willingness to respond
   C. Satisfaction
 III. Valuing
   A. Acceptance of a value
   B. Preference for a value
   C. Commitment (conviction)
 IV. Organization
   A. Conceptualization of a value
   B. Organization of a value system
 V. Characterization by a Value or Value Complex
   A. Generalized set of values
   B. Characterization or philosophy of life

Source: David R. Krathwohl et al. *Taxonomy of educational objectives: Handbook II: Affective domain.* Copyright © 1964 by Longman. Reprinted by permission.

Figure 2.5. Taxonomy of the Self-Control Curriculum

 I. Selection: Accurate Perception
   A. Focusing and concentration
   B. Mastering figure-ground discrimination
   C. Mastering distractions and interference
   D. Processing complex patterns
 II. Storage: Retention of Information
   A. Developing visual memory
   B. Developing auditory memory
 III. Sequencing and ordering: Organizing and planning actions
   A. Developing time orientation
   B. Developing auditory-visual sequencing
   C. Developing sequential planning
 IV. Anticipating Feelings: Identification and Constructive Use of Affective Experiences
   A. Developing alternatives
   B. Evaluating consequences
 V. Appreciating Feelings: Identification and Constructive Use of Affective Experiences
   A. Identifying feelings
   B. Developing positive feelings
   C. Managing feelings
   D. Reinterpreting feeling events
 VI. Managing Frustration: Coping with Negative Feelings
   A. Accepting feelings of frustration
   B. Building coping resources
   C. Tolerating frustration
 VII. Inhibition and Delay: Postponing Actions
   A. Controlling action
   B. Developing partial goals
 VIII. Relaxation: Reducing Internal Tensions
   A. Developing body relaxation
   B. Developing thought relaxation
   C. Developing movement relaxation

Source: S. A. Fagen, N. L. Long, and D. J. Stevens. *Teaching children self-control.* Columbus, OH: Merrill Publishing Company, 1975.

lum is based is depicted in Figure 2.5. Built on a humanistic perspective, the Self-Control Curriculum concentrates first on developing the cognitive processes of attention, perception, memory, cognition, and expression. This sets the foundation for skill development in the affective areas of appreciating feelings, managing frustrations and inhibitions, and learning to relax.

If one of the aims of education is to develop good citizenship it is important that affective education be included. Positive attitudes, higher self-concepts, acceptance of responsibility for one's actions, ability to use leisure time to pursue one's interests successfully, and commitment to one's society can and must be taught. How one gets along with others is determined in large part by affect. The link between affect and social skills is explored next.

THE SOCIAL DIMENSION

If one were faced with the very difficult task of having to decide if it is better to train either social skills or cognitive skills, the decision could not be made without some degree of agonizing. Traditionally, educators have been more inclined to concentrate on academics, with less effort expended on social skills training. Perhaps educators think that social skills will be learned in incidental fashion. Perhaps they think the teaching of social skills is a job best accomplished outside of the schools.

Although it is possible to argue that one can get along better in life without cognitive skills than without social skills, it is clear that both academic and social competence are necessary for optimal success in adult life. One of the reasons most often cited by employers for termination of mildly handicapped workers is their

Figure 2.6. Taxonomy of Social Skills

I. Environmental Behaviors
  A. Care for the environment
  B. Dealing with emergency
  C. Lunchroom
  D. Movement around environment
II. Interpersonal Behaviors
  A. Accepting authority
  B. Coping with conflict
  C. Gaining attention
  D. Greeting others
  E. Helping others
  F. Making conversation
  G. Organized play
  F. Positive attitude toward others
  G. Plays informally
  H. Property: Own and others'

III. Self-Related Behaviors
  A. Accepting consequences
  B. Ethical behavior
  C. Expressing feelings
  D. Positive attitude toward self
  E. Responsible behaviors
  F. Self-care
IV. Task-Related Behaviors
  A. Asking and answering questions
  B. Attending behavior
  C. Classroom discussion
  D. Completing tasks
  E. Following directions
  F. Group activities
  G. Independent work
  H. On-task behavior
  I. Performing before others
  J. Quality of work

Source: T. M. Stephens. *Social skills in the classroom.* Copyright © 1978 by Cedars Press. Reprinted by permission.

Figure 2.7. Skillstreaming Curriculum

I. Beginning Social Skills
    A. Listening
    B. Starting a conversation
    C. Having a conversation
    D. Asking a question
    E. Saying thank you
    F. Introducing yourself
    G. Introducing other people
    H. Giving a compliment
II. Advanced Social Skills
    A. Asking for help
    B. Joining in
    C. Giving instructions
    D. Following instructions
    E. Apologizing
    F. Convincing others
III. Skills for Dealing with Feelings
    A. Knowing your feelings
    B. Expressing your feelings
    C. Understanding the feelings of others
    D. Dealing with someone else's anger
    E. Expressing affection
    F. Dealing with fear
    G. Rewarding yourself

IV. Skill Alternatives to Aggression
    A. Asking permission
    B. Sharing something
    C. Helping others
    D. Negotiation
    E. Using self-control
    F. Standing up for your rights
    G. Responding to teasing
    H. Avoiding trouble with others
    I. Keeping out of fights
V. Skills for Dealing with Stress
    A. Making a complaint
    B. Answering a complaint
    C. Sportsmanship after the game
    D. Dealing with embarrassment
    E. Dealing with being left out
    F. Standing up for a friend
    G. Responding to persuasion
    H. Responding to failure
    I. Dealing with contradictory messages
    J. Dealing with an accusation
    K. Getting ready for a difficult conversation
    L. Dealing with group pressure
VI. Planning Skills
    A. Deciding on something to do
    B. Deciding what caused a problem
    C. Setting a goal
    D. Deciding on your abilities
    E. Gathering information
    F. Arranging problems by importance
    G. Concentrating on a task

From *Skillstreaming the adolescent: A structured learning approach to teaching prosocial skills* (pp. 84–85), by A. P. Goldstein, R. P. Sprafkin, N. J. Gershaw, & P. Klein, 1980, Champaign, IL: Research Press. Copyright 1980 by the authors. Reprinted by permission.

inability to get along with their coworkers. Students need to start adult life equipped with the necessary social skills to get along with others. If educators do not take increasing responsibility in this area, the job may not get done adequately.

Stephens (1978) proposed a social skills taxonomy, which is reproduced in Figure 2.6. It is congruent with the efforts of those who have developed career education programs designed to be infused into the regular curricula. Secondary educators may wish to view the Stephens taxonomy as a list of entry skills that students would be expected to bring with them to secondary school. It is reproduced here because it is reasonable to assume that not all students will have advanced through the end of the taxonomy by the time they start middle school or junior high school.

Although Goldstein, Sprafkin, Gershan, and Klein (1980) called their adolescent skillstreaming model a curriculum, it is reproduced here as Figure 2.7 because it more closely resembles a taxonomy. Either the social skills taxonomy or the skillstreaming model could form the basis for a social skills curriculum. Two distinct advantages of teaching social skills are obvious. First, social skills training could be integrated into ongoing programs without subtracting time needed for academic pursuits. Second, systematic teaching of social competencies would lessen the chance that students would be forced to make the transition from school to adult life with gaps in their abilities to get along with others.

Social competence is based on knowing how to interact with others. Guidance in one's actions is obtained in part from the ability to deal with right and wrong, a function of morals. Social skills are studied further in Chapters 3 and 5.

THE MORAL DIMENSION

According to Kohlberg (1981), humans may go through up to six stages of moral development on three levels, as depicted in Figure 2.8. Not everyone is able to attain the highest level. Moral development is highly dependent on cognitive development. As one advances in the hierarchy, one is increasingly able to see another's point of view and objectively appraise potential outcomes and consequences.

Preconventional Level

At the Preconventional level, children are oriented toward the tangible consequences of getting rewarded and avoiding punishment. In the first stage, good is behavior that is rewarded or not punished. In the second stage, good is satisfying one's own needs and those of others who will reciprocate with tangible reinforcers.

Conventional Level

At the Conventional level, the emphasis is on social conventions and expectations, which may include stereotyping and unthinking conformity. In the third stage, good is associated with peer approval. In the fourth stage, good is conforming to rules, laws, mores, and authority.

Figure 2.8. Stages of Moral Judgment

   I. Preconventional Level (birth–9 years)
       A. Reward and punishment
       B. Needs exchange
  II. Conventional Level (ages 9–15)
       A. Peer approval
       B. Law and order
 III. Postconventional Level
       A. General rights and standards
       B. Self-chosen ethics and principles

Source: Excerpt from *The philosophy of moral development* by Lawrence Kohlberg. © 1981 by Lawrence Kohlberg. Reprinted by permission of Harper & Row, Publishers, Inc.

Postconventional Level

At the Postconventional level, the individual searches for universal principles in the establishment of a personal set of moral principles. In the fifth stage, good occurs when due process is followed, no matter what the outcome or consequence. In the sixth stage, good is what is consistent with one's self-chosen ethics and principles.

Not all individuals develop the same set of ethics and moral principles. Experiences shape one's interpretation of what is good. The question of whose value system should be taught often arises. A story about the clash of values is illustrative.

CASE STUDY 5

Ms. Smith believes that it is wrong to steal and naturally assumes that everyone shares this value. One of her students, Johnny, was caught stealing a watch that Mark had just received for his birthday. The incident happened during a physical education class in the locker room. When questioned, Johnny stated that the experience would make Mark a better person. Johnny went on to explain that the watch was relatively cheap and that Mark had been careless in leaving it on the bench in front of his locker during the time he was showering. By taking it, Johnny was teaching Mark a valuable lesson. In fact, Johnny implied that it was his duty to help Mark learn about how life works so that he would be more careful in the future and not lose something of real value to theft. Johnny was serious and blamed Mark when he was punished for stealing. Ms. Smith was shocked, but she started locking her purse in the file drawer of her desk the very next day.

Morality development may occur in stages, but there is no guarantee that everyone will exit each stage with the same set of morals. It is not enough to make sure that cognitive development is proceeding on schedule. Decisions about whether to teach morals in school—and, if so, whose morals to teach—have to be made. For students with mild handicaps, awareness of what constitutes middle-class morality and how to deal with it are necessary. From a pragmatic standpoint, the student is more likely to work for an employer with values similar to those held by educators. It is more than likely that the employer will not change his or her value system if it does not conform to that held by his or her mildly handicapped employee.

Morals development depends on cognitive development. Moral behavior does not exist in a vacuum. Perhaps one is more likely to be guided by "higher" moral standards if one feels more personally secure. This is most likely to occur when psychological needs are being met.

THE PSYCHOLOGICAL DIMENSION

Both Maslow (1970) and Erikson (1950) have investigated psychological needs.

Maslow's Hierarchy

The Maslovian hierarchy is shown in Figure 2.9. As low-level human needs are satisfied, it is theorized that the individual is motivated to satisfy higher order needs until the Self-actualization level is approached. Self-actualization can never be satis-

Figure 2.9. Maslow's Hierarchy of Human Needs

I. Physiological
   A. Food
   B. Water
   C. Air
   D. Sleep
   E. Elimination
   F. Sex
II. Safety
   A. Security
   B. Protection from physical harm
III. Love, Affection, and Intimacy
    (Belongingness)
   A. Friendship
   B. Affection
   C. Acceptance

IV. Achievement
   A. Knowledge
   B. Skills
   C. Exploration
   D. Mastery of environment
V. Self-Esteem
   A. Self-respect
   B. Respect of others
   C. Recognition
IV. Aesthetic
   A. Beauty
   B. Acquisition of art
   C. Symmetry
VII. Self-Actualization
   A. Leadership
   B. Reputation
   C. Distinction
   D. Eminence

Source: Excerpt from *Motivation and personality* by Abraham H. Maslow. © 1970 by Abraham H. Maslow. Reprinted by permission of Harper & Row, Publishers, Inc.

fied and provides continuous motivation because there is always some facet of the psyche that can be enhanced.

Speculation abounds as to why adolescents behave as they do. From a needs hierarchy position, one interpretation of adolescent behavior is that the adult world is demanding that adolescents function at the Achievement level or above but is not accepting them as worthwhile individuals. According to Maslow, one must satisfy the lower level needs before upper level needs can be addressed. The dilemma into which adolescents are put is that they are struggling to belong (i.e., enjoy recognition and dignity) while expected to attain higher level goals. This is not possible in the theoretical orientation of Maslow. Assessment should center on determining which needs have and have not been met so that intervention may be adjusted. This task is legitimately beyond the scope of the secondary school.

Erikson's Stages

Erik Erikson takes a different perspective. His eight maturing stages are depicted in Figure 2.10. The successful individual integrates his or her individual needs and experiences with societal mores and finds personal and cultural fulfillment. Stages 4 to 8 are of most concern to the secondary teacher. If the individual is successful in the quest for "Industry," he or she learns to be productive. Childhood ends when an identity is determined and one projects a predictable persona to the world. At this time, career preparation is important. Intimacy allows the young adult to share his or her identity with others. The adult wishes to prepare the next generation. Ego identity occurs when one accepts his or her life and is the fruition of the previous stages. Those who are successful accept death as the culmination of a fruitful life. Are

Figure 2.10. The Eight Maturing Stages of Erikson

    I. Trust vs. mistrust
    II. Autonomy vs. shame and doubt
  III. Initiative vs. guilt
  IV. Industry vs. inferiority
    V. Identity vs. role confusion
  VI. Intimacy vs. isolation
 VII. Generativity vs. stagnation
VIII. Ego integrity vs. despair

Source: Erik H. Erikson, *Childhood and society.* (1950, 1963.) W. W. Norton & Company, Inc.

industry, identity, intimacy, generativity, and ego identity fit areas for a secondary curriculum? The answer is that career-education programs include instruction related to personal attributes such as aptitude, interests, and values. Developers of career-education curricula posit that the best chance for life satisfaction comes when the individual can find the occupation and then specific jobs that most closely match his or her traits. This perspective is consistent with Erikson's maturational stages and can be reconciled with each of the theoretical orientations presented in each of the dimensions.

For many adolescents, the transition from school to adult life proves to be a period of great difficulty. From a youth's perspective, it may appear that adult behavior is increasingly expected; yet the granting of adult privileges occurs only sparingly and grudgingly. In the next section, issues important to the transition to adult life are addressed.

FROM SCHOOL TO LIFE: JOB-RELATED SKILLS

Recent surveys (Rusch & Phelps, 1987) have shown that about two-thirds of adults with handicapping conditions are not working. Of the one-third who do work, about three-quarters are employed part time. Okolo and Sitlington (1986) reported that employment problems among the mildly handicapped seem due to (1) lack of interpersonal skills, (2) lack of job-related academic skills, and (3) lack of specific vocational skills.

Not surprisingly, the lack of interpersonal skills was found to be the most crucial factor in lack of success. Factors such as trustworthiness, working flexibility, personal appearance, hygiene, respectfulness, and cooperativeness were found to be highly related to job success (Gustafson, 1978). Brown (1976) found ten reasons why employers rejected job applicants after the job interview:

1. Poor reasons for wanting a job
2. Past history of job hopping
3. Inability to communicate during job interview

4. Poor health record
5. Immaturity
6. Poor personal appearance
7. Poor manners and mannerisms
8. Wrong personality traits
9. Lack of specific job skills
10. Poorly filled-out job application

In the same study, employers cited five primary causes of employee termination:

1. Absenteeism
2. Lack of interest
3. Continuous making of costly mistakes
4. Not following directions
5. Unwillingness to learn

In the area of job-related academic skills, Okolo and Sitlington (1986) determined that although it was necessary to have basic competencies in reading, writing, and mathematics, it was also important to be able to employ those skills to meet situation-specific demands. Educators refer to this as *transferability of training* and provide for this by giving students the same problem or type of problem in several different contexts and teaching them to use metacognitive skills to arrive at acceptable solutions. At first, the teacher makes the students use their skills in simple transfers of context such as changing the form of an arithmetic problem from a vertical format

$$\begin{array}{r} 5 \\ +\ 3 \\ \hline ? \end{array}$$

to a horizontal format $5 + 3 = ?$. Later, the teacher adds story problems, distractors, and different operations. Transferability as a skill is temptingly easy to assume, but skills often seem to vanish from mind as the student transfers from location to location, worksheet to worksheet, subject to subject, and text to text. Without tutelage, the student may find it easy to assume that a skill learned in social studies is not applicable in English class.

Specific vocational skills are so diverse that it is difficult to discuss them succinctly (Chapter 8, however, outlines a basic curriculum.) In general, Okolo and Sitlington (1986) determined that *the ability to use tools and equipment* normally found on the job is helpful. Cooperation with outside agencies may be necessary to meet this need. Students should probably exit school familiar with tools and equipment commonly found in the occupational cluster or clusters they have chosen to pursue as part of their career education programs. Experience with office equipment, hand tools, drafting tools, and telecommunications equipment are just a few of the examples of general skills that could be taught in conjunction with outside agencies.

Checklists could be included in each student's folder of tools and equipment to which the student had been exposed, was mastering, and had mastered. Ordinarily, there is not enough time nor is it wise to teach specific jobs in the secondary school as jobs become obsolete over time and new job categories with corresponding new demands are constantly being created. An understanding that school will turn out a worker with basic skills that need to be enhanced with on-the-job training for specific job needs will have to be reached with the business, industrial, service, and other sectors.

Services to Aid Transition

Even with full-service secondary school programs, which include instruction in traditional academics, prevocational and vocational skills, interpersonal skills, functional academics, and home living skills, it is apparent that youth will need additional transition services. The call to bridge the gap between the foundation of school preparation and adult services has been strongly made (McDonnell et al., 1983). Will (1984) talks of three bridges:

1. Transition without special services
2. Transition with time-limited services
3. Transition with ongoing services

Individuals would receive the level of service commensurate with their needs as determined by a cooperative assessment and intervention effort between school and vocational rehabilitation services.

The question of what the secondary school system must do to allow students to take full advantage of existing transitional services is constantly in need of resolution because the dynamic nature of the work world necessitates continual reappraisal of the role of the schools. It has been implied (Lichtenstein, 1987) that the focus of high school should be the provision of marketable skills and the securing of employment. Less emphasis would be placed on academic remediation and graduation requirements. In this context, the high school would change, perhaps taking on some of the functions of an employment agency.

Halpern (1985) looked beyond employment to a curriculum in which the overall goal is successful living in one's community. In this approach, there are three areas of focus: the residential environment, employment, and social and interpersonal networks. Considerations in the residential environment include quality of living, safety, and proximity to work, family, recreational interests, and so on. Hasazi, Gordon, and Roe (1985) reported that individuals with handicaps were much more likely to find employment when they used their self-family-friend networks. This reveals the importance of skills to deal successfully with social and interpersonal networks. Relevant factors here include competence in daily communications, degree of self-esteem, amount of family support, emotional maturity, ability to seek and keep friends, and traits necessary to handle intimate relationships.

Mithaug, Martin, and Agran (1987) argued that school personnel need to teach problem-solving skills to meet the need to learn how to adapt to changes in the work environment while maintaining acceptable levels of work performance. Their prescription involves less use of direct instruction and an increased student-centered teaching orientation.

Can the entrance of additional vocational and transitional service considerations into the secondary school arena be reconciled with the provision of traditional secondary services? Beginning with a look at the very purpose of schooling, we now examine the other four keys to success in helping students in their efforts to enter and enjoy competence in the adult world; the aims of schooling, curriculum, career education, and climate.

THE AIMS OF SCHOOLING

From treatises on educational history and philosophy we learn that the aims or purposes of education have been debated since ancient times. In more recent history, the debate has settled on the resolution of where education should land on a continuum bound by two extremes:

1. Education should train the mind. The more one's mind is exercised, the stronger it becomes. People who believe in a classical education lean to this side of the continuum.
2. Education should be relevant. Schooling does no good if it cannot be used to get and keep a job.

Complicating the debate is the dynamic nature of knowledge. More than 90 percent of all scientists who ever lived are living today. It is no surprise that knowledge is exploding at a tremendously accelerating rate. During the early part of the Middle Ages, it seemed possible to commit to memory all existing knowledge. Scholars were literally walking encyclopedias. In contrast, by the second half of the twentieth century, it has become impossible even to stay current in one's own very narrow discipline.

Specialization has become the rule, and the number of disciplines keeps increasing yearly. Information management, rather than acquisition, is spurring a tremendous commitment to information storage and retrieval. Experts even fear loss of a common set of experiences that forms the basis for meaningful communication. How schools meet these and other challenges has a direct bearing on the development of instructional strategies that will meet the needs of students who are mildly handicapped.

Those who have advocated the identification of a core of skills that each student would attempt to master have been persuasive. There is merit in establishing a common set of academic experiences. In 1892, the Committee of Ten was formed to resolve the issue of whether secondary school should serve the masses or function as an academy for college preparation (National Education Association, 1893). Their answer was that there really was no conflict and that both terminal and college-bound students could profit from the same programs. Mental discipline was stressed, and it was thought that all students could benefit from training in observation, memory, reasoning, and expression. Operationally, four curricula were recommended: classical, Latin-scientific, modern language, and English. Each curriculum included prescribed choices in basic courses in foreign languages, mathematics, sciences, English, and history. As proposed, this approach was basically designed for those going on to college.

Within a few years, this approach was challenged by the demands that higher levels of technology exact on the labor force. In 1918 the Cardinal Principles were published (Commission on the Reorganization of Secondary Education, 1918) based on the earlier work of Spencer (1881). The Cardinal Principles were derived from a need to educate the whole child and included (1) Health, (2) Command of Functional Processes, (3) Worthy Home Membership, (4) Vocation, (5) Civic Education, (6) Worthy Use of Leisure, and (7) Ethical Character.

In 1938 the National Education Association published a report in which the aims of education were reduced to four (Educational Policies Commission, 1938).

1. Self-realization (basic skills)
2. Human relations
3. Economic efficiency (career education)
4. Civil responsibility.

This was followed by another report (Educational Policies Commission, 1944) in which the commission urged that ten imperative needs would be met.

1. Develop salable skills and those understandings and attitudes that make the worker an intelligent and productive participant in economic life. To this end, most youth need supervised work experience as well as education in the skills and knowledge of their occupations.
2. Develop and maintain good health and physical fitness.
3. Understand the rights and duties of citizens of a democratic society and be diligent and competent in the performance of their obligations as members of the community and citizens of the state and nation and of the world.
4. Understand the significance of the family for the individual and society and the conditions conducive to successful family life.
5. Know how to purchase and use goods and services intelligently, understanding both value received by the consumers and the economic consequences of their acts.
6. Understand the methods of science, the influence of science, the influence of science on human life, and the main scientific facts concerning the nature of the world and man.
7. Have opportunities to develop their capacities to appreciate beauty in literature, art, music, and nature.
8. Be able to use their leisure time well and budget it wisely, balancing activities that yield satisfaction to the individual with those that are socially useful.
9. Develop respect for other persons, grow in their insight into ethical values and principles, and be able to live and work cooperatively with others.
10. Grow in their ability to think rationally, express their thoughts clearly, and read and listen with understanding.

By the mid-1970s, the aims of education were expressed in five broad domains (U.S. Office of Education, 1976).

1. Personal values
2. Citizenship education
3. Arts
4. Humanities
5. Career education

The six dimensions discussed earlier in this chapter spill into and form the basis for curriculum development in each of these five domains. It is possible to achieve these or similar aims, meet the developmental needs of students, and prepare students whose exit behaviors will serve them well in the job market. A good career-education program may be the key to successful transition to adult life.

THE CURRICULUM AND CAREER EDUCATION

One viable way to answer the set of questions posed at the beginning of this chapter about programming to meet the adult needs of students is to infuse a career-education program *into* a curriculum designed to meet the developmental and individual needs of each student. There are many education programs available. Chapter 8 provides guidelines. Adapting one or several to meet the unique needs of each situation is a task that is ongoing but worthwhile in that students have a better chance in the adult world when systematic preparation designed to meet their needs has been provided.

Clark (1979) proposed a model for constructing elementary career-education programs. It is mentioned here because of the importance of putting into place K–12 and beyond career-education programs. Learning to make decisions and awareness of the world of work are goals that must be mastered by the end of the elementary level if an optimum career-education program is to function.

Brolin and Kokaska (1979) discussed a curriculum in which twenty-two competencies are expressed in the areas of daily living skills, personal social skills, and occupational guidance and preparation. Part of the curriculum is reproduced as Figure 2.11. Although the total program appears intimidating at first because there are more than 100 objectives, there is a great deal of overlap with the dimensions. The infusion of these competencies into a good secondary school curriculum can be accomplished with little fundamental restructuring of goals or objectives. A staff can develop a matrix of required courses and determine where each objective will be taught. Each student can have a checksheet in his or her folder with both the mastered objectives marked each grading period and progress noted on which objectives are being attempted. This process also has ramifications for individualized educational program (IEP) construction and vocational rehabilitation record keeping.

Waugh and associates (1982) have developed a comprehensive career-education assessment and curriculum guide for special education students. It includes objectives, activities, materials, and assessment resources for each of six goal areas:

Figure 2.11. Career-Education Curriculum Competencies

I. Daily Living Skills
   A. Managing family finances
   B. Selecting, maintaining, and managing a home
   C. Caring for personal needs
   D. Raising children, family living
   E. Buying and preparing food
   F. Buying and caring for clothing
   G. Engaging in civic activities
   H. Utilizing recreation and leisure
   I. Getting around the community

II. Personal Social Skills
   A. Achieving self-awareness
   B. Acquiring self-confidence
   C. Achieving socially responsible behavior
   D. Maintaining good interpersonal skills
   E. Achieving independence
   F. Achieving problem-solving skills
   G. Communicating adequately with others

III. Occupational Guidance and Preparation
   A. Knowing and exploring occupational possibilities
   B. Selecting and planning occupational choices
   C. Exhibiting appropriate work habits and behaviors
   D. Exhibiting sufficient physical-manual skills
   E. Obtaining a specific occupational skill
   F. Seeking, securing, and maintaining employment

Adapted with permission of Merrill, an imprint of Macmillan Publishing Company, from *Career Education for Handicapped Individuals, Second Edition* by Charles J. Kokaska and Donn E. Brolin, Copyright © 1985 Merrill Publishing Company, Columbus, Ohio.

1. To develop self-appraisal skills
2. To develop interpersonal skills
3. To develop decision-making skills
4. To explore career, school and work meanings, life-style options, and values
5. To clarify school and work meanings and values
6. To acquire the skills necessary to carry out career plan upon high school exit

Each of the goals areas is divided into the levels of awareness, acceptance, exploration, and preparation. Although much too comprehensive to reproduce here, it provides a model that can be used to supplement existing instruction or can stand alone as a self-contained career-education package.

For those dealing with secondary-aged youth who have not experienced the full benefits of comprehensive K–12 career-education programming and who are getting uncomfortably close to the time when they will have to shoulder their share of adult responsibilities, Izzo and Drier (1987) have prepared a monograph containing descriptions of nineteen programs designed to provide career guidance to high-risk youth. Each of the agencies is a participant in the Job Training Partnership Act of 1982 (JPTA). Oriented toward employment counseling, these programs attempt to help bridge the gap between school and work. Some attempt to compress career-education programs into shorter time frames. Others help unwed mothers, bring business and industry closer to education, encourage students to finish high school, build on existing skills, provide summer employment, assess current skills, and provide career assistance to ex-offenders.

Existing programs can be tapped to provide resources for establishing K–12 and beyond career-education programming. The examples provided here are representative of the many different approaches that can be used to meet developmental needs as expressed in the dimensions and scholastic needs as expressed in the aims. In combination, the goal of meeting the adult needs of former students can be realized.

THE SCHOOL CLIMATE

There is one more piece of the puzzle that needs to be put into place. Students are dropping out of school because forces influencing them to leave school are stronger than the motivation to stay in school. Many of those who do stay are not getting enough out of their educational experiences to justify the resources that are being expended on their programs. In assessing their needs, it is apparent that they struggle with the demands of adult life. They may give verbal support to the importance of school when asked, but there is a discrepancy between what they say and their behavior on a day-to-day basis.

Students need to be involved personally with their educations. No student should feel that school is a place where the student does what he or she is told without complaint or question. It is not enough to inform students that educators know what is best. The attitude that students are products or consumers of a product called education is demeaning to both student and school. Adults must demonstrate that they believe each individual has worth and is worth caring about. The contradiction is that school must teach its students independence while also nurturing them. Sometimes the vision needed to serve students is lost, and school may become a place where students are processed as objects. Students may feel they are victims of an uncaring, monolithic bureaucracy and try to rebel against a system that should be supporting their efforts to grow into responsible adults. Their relative lack of experience and understandable yearn for immediate gratification may cause them to seek the most immediate short-term solutions when they should be looking ahead to their futures.

Adjusting the curriculum is not enough. Schools must be humane places where students know they are valued. The resulting rise in morale would further motivate students to stretch themselves in all of the dimensions.

SUMMARY

Five keys to meeting the future needs of students can be identified: dimensions, aims, curriculum, career education, and climate. The six dimensions—cognitive, psychomotor, affective, social, moral, and psychological—constitute the developmental patterns and needs that children and youth bring to school. This chapter explored the six stages and offered taxonomies for each. *Aims* are purposes that schools are designed to fulfill. *Curriculum* specifies what is to be taught. *Career education* helps people determine who they are and what they want to accomplish. *Climate* is the glue that holds the whole enterprise of school together.

Once a clear understanding of what these keys involve and how they interact to become "school" has been reached, programming for youth with mildly handicapping conditions can be structured to help them to cope better with life and what it holds. The inescapable conclusion is that educators are being increasingly asked to take a holistic approach. This whole child commitment is best fulfilled when the curriculum is structured to account for each of the six dimensions (cognitive, psychomotor, affective, social, moral, and psychological).

Educators continue their commitment to youth when they assist in their transitions from school to adult life. Development of interpersonal skills, the ability to transfer training to meet the demands of new situations, and a grasp of basic skills will assist students in meeting their overall goal of successful living in their communities. Continued discussions of what schools should be and what services they should offer are still needed.

The examinations of comprehensive curricula in Chapters 8 and 9 will help clarify issues raised here and elsewhere. Note there how the different developmental needs of students can be met in a phased vocational curriculum.

STUDY QUESTIONS

1. What philosophical issues are important in secondary programming?
2. What is the role of theory in education?
3. Should schools go beyond academic programming?
4. What is needed to develop curricula in each of the six dimensions: cognitive, psychomotor, affective, social, moral, and psychological?
5. Why aren't more adults with handicaps employed and what can be done about it?
6. What is transition and how does it work?
7. What are the aims of education?
8. What are the options for meeting the needs of exceptional students?
9. What can teachers do to motivate students?
10. How do you know that what you are doing will meet the needs of students?

REFERENCES

Adelman, H. S., & Taylor, L. (1983). Enhancing motivation for overcoming learning and behavior problems. *Journal of Learning Disabilities, 16*, 384–392.

Bloom, B. S., Engelhardt, M. D., Furst, E. J., Hill, W. H., & Krathwohl, D. R. (1956). *Taxonomy of educational objectives, Handbook I: Cognitive domain*. New York: McKay.

Briggs, C., & Elkind, D. (1973). Cognitive development in early readers. *Developmental Psychology, 9*, 279–280.

Brolin, D. E., & Kokaska, C. J. (1979). *Career education for handicapped children and youth*. Columbus: C. E. Merrill.

Brown, K. W. (1976). What employers look for in job applicants. *Business Education Forum*, *30*(7), 7.

Clark, G. M. (1979). *Career education for the handicapped child in the elementary classroom*. Denver: Love.

Commission on the Reorganization of Secondary Education. (1918). *Cardinal principles of secondary education* (Bulletin No. 35). Washington, DC: U.S. Government Printing Office.

Educational Policies Commission. (1938). *The purposes of education in American democracy*. Washington, DC: National Education Association.

―――. (1944). *Education for all American youth*. Washington, DC: National Education Association.

Erikson, E. H. (1968). *Childhood and society* (2nd ed.). New York: Norton.

Fagan, S. A., Long, N. J., & Stevens, D. J. (1975). *Teaching children self-control*. Columbus: C. E. Merrill.

Flavell, J. H. (1963). *The developmental psychology of Jean Piaget*. New York: D. Van Nostrand.

Furth, H. G. (1969). *Piaget and knowledge: Theoretical foundations*. Englewood Cliffs, NJ: Prentice-Hall.

Ginsburg, H., & Opper, S. (1969). *Piaget's theory of intellectual development: An introduction*. Englewood Cliffs, NJ: Prentice-Hall.

Goldstein, A. P., Sprafkin, R. P., Gershaw, N. J., & Klein, P. (1980). *Skillstreaming the adolescent: A structured learning approach to teaching prosocial skills*. Champaign, IL: Research Press.

Halpern, A. S. (1985). Transition: A look at the foundations. *Exceptional Children, 51*(6) 479–486.

Harlow, A. J. (1972). *Taxonomy of the psychomotor domain: A guide for developing behavioral objectives*. New York: McKay.

Hasazi, S. B., Gordon, L. R., & Roe, C. A. (1985). Factors associated with the employment status of handicapped youth exiting high school from 1979 to 1983. *Exceptional Children, 51*(6), 455–469.

Izzo, M. V., & Drier, H. N., (1987). *Career guidance within JTPA for high risk populations: Programs, methods and products*. Columbus: National Consortium of State Career Guidance Supervisors, Ohio State University and National Center for Research in Vocational Education (ERIC Document Reproduction Service No. ED 278 869).

Inhelder, B., & Piaget, J. (1958). *The growth of logical thinking* (A. Parsons & S. Milgram, Trans.). New York: Basic Books.

Kohlberg, L. (1981). *The philosophy of moral development*. San Francisco: Harper & Row.

Krathwohl, D. R., Bloom, B. S., & Masia, B. (1964). *Taxonomy of objectives, Handbook II: Affective domain*. New York: McKay.

Lichtenstein, S. (1987). *Transition issues: Post-school employment patterns of handicapped and nonhandicapped graduates and dropouts*. Washington, DC: Education Department, Office of Special Education and Rehabilitation Services (ERIC Document Reproduction Service No. ED 287 243).

Maslow, A. H. (1970). *Motivation and personality* (2nd ed.). New York: Harper & Row.

McDonell, J. J., Wilcox, B., & Boles, S. M. (1983). *Issues in the transition from school to adult services: A study of parents of secondary students with severe handicaps*. Eugene: University of Oregon, Center on Human Development, Specialized Training Program Model School and Community Services for People with Severe Handicaps (ERIC Document Reproduction Service No. ED 240 381).

Mithaug, D. E., Martin, J. E., & Agran, M. (1987). Adaptability instruction: The goal of transitional programming. *Exceptional Children, 53*(6) 500–505.

Muus, R. E. (1968). *Theories of adolescence* (2nd ed.). New York: Random House.

National Education Association. (1983). *Report of the Committee on Secondary School Studies.* Washington, DC: U.S. Government Printing Office.

O'Brien, T. C. (1989, January). Some thoughts on treasure-keeping. *Phi Delta Kappan, 70*(5), 360–364.

Okolo, C. M., & Sitlington, P. (1986, Spring). The role of special education in LD adolescents' transition from school to work. *Learning Disability Quarterly, 9,* 141–155.

Phillips, J. L. (1975). *The origin of intellect: Piaget's theory* (2nd ed.). San Francisco: W. H. Freeman.

Piaget, J. (1950). *The psychology of intelligence.* New York: Harcourt, Brace, Jovanovich.

Rusch, F. R., & Phelps, L. A. (1987). Secondary special education and transition from school to work: A national priority. *Exceptional Children, 53*(6), 487–492.

Spencer, H. (1881). *Education: Intellectual, moral, and physical.* New York: Appleton.

Stephens, T. M. (1978). *Social skills in the classroom.* Columbus: Cedar Press.

U.S. Office of Education. (1976). *The education of adolescents.* Washington, DC: U.S. Government Printing Office.

Waugh, J., et al. (1982). *Assessment and curriculum guide for special students.* Fort Dodge, IA: Arrowhead Area Education Agency and Learning Research Center: Iowa Central Community College (ERIC Document Reproduction Service No. ED 228 402).

Will, M. (1984, March–April). Bridges from school to working life. *Programs for the Handicapped.* Washington, DC: Clearinghouse on the Handicapped.

Youth and America's Future: The William T. Grant Commission on Work, Family, and Citizenship. (1988). *The forgotten half: Pathways to success for America's youth and young families.* Washington, DC.

CHAPTER 3

Assessment for Instructional Planning

When teaching is driven by individualized assessment results, deciding what to teach and finding a stimulating introduction to content can be based on student need rather than whim or chance. In this chapter assessment as an integral part of the teaching process is examined in detail. Assessment of students' needs—of how far they have come in acquiring basic academic and vocation-related skills—lets the teacher intelligently plan a mode of delivery. Assessment may be viewed as a bridge to setting annual and short-term objectives. For the teacher of secondary mildly handicapped students, the other important function of assessment is the monitoring of individual student progress. This chapter focuses on those two functions and includes samples of both diagnostic and evaluative reports. Not overlooked are the issues in assessment that are important to all educators. The special focus here is on the Curriculum Based Assessment approach, which is an application of the Diagnostic-Prescriptive Teaching process (presented in Chapter 4). Rationale, guidelines, and specific examples are included.

As the body of knowledge grows, teachers are increasingly adopting the perspective that it is not only possible but desirable to provide equal educational opportunities for all students geared to their individual needs, interests, and career goals. In special education, this ideal is being addressed through individualized instruction. As special education and regular education continue to function interdependently, the outcomes include greater individualization of programming for regular education students and an educational environment closer to normal for handicapped students. For all students, the rationale for intervention becomes grounded in a data-based approach.

WHAT IS ASSESSMENT?

Assessment is the process of collecting and interpreting relevant educational information about a student. Scores from screening instruments, checklists, normative tests, and criterion-referenced tests often become part of the assessment collection. Assessment information may also include anecdotal reports, developmental histories, educational histories, medical reports, psychological reports, and other information that will be used to help the student succeed in school.

Testing is a subset of assessment. When test instruments are administered and scored, testing is complete. The sole product of testing is a score or collection of scores, which may include hearing, vision, behavior, aptitude, and achievement. Test instruments may be administered individually or to groups and may be used for various purposes. In any event, tests have educational relevance only *after they are interpreted*, which is a function of assessment.

Assessment is conducted for five major purposes. Secondary special education teachers are most concerned with assessment that can be used to provide direct services to students. The purposes of assessment are:

1. Screening. A regular education function, screening is conducted to determine who is at risk in the areas of vision, hearing, aptitude, achievement, and psychomotor skills. Secondary special educators are not often involved with screening. For a more thorough discussion, see Salvia and Ysseldyke (1988).
2. Classification/Eligibility for Special Education. PL 94-142 has specific guidelines for determining and maintaining eligibility for special education. Operationalization of these guidelines may be found in state plans. Because of its more administrative nature, a discussion of eligibility is beyond the scope of this text.
3. Educational Planning. How does a teacher derive lesson plans from assessment data? This part of the teaching process is addressed in Individualized Educational Program (IEP) development, mandated by PL 94-142 to serve students with specific needs that go beyond the curriculum. One of the most promising ways is through Curriculum-Based Assessment (Bigge, 1988; Gickling & Havertape, 1987), which is discussed later in this chapter.
4. Monitoring Individual Student Progress. Once lesson plans are written, it is up to the teacher to carry them out. After that, it is necessary to judge the effectiveness of each plan by monitoring individual student progress. Lesson plans are then modified as needed. Because it was developed with a focus on practicality, Curriculum-Based Assessment (CBA) is a good choice for documenting individual progress.
5. Program Evaluation. Summative in nature, program evaluation determines the efficacy of a program such as the strategies-intervention approach. Curriculum, methods, materials, and activities are included in this comprehensive evaluation. Whether or not the program is viable for groups or for types of handicapped students is investigated. Further discussion may be found in Maher and Bennett (1984), Howe (1981), and Gagne and Briggs (1979).

The overriding purpose of assessment is to help students succeed in school. Nothing is more important than this. A role that all special educators must play is that of student advocate. To function most efficiently in this role, it is critical to be aware of what assessment can do, the responsibilities of those who engage in it, and the dangers inherent in it. What is done at any point in assessment may affect the student for the rest of his or her life. This is a tremendous responsibility and must not be taken lightly by any educator.

School success leads to later success in adult life. Success in special and regular education is dependent on the ability of educators to understand individual performances, to acquire information that will assist with the resolution of presenting problems, and to make decisions. The results of assessment are used to determine what is needed in each of those areas.

Formal assessment is routinely performed in the affective, cognitive, and psychomotor domains, which were among the dimensions examined in Chapter 2. When psychological tests are used to resolve educational problems, the result is a psychoeducational assessment. This often occurs in the areas of aptitude, achievement, and personality. Aptitude is most often associated with the concept of potential or intelligence quotient (IQ), achievement with performance in various subject areas, and personality with adaptive behavior. *Informal assessment* is also part of the total assessment process. It occurs most often in areas directly associated with the curriculum. Teachers must know what specific objectives students have and have not mastered so that lesson plans can be constructed. How this process occurs is guided by a set of ethics that every educator should follow.

ETHICAL CONSIDERATIONS

In any discussion on assessment, ethics must be included. Ethics guides practitioners in what they should and should not do. The American Psychological Association (1979) has developed a set of ethics almost universally recognized and accepted in practice. Ten ethics are included in the set, of which eight are relevant to the special educator. All educators who are involved in assessment or testing should observe these ethics. They are a guide to best practices and are consistent with legal obligations assumed by those who engage in testing. The eight areas of concern in special needs assessment are:

1. Responsibility. Those who assess alter the lives of others. They must accept responsibility for the consequences of their acts and make every effort to insure that their services are used appropriately. In order of priority when issues of conflict of interest arise, examiners are primarily responsible to their discipline and clients first and then to their employing agencies.
2. Competence. Those who assess render only those services they are qualified to provide by training and experience. For educators, this means that a student must not be punished or misplaced as a result of the assessment process. As individuals, those who assess do not test a student if the presenting problem (i.e., reason for referral) is beyond their professional ability. The welfare of the student comes first.
3. Moral and Legal Standards. Those who assess must always consider the

effect their personal behavior could have on their educational responsibilities. One's ability to practice effectively is directly related to credibility and reputation. Practitioners must also be conscientious to affirm policies of fairness and nondiscrimination.

4. Public Statements. Discussions of qualifications and services provided must be made so that consumers of the services will be able to make fair and informed choices.

5. Confidentiality. Those who assess work in the best interests of their clients. Test results are confidential and may only be used for their stated purposes. Release of test results to third parties is allowed only upon written consent of the student, parent, or guardian.

6. Welfare of the Consumer. Those who assess respect the integrity and protect the welfare of the students and parents with whom they work. Services are terminated when they are no longer necessary or productive.

7. Professional Relationships. Those who assess respect the prerogatives and obligations of other practitioners and their institutions. They make full use of resources that serve the best interests of students.

8. Assessment Techniques. The welfare and best interests of the student must be protected. Before testing, the practitioner determines what is to be gained from the proposed test and why testing in this area is being done. "What more will you know than you knew before you started testing?" and "How will this help?" are the questions that should always be answered satisfactorily before testing begins.

The Dangers of Testing

Ethics protects students from the dangers associated with misuse or abuse of tests. Considerable controversy has been associated with testing because of past experience and the ever-present potential it has to affect students adversely for the rest of their lives. With this in mind, the ethical educator is especially cognizant of four specific dangers (Salvia & Ysseldyke, 1988).

1. Invasion of Privacy. Only areas that directly impact on educational progress are to be assessed. The one exception to this rule is the mandated reporting of child abuse that exists in most states.

2. Invasion of Confidentiality of Results. In too many schools, it is possible to follow educators in the hallways or sit in the teachers' lounge and overhear some interesting discussions about students. Only those who have a need to know are privy to test results. Everyone else is considered to be a third party and must get written permission from the student, parent, or guardian before test results can be released.

3. Creation of Anxiety. In testing, the examiner accepts student responses. It is important to withhold judgment until the results are in and evaluated. Emotion-laden terms should not be used to report results, and the examiner must maintain good working relationships with all parties involved

4. Negative Implications of Invalid Results. A normally functioning student who is incorrectly labeled as handicapped receives an inappropriate education. This violates his or her constitutional rights to pursue life, liberty, and property, an offense of the most serious nature. The issue of educational malpractice is increasingly debated as education becomes more professionalized. Although it is the responsibility of students to learn, educators must provide atmospheres in which learning can take place. In the case of a handicapped student, the provision of a free, appropriate, public education is guaranteed.

Everyone involved in the assessment process must realize that testing affirms or refutes the teacher's clinical judgment about a student. When testing results are in conflict with teacher judgment, further investigation must be done to resolve the discrepancies and insure the student fair treatment. Tests are not infallible. To be valid, tests must meet five assumptions (Salvia & Ysseldyke, 1988).

1. Skilled tester. Four criteria are necessary to meet this assumption. The examiner must have the ability to develop rapport, provide a standardized test administration, score the test properly, and interpret the results correctly.
2. Errors will be present. All tests contain errors. Scores that are derived from testing should never be thought of as absolute. With formal tests, the most accurate way to report results is with a range of scores in which the true score is thought to be captured (Horvath, 1985). This is a question about the reliability of a test.
3. Acculturation is comparable. This boils down to one question: On a normed test, does the student who is being tested have a similar experiential background as those students on whom the test was normed? It is the responsibility of the person who administers the test to make this determination.
4. Adequate behavior sampling. Two areas are considered in this assumption. The first is that there will be enough items to draw conclusions about the student's proficiency in any given skill area. The second is that the items will actually measure what the authors claim it measures. This is a question of the validity of the test.
5. Present behavior is observed. Future behavior is inferred. Testing samples a slice of behavior at a given time. From that sample, predictions are often made about behavior that will occur at a later time. Because of the complexity of human behavior, it is important to remember that prediction is an inexact undertaking. Students change. They bloom late, lose their motivation, fall in love, or are affected by the myriad of other variables inherent in everyone's lives.

The most powerful diagnostic procedures combine clinical judgment with testing. Neither clinical judgment nor testing by itself is sufficient to determine the educational fate of a student. Educational intervention must be based on a careful evaluation of all quantitative and qualitative data that are relevant to the delivery of instruction.

REPORTING THE RESULTS

Because the assessment process is highly individualized, each report will reflect the differences inherent in meeting the needs of individual students. Not all reports need to contain all possible components. The concern is that each report will be useful to those who are its consumers—direct service providers. Goals, objectives, and lesson plans are the outcomes of report writing. To achieve that, the diagnostic report must be practical.

A complete diagnostic prescriptive assessment report includes nine components (Horvath, 1985).

1. Personal Data. Name, address, date of birth, and other relevant information are collected here. It is important to date each report.
2. Presenting Problem. This is a statement of the educational and/or behavioral problem or problems the student is experiencing. More specific statements help those who provide service direct access to necessary remedial strategies.
3. Background Information. Observable facts may be presented in three areas: family background, physical and developmental history, and school history. It is sometimes useful to know what has occurred in the life of a student, what has been tried previously, and what the results have been.
4. Prior Testing. Curricular changes may lead to demands for which the student may not be equipped to cope. This may be shown in the test history. Information about learning style, motivation, and methodology may be useful in educational planning.
5. Present Testing. Scores should be reported as completely as possible. If the test is norm referenced, standard scores such as percentiles should be reported for the total test and each of the subtests. Date of the test and the student's chronological age should be reported also. For criterion-referenced testing, a complete description of what objectives the student has and has not mastered should be provided.
6. Clinical Observations. Traits such as test behavior, reaction to stress, emotional involvement, hidden abilities, relevant personal assets and deficits, and motivation are reported.
7. Interpretation. This section answers the question of why the student behaves in such a way as to call attention to the behavior. Student performance is described as a function of the examiner's theoretical orientation in a way that is understandable to those who are likely to read the report.
8. Diagnosis. What label can be applied to the student and why? Any consistencies that appear as part of the assessment process should be discussed.
9. Recommendations. This is a critical part of any report. Educationally relevant solutions to deal with the presenting problem(s) are proposed. Specific methods and materials are described in detail. Direct service providers should find enough guidance here to either write goals, objectives, and lesson plans or proceed to informal assessment activities that are the forerunners of lesson plans. See Appendix 3.1 at the end of this chapter for an

example of a diagnostic/prescriptive assessment report; study questions are included to guide you in use of the report.

Once the development of goals, objectives, and lesson plans in each subject area is accomplished, lessons can be delivered and individual student progress monitored. The rest of this chapter focuses on educational planning and the monitoring of individual student progress.

USING ASSESSMENT TO TEACH

Norm-referenced testing gives the teacher an approximate starting point for criterion-referenced testing, which helps the teacher make day-to-day decisions about what to do. (Norm-referenced tests give results measured against predetermined answers gathered by looking at how groups of other students answered these questions. Against these knowns one sets up criteria based on the needs of the population being tested with criterion reference.) The whole teaching process is a test-teach-test-teach cycle (Lerner, 1985), a formative or ongoing attempt to provide relevant instruction.

Present Level of Functioning and the Curriculum

The present-level-of-functioning component on the Individualized Education Program (IEP) is required by PL 94-142 and good teaching practices. Appendix 3.2 at the end of this chapter is an example of a present-level-of-functioning statement; it is based on the Appendix 3.1 diagnostic precriptive assessment report on Sidney Johnson. (Some of the other required components of an IEP include the duration of services, amount of time spent in regular education, goals and objectives stated objectively, related services to be provided, and who is responsible for delivery of services.)

Present functioning is a summary of assessment results. For the teacher, this section is critically important because it is the real basis for developing goals, objectives, and lesson plans. A viable present-level-of-functioning section is derived from the diagnostic/prescriptive assessment report and additional information collected by the multidisciplinary team; special education teachers usually take primary responsibility for this section. Its greatest usefulness is in stating what the student has mastered and has not mastered in relation to the curriculum in each area. The first step, then, is to have a curriculum in place.

The development of a curriculum is not meant to be the absolute rule of what is to be taught. Rather, it gives focus to what the teacher is trying to do and gives others an idea of what is planned. As the student progresses, this curriculum can be used as an outline of a history of what has been taught.

Smith and Payne (1980) proposed a secondary curriculum composed of six major sections.

I. Language Arts
   A. Reading
   B. Verbal expression

      C. Written expression
      D. Spelling
  II. Mathematics
      A. Computation
      B. Application
 III. Social, Emotional, Personal
      A. Family life
  IV. Career/Vocational
   V. Physical Education
  VI. Survival Skills
      A. Consumer skills
      B. Daily living skills
      C. Leisure skills

For secondary students, it may be more realistic to infuse elements of the Smith and Payne curriculum into their existing curriculum to assess how the student is doing. This infusion will allow the teacher to measure the skill levels attained in these areas by the student.

Setting Goals and Objectives

Goals flow from the present-level-of-functioning section of the Individualized Education Program, reflect the existing curriculum, and encompass a one-year time frame. One method for goal writing is to use an increase/decrease + from + to + measurement formula. This is a refinement of the long-term-objective format proposed by Thompson (1977). An example of this is: The student will increase employability skills from the ability to follow two-step directions and use basic psychometric skills to the ability to use hand tools in the designated work situations, as measured by the percentage of successfully finished products in a given time frame.

    Objectives for individualized educational programs can be thought of as units of instruction (Meyen, 1980), each encompassing a one-to-nine-week period. Three to eight objectives can be written for each goal. As with goals, objectives are written to reflect the existing curriculum. Complete objectives contain four elements (Leles & Bernabie, 1969).

1. A description of the conditions under which the desired behavior will be demonstrated, for example, given a sheet of fifty sentences, each containing one punctuation error, . . .
2. A description of the learner, for example, the 7th-grade educable mentally retarded (EMR) student . . .
3. The specific behavior to be elicited, for example, . . . will write the correct punctuation . . .
4. Criterion for acceptable performance, for example, . . . with 90 percent accuracy within a five-minute period . . .

The complete objective: Given a sheet of fifty sentences, the seventh-grade EMR student will write the correct punctuation with 90 percent accuracy within a five-minute period. Often a description of the learner is omitted because it is assumed that this is redundant.

Lesson Plans

From the goals and objectives required by the Individualized Educational Program, the teacher should be able to construct daily lesson plans. These plans are required by good teaching practice but are not mandated as part of the IEP process. Lesson plans are highly individualistic but should contain specific objectives that describe student behavior, are objectively written, and communicate to others what is expected from the student. Note that when teachers list page numbers as guidelines to teaching, it is a shorthand way to refer to objectives. The pages are never objectives in themselves but only represent the objectives that appear on the pages.

One danger in using workbooks is that there are often several skills presented on one page. The discerning teacher must be careful to cull from the page only those items that match the objective(s) that the student is currently attempting to master.

How the educator moves from assessment to lesson plans is further studied in Chapter 4, which presents several instructional models.

CURRICULUM-BASED ASSESSMENT

The gathering of data and its use in planning and decision making are crucial in teaching. One data-based approach that has been found to be successful is Curriculum-Based Assessment (CBA). It goes hand in hand with the generic diagnostic/prescriptive teaching process that is presented in Chapter 4. Gickling and Havertape (1981) defined *CBA* as "a procedure for determining the instructional needs of a student based on the student's ongoing performance in existing course content" (p. R4). To reflect more fully the importance of the teacher's ability to match student skills to task demands and thereby decrease curriculum casualties, Gickling (1988, personal communication) redefined *CBA* as "a system for determining the instructional needs of a student based upon the student's ongoing performance within existing course content and for delivering instruction as effectively and efficiently as possible to meet those needs." This is accomplished by challenging each student at his or her instructional level, a type of individualization based on placement of students in their proper places in the curriculum.

At the secondary level, it is not possible to excuse a student from competencies or courses required for graduation. One option is to adjust the reading level to the student's instructional level without reducing the content. The resulting instructional match offers students tasks that are sufficiently familiar but challenging enough to provide optimal learning. Gickling and Havertape (1981) divided instruction into two basic types of activities: reading and drill. *Reading* is the recognition of words in context and the accompanying comprehension of the meaning of what is read. *Drill* is anything that is not reading and includes computational skills, writing and spelling activities, science, social studies, responses to teacher questions, and even the subskill areas of reading such as phonics instruction, word-attack procedures, and sight word recognition.

Figure 3.1 is the Instructional Delivery Model developed by Gickling (1977). The model contends that an optimal teaching/learning condition exists in reading when the student knows a minimum of 93–97 percent of the words. One is challenged by no more than 3–7 percent of new words and maintains a minimum of 75 percent comprehension. When these conditions exist, the student is on his or her instructional level and a good instructional match has been made. To accomplish this, a teacher may have to rewrite the text or, if the curriculum is a spiral one, have the student read from a lower grade level reader supplemented by lecture and class discussion. Rather than reinventing the wheel and constructing a new curriculum, the existing curriculum is modified. The CBA focuses on student performance in the regular curriculum.

In drill activities, the student is challenged and a good instructional match occurs when 15–30 percent of the words are hesitants or unknowns (hesitants and unknowns together are called areas of challenge). This is depicted in Figure 3.2. Curricular studies indicate that average and above-average students are challenged at their instructional levels or independent levels in the existing curriculum at these rates. Slow learners and mildly handicapped students, however, experience frustration by being required by the curriculum to function at much lower rates. The CBA adjusts the curriculum so that every student functions at the appropriate instructional level.

To illustrate how assessment works in actual practice, Curriculum-Based Assessments (CBAs) in reading, mathematics, and language arts are presented next. Following this, assessment in the areas of career education and social skills is discussed.

Figure 3.1. Instructional Delivery Model

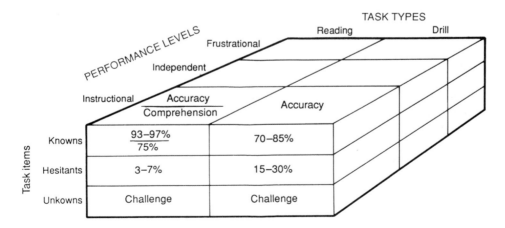

Source: E. E. Gickling. (1977). Controlling academic and social performance using an instructional delivery model. *Programs for the emotionally handicapped: Administrative considerations.* Washington, DC: Coordinating Office of the Regional Resource Centers.

Figure 3.2. Maintaining a Good Instructional Match

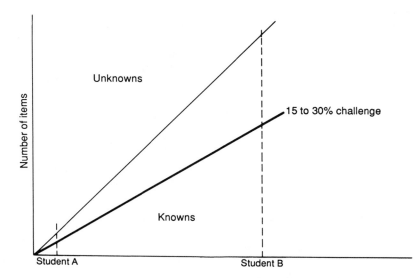

Source: E. E. Gickling and J. F. Havertape. (1981). Curriculum-based assessment, in J. A. Tucker (Ed.), *Non-test-based assessment: A training module.* Minneapolis: National School Psychologist Inservice Training Network, University of Minnesota.

Figure 3.3 depicts the steps leading to mastery (Gickling & Thompson, 1988). The course of instruction occurs over three steps or stages. The first stage is exposure. New concepts and content are presented. The second stage is accuracy. Systematic drill is provided. The third stage is automaticity. Practice to achieve habituation of the skill is offered.

To summarize, here are the basic principles upon which the CBA was founded, as listed by Gickling and Havertape (1987):

CBA aligns assessment practices with what is actually taught in the classroom.
CBA starts instruction with what a student knows.
CBA controls the task variability, demand, and pace of instruction.
CBA strives for uniformity among students' scores.
CBA enhances student success by structuring optimum learning conditions.
CBA allows for the direct measurement of student progress.

Reading CBA

One complaint about many secondary programs for the mildly handicapped is that they are upward extensions of the basic skill programs found at the elementary levels. Whereas the focus of their nonhandicapped peers shifts to content skills, handicapped

Figure 3.3. Steps Leading to Mastery

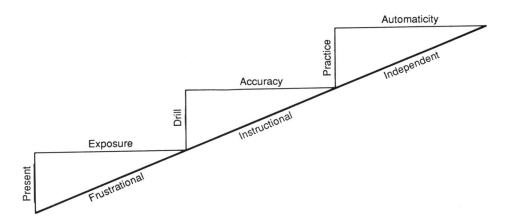

Source: E. E. Gickling and V. P. Thompson. "Optimizing instruction via curriculum-based assessment." Paper presented at the 66th Annual Convention of the Council for Exceptional Children, Washington D.C., March 1988. Reprinted by permission.

learners may continue to learn their arithmetic tables, spell words from the Dolch list, or formulate manuscript letters.

The continuation of reading instruction at the secondary level is justifiable because of its importance. Educators are fond of saying that success in school ultimately depends on one's ability to read. This is magnified at the secondary level because so much of what is learned is acquired through the derivation of meaning from the printed page. Reading is important, and no one questions the need to develop greater reading proficiency. How to achieve the reading goals is where the controversy lies. A look at successful programs for the mildly handicapped indicates that most success occurs when the model used is something other than a basic skills approach. Reading has to be taught in the context of the content areas that the student is required to take. If the student is capable, it is better to develop greater reading proficiency through practice in the assigned geography materials than in a flashcard drill and practice session on isolated nouns. One way to accomplish this is through a strategies-intervention approach, discussed in Chapter 4, combined with the CBA. By having several options, the teacher will be able to balance the demands for passing tests in regular classes, making progress in reading and developing the functional skills necessary for greater success beyond the school years.

There are three steps in a CBA for reading (Gickling & Havertape, 1987; Gickling & Thompson, 1988). The whole process is designed to emphasize task success. With the CBA, the student is challenged at his or her presumed instructional level in the testing phase and taught from the same materials. Teachers often say that assessment is too traumatic for students because it frustrates them tremendously and the resulting carryover into instruction leads to low achievement and affective resistance. The CBA offers a way to assess without the resulting student anxiety.

1. Select a Workable Passage. Photocopy several pages from the assigned text or from optional texts if necessary. Conduct a word search by selectively pointing to several words of varying difficulty and asking the student to read them. Ask the student to define selected words. Word search has a threefold purpose: to check for sight vocabulary, to check for word-recognition strategies, and to check for word meaning. If the level of challenge (number of hesitants and unknowns) does not exceed the student's ability to comprehend the passage, the passage is workable. If the error rate is not too excessive, the passage is workable.

2. Sample Oral and/or Silent Reading. Time and record the number of words read per minute. Deno (1985) suggested one-minute probes, but this is up to the teacher. In oral reading, note the known words and monitor word-recognition errors. In silent reading, observe student mannerisms. During the sample, it is important to get the student to verbalize about the task to determine student understanding in three areas:
   a. Check for prior knowledge and vocabulary.
   b. Determine basic recall information regarding who, what, when, where, and how.
   c. Determine use of metacognitive strategies used before, during, and after reading.

3. Teach to the Passage Adjusting to Student Need. The teacher has six tasks to accomplish:
   a. Establish the purpose for reading by encouraging questioning and predicting.
   b. Develop word accuracy by "sandwiching" unknown words among those that are known.
   c. Build basic vocabulary understanding.
   d. Practice phrasing techniques for fluency.
   e. Reread for holistic practice.
   f. Repeat timed reading samples to measure again.

By the time a nonhandicapped student enters 7th grade, the expectation is that he or she will be able to read orally more than 160 words per minute. Expected sight-word vocabulary for this student is more than 8,000 words. Mildly handicapped students do not often meet these expectations. No wonder so much of the effort at this level focuses on reading instruction. It is the key to success in all areas of the secondary curriculum.

Mathematics CBA

Next to reading, mathematics instruction presents the greatest challenges in teaching. Blankenship (1985) presented a series of eleven steps for general CBA and a sample mathematics CBA.

   1. List the skills presented in the material selected.
   2. Examine the list to see if all important skills are presented. This step

determines if the material selected matches the goals, objectives, and lesson plans selected for instruction. If not, it will be necessary to modify the materials accordingly.

3. Decide if the resulting, edited list has skills in logical order. Rearrange as needed.
4. Write an objective for each skill on the list.
5. Prepare items to test each listed objective.
6. Prepare testing materials for student use.
7. Plan how the CBA will be given.
9. Determine degree of mastery of prerequisite skills and target skills.
10. After instruction, readminister the CBA. Evaluate the progress and modify instruction as needed.
11. Assess for long-term retention of material by periodically readministering the CBA during the year.

In her example of a mathematics CBA, Blankenship presented information on metric measurement. Although the instruction was aimed at 4th graders, this task is appropriate for many secondary students. The teacher first made a list of all skills that were presented in a chapter on metric measurement. After making sure that the skills presented were completed and logically arranged, she wrote objectives for the skills she wanted to assess. The next steps were to prepare test items and put them in a form for student use. This was done with dittoed sheets that contained problems for each objective. Before the test was given, the teacher planned the schedule and administered the test before instruction began. Intervention planning was done after an analysis of the test results revealed the degree of mastery exhibited on the test items. After instruction, the teacher used an alternate form of the test to check progress. Once sufficient mastery had been achieved, the teacher moved on to other objectives and periodically checked to be sure metric-measurement skills had been retained.

Gickling and Havertape (1981) recommended task analysis and product analysis in their mathematics-curriculum-based assessment. The goal is to get to assignments on the instructional level of students. As in reading, direct assessment provides data that can immediately be converted into curriculum decisions.

Task analysis is defined by Gickling and Havertape as "the enumeration of the sequence of prerequisite skills necessary to complete the task(s) successfully" (1981, p. R29). By breaking a task into its component parts and checking for student mastery of each part, missing concepts, facts, or procedures are located. The teacher then provides instruction in the deficit areas until the student is able to complete the task sequence.

Product analysis includes error analysis (Ashlock, 1972) and other informal procedures designed to determine how a student arrives at an outcome. A wide range of latitude exists in error analysis. Ashlock (1972) described more than twenty-five types of errors that students make. Gickling and Havertape proposed a list of four common sources of error: using wrong operations, using incorrect algorithms, problems with place value, and random responses and assumptions. Each teacher will have to decide which items will be analyzed. Other informal product analysis procedures include: examination of completed assignments, interviews regarding responses, and an assessment of the suitability and ease of student performance, measured by the rate of fluency (proficiency or speed).

After having gone through either task analysis or product analysis or both, the teacher is ready to provide instruction derived directly from the curriculum. Students are given assignments at their instructional level. In the case of mathematics, the problems provided should include 70–85 percent known items and 15–30 percent challenge items as depicted in Figure 3.4. As in reading, the teacher should provide instruction that displays a high number of known items in relation to the number of challenging items for each student assignment.

Language-Arts CBA

For each area of the curriculum, daily progress should be monitored in the areas of acquisition rate, fluency rate, and knowledge and comprehension (Gickling & Havertape, 1981). The teacher must determine what the student can learn and retain from each day's instruction and set the level of challenge just slightly above that rate. Collecting baseline data will help to determine the initial level of challenge, but this will change over time as the student develops greater proficiency in learning. Intervention may take the form of curriculum challenges and learning strategies designed to boost student success.

As student success increases, one of the differences will be a change in student rate of fluency. A faster response time will be noted. The student will also seem to feel more comfortable with the material, and this increased confidence will translate into a greater willingness to take the chances and make the inferences successfully, both of which are characteristics of good learners.

Drills in spelling, writing, and other language-arts skills are necessary to achieve

Figure 3.4. Instructional Delivery Model—Mathematics

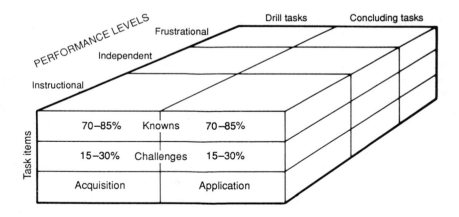

Source: E. E. Gickling and J. F. Havertape. (1981). Curriculum-based assessment, in J. A. Tucker (Ed.), *Non-test-based assessment: A training module.* Minneapolis: National School Psychologist Inservice Training Network, University of Minnesota.

acquisition and fluency. As a means to the end of knowledge and comprehension, it is often necessary to engage students in drill activities that may appear meaningless to the student. Depending on the needs of the students, at some time in the sequence of instruction it will be necessary to teach for understanding of why the instruction is being provided and to what end the instruction can be used. For some students, this will be most appropriate at the beginning of instruction. Others may be more comfortable practicing a skill before discovering how it can be used to advantage. It is important that the teacher be attuned to student need in this area and remember that learning proceeds in stages from acquisition to maintenance to generalization (Smith & Payne, 1980).

CAREER ASSESSMENT

Curriculum-Based Assessment can also be used with all career-education curricula. To get to the level of readiness expected by employers, students should go through one of the available career-education programs, which can be infused into the existing curriculum. Assessment consists of checking to see if curricular items have been mastered. As with all teaching, a curriculum must exist, a student must be placed somewhere within it, and records of progress must be maintained to assist in the decision-making process. Good starting points are the elementary education curriculum of Clark (1979), the life-management curriculum of Bigge (1988), the career-education curriculum competencies of Brolin (1976) and Brolin and Kokaska (1979), and the awareness, exploration, and preparation stages of Phelps and Lutz (1977).

The life-management curriculum includes the areas of domestic and family living, education, community living, work, and communication. Brolin (1976) and Brolin and Kokaska (1979) presented a different curriculum based on twenty-two competencies. No matter what approach is used, career education should start as early as possible (Clark, 1979). Secondary programming in an ideal world should be a continuation of programming started in the preschool years. Phelps and Lutz (1977) described a career education approach that includes the three phases of awareness, exploration, and preparation. Exploration starts with the junior high or middle school years. Preparation is reserved for the high school years.

Assessment considerations ultimately involve a student's readiness to exhibit necessary functional skills. Burton and Bero (1984) surveyed employers to determine skills they perceived as important among handicapped employees and problems that those employees brought to the workplace. The results are reproduced in Figure 3.5.

Since the creation and implementation of PL 94-142, a common complaint among special education teachers is the questionable value of the individual education plan; that is, considering the time that is spent preparing them, do they really have a purpose?

The utility of the IEP at the secondary level may have become greater since the passage of the Carl Perkins' Vocational Education Amendments in 1989 (see Chapter 8). Among the elements of the law is the need to show progress toward employment. This can be done if a curriculum is in place and a student's progress is measured regularly against the expected skills.

Figure 3.5. Employer Expectations and Problems

Expectations	*Problems*
Get along with people.	Nonpunctual
Communicate with public.	Difficulty communicating with public
Be on time/dependable.	Lack of transportation
Stand on feet/stamina.	Lack of respect for supervision
Cope with stress/work under pressure.	Inflexibility
Care about the job.	Lack of endurance
Be willing to learn.	No enthusiasm for the job
Be neat and clean.	Social life interferes
Be able to load, stack, and/or stuff.	Unable to move quickly
Have common sense.	Poor physical coordination and strength

Source: L. Burton and F. Bero. (1984, March). Is career education really being taught? A second look. *Academic Therapy, 19*(4), 389–395.

Such a system has been in place for more than three years in the special education program at United Township High School. Upon completion of a course, students are evaluated on the skills taught or outcomes they are expected to have mastered. The student is evaluated on general skills (i.e., ability to follow directions, work cooperatively, be prepared) that extend beyond a content area.

The system is beneficial to the teachers, the students, and the students' parents in that it provides information on a student's current knowledge and progress within the curriculum. Beyond the content areas a student can be compared on generalized skills that have been determined important for employment.

Formal assessment in the vocational education area is often helpful. A representative list of instruments that may be helpful for secondary teachers to know includes:

1. Comprehensive Occupational Assessment and Training System (COATS), by Prep, Inc., 1575 Parkway Avenue, Trenton, NJ 08628. Designed for secondary students, COATS has four components with twenty-six work samples. Administration time is between fifty-two and ninety-three hours. Directions are specific and presented in audiovisual fashion. No training is required to administer COATS, and clients time themselves. The test gives occupational information that can be used to design programs of study.
2. McCarren-Dial Work Evaluation System by McCarren-Dial Systems, P.O. Box 45628, Dallas, TX 75245. Designed for the mentally ill, mentally retarded, and learning disabled, this test is composed of five areas with seventeen work samples. It is administered over a two-week period. Directions are clear, but training before administration is required. Although it is timed, quality is more heavily weighted in score determination. This test is technically adequate.
3. Philadelphia Jewish Employment Service Work Sample System (JEVS), Vocational Information and Evaluation Work Samples (VIEWS), and Vocational Interest Temperament and Aptitude System (VITAS) by Vocational Research Institute, Jewish Employment and Vocational Service, 1700 Sansom Street,

9th Floor, Philadelphia, PA 19103. Designed respectively for the disadvantaged, mentally retarded, and employment-service applicants, these tests are related to the U.S. Department of Labor *Dictionary of Occupational Titles* (DOT) classification system. Each has several work samples, and each requires training before administration. The JEVS takes six to seven days to administer, VIEWS can take up to thirty-five hours, and VITAS requires fifteen hours. Tasks are realistic, directions are clear, and both time and quality receive equal weight in scoring.

4. Singer Vocational Evaluation System by Singer Educational Division, Career Systems, 80 Commercial Drive, Rochester, NY 14623. Designed for the special needs population, Singer contains twenty-five work samples. Supplies to replenish those used during administration can be obtained locally. Each sample requires two and a half hours to complete, and directions are clear. No training is required to administer the test. Time and quality are weighted equally in scoring. Extensive client involvement is required. Information on twenty factors is provided.

5. Talent Assessment Programs (TAP) by Talent Assessment, Inc., P.O. Box 5087, Jacksonville, FL 32207. Designed for 14-year-old and older mildly handicapped and normal students, the TAP contains ten work samples and takes about two and a half hours to administer. Directions are general. The client is timed, and time is most heavily weighted in scoring. Training is required before one can administer this test. Counselors will probably get the greatest benefit from the results.

6. Tower System (and also Micro-Tower) by ICD Rehabilitation and Research Center, 340 East 24th Street, New York, NY 10010. Designed respectively for the physically/emotionally disabled and the general rehabilitation population, Tower and Micro-Tower are somewhat different. Tower contains ninety-three work samples divided into fourteen areas and takes three weeks to complete. It is a comprehensive test that requires three weeks of training before one is qualified in its administration. Specific directions are provided, and the examiner is requested to make frequent observations. Micro-Tower contains thirteen work samples divided into five groups and requires about twenty hours to complete. It is related to the DOT classification system, and all supplies can be obtained locally. No training is required to administer Micro-Tower. Directions are provided on audiocassette and are clear. Samples are timed, and frequent examiner observation is required.

7. VALPAR Component Work Sample Series by Valpar Corporation, 3801 East 34th Street, Tucson, AZ 85713. Designed for the general population, the VALPAR contains sixteen work samples, each requiring about one hour. Directions are clear. This test is timed, and the client is rated on seventeen factors.

8. Vocational Skills Assessment and Development Program by Brodhead-Garrett Company, 4560 East 71st Street, Cleveland, OH 44105. Designed for the handicapped and disadvantaged, this test contains eighteen work samples. Time and quality are weighted equally. No training is required to administer this test, and it gives information on thirty-six work behaviors.

SOCIAL SKILLS ASSESSMENT

Secondary-aged students as a class are noteworthy for their struggles in the transition into adulthood. Although they are expected to take greater responsibility for their actions and are being held increasingly accountable for their utterances, at times they need the security that childhood guarantees. They are confused, frustrated, and often do not know what they want. Adults around them may not know when to treat a juvenile as an adult or to provide the protective shelter of childhood. Adolescents are striving to assert their independence at the same time the herd instinct is strongest.

The struggle to reconcile locus-of-control problems is often evident. *Locus of control* may be thought of as the perceived ability of individuals to influence outcomes as a direct result of actions on their part. Adolescents may sometimes feel that nothing they do makes a difference in their lives. Mood shifts, depression, and helplessness may be noted. Teens may develop an attitude of fatalism and extreme passivity as the result. Ultimately, they have to learn to regulate their attitudes depending upon situations that they encounter. Each person must learn to be the captain of the ship or drift with the tide as required.

Secondary students may not mean to be insulting but sometimes lack the social skills to know when they are hurting those around them. Some teachers even view their adolescent students as similar to the behavior disordered. The idea is that the acts of behavior-disordered students are a function of the handicapping condition and not the real person inside. In the case of juveniles, the behavior is a function of the hormones and not the real person struggling to emerge.

Besides social awkwardness, teenagers appear to be gangly, uncoordinated creatures with limbs out of proportion to the rest of their bodies. They seem to be at various and unmatched stages of development in the affective, psychomotor, and cognitive domains. Lack of common sense is one of the laments of parents and teachers alike. For mildly handicapped and slow-learning students, the problems may be worse. They often fail to perceive social cues, facial expressions, body language, emotional states, and gestures. Even when social perception is more or less in place, some students do not know how to act in a socially acceptable manner. *Deviant, bizarre, unfeeling,* and *maladroit* are just some of the terms used to describe behavior exhibited by handicapped adolescents.

Deviant behavior is often defined and measured in relation to the perceiver of the behavior. One adult may find behavior intolerable whereas another may not. Assessing and dealing with behavior in the grey area between severely normal and mildly abnormal is a subjective undertaking.

Teachers rightfully assume that their primary role is to provide instruction in the academic realm. Most teachers do not feel as comfortable in the affective domain as they do in the cognitive domain because of the training and experience they have had. Treating deviant social behavior is thought of as a prerequisite to the attainment of additional academic skills. Wise teachers prefer to structure meaningful academic successes so that the frustrated or defensive student can gain self-confidence, enhance self-concept, and motivate himself or herself to higher levels of achievement. For some students, this may be enough. Increasing the levels of academic competency seems to have a positive effect on the development of social skills. For other students, social skills will have to be taught in a systematic fashion.

It is more difficult to assess in the social skills realm than in the academic. Handicapped students often do not learn in an incidental fashion, and the teacher must systematically test every item in the social skills curriculum. Probably, the most appropriate procedure for the teacher to follow is to target a behavior that should be increased or decreased and reward or ignore that behavior as appropriate. Some teachers start with training in self-control (Stephens, Blackhurst, & Magliocca, 1988) as a vehicle for developing better social skills and achieving higher grades. Most experts recommend that no more than two or three behaviors be targeted at one time.

For those who do not feel comfortable with that approach or who have students who have greater needs, other members of the multidisciplinary team may be called on to contribute their expertise in designing a program for social skill enhancement. Attributing the source of the problems solely to the environment or solely to the student is giving way to an ecological approach in which the student is viewed as interacting with the environment (Rhodes & Tracey, 1974). Assessment is comprehensive in that the whole ecology is examined. This may include the use of tests, rating scales, sociograms, projective devices, anecdotal reports, and self-report instruments. For further discussion of these instruments, see Swanson and Watson (1982), Anastasi (1982), and Taylor (1989). Data collected during the ongoing assessment process is then used to design a program in which the teacher may combine forces with other members of the multidisciplinary team and other experts outside the school such as medical and mental health experts.

Developing a social skills curriculum and assessing in this area requires support. Help is provided by Krathwohl, Bloom, and Masia (1964); Kauffman (1985); the Committee on Child Psychiatry of the Group for the Advancement of Psychiatry, commonly referred to as GAP (1966); Kohlberg (1964); Dreikurs (1968); Long, Morse, and Newman (1976); Shea (1978); and Erikson (1968).

SUMMARY

Teaching as a process involves the collection of data from which lessons emerge. Delivery of instruction is a function of assessment, of which testing is a component. To be useful, assessment must be relevant, practical, and conducted in an ethical manner. Ideally, the individualized education program is used in this fashion: assessment results are stated in terms of specific curriculum objectives that have been and have not been mastered in the present-level-of-functioning section. These data are used to write annual goals. One-to-nine-week short-term objectives derived from annual goals are then constructed. These objectives may be thought of as units of instruction.

From the present-level-of-functioning section, goals section, and objectives section of the Individualized Education Program, teachers write daily and weekly lesson plans. This process is based on the assumption that a curriculum is in place before assessment and instruction begin.

At the secondary level, Curriculum-Based Assessment goes hand in hand with the strategies-intervention model presented in Chapter 4. The combination allows students to experience meaningful instruction that will be relevant to them as adults. This chapter described Curriculum-Based Assessment processes for reading, mathematics, and language-arts and components of assessment in the areas of career education and social skills.

The guidelines for developing a curriculum—along with resources that will enable you to use what has been already developed—were explored in this chapter. Specific questions regarding the goal of teaching and the measurement of what has been taught have also been addressed.

STUDY QUESTIONS

1. Why should assessment be used as a basis for teaching?
2. How is testing different from assessment?
3. What is the purpose of an assessment report?
4. What should be included in a useful assessment report?
5. Why are ethics important?
6. What is required in an IEP?
7. What is the role of curriculum in the teaching process?
8. What should be included in goals and objectives?
9. How do you get from assessment to lesson plans?
10. What is Curriculum-Based Assessment?

REFERENCES

Anastasi, A. (1982). *Psychological testing* (5th ed.). New York: Macmillan.

Ashlock, R. B. (1972). *Error patterns in computation*. Columbus: C. E. Merrill.

Bigge, J. (1988). *Curriculum-based instruction for special education students*. Mountain View, CA: Mayfield.

Blankenship, C. S. (1985). Using curriculum-based assessment to make instructional decisions. *Exceptional Children, 52*(3), 233–238.

Boning, R. (1970). *Specific skills series*. Boston: Barnell-Loft.

Brolin, D. E. (1976). *Vocational preparation of retarded citizens*. Columbus: C. E. Merrill.

Brolin, D. E., & Kokaska, C. J. (1979). *Career education for handicapped children and youth*. Columbus: C. E. Merrill.

Burton, L., & Bero, F. (1984, March). Is career education really being taught? A second look. *Academic Therapy, 19*(4), 389–395.

Clark, G. M. (1979). *Career education for the handicapped child in the elementary classroom*. Denver: Love.

Deno, S. (1985). Curriculum-based measurement: The emerging alternative. *Exceptional Children, 52*(3), 219–232.

Dreikurs, R. (1968). *Psychology in the classroom: A manual for teachers* (2nd ed.). New York: Harper & Row.

Erikson, E. (1968) *Identity, youth, and crisis*. New York: Norton.

Gagne, R. M., & Briggs, L. T. (1979). *Principles of instructional design* (2nd ed.). New York: Holt, Rinehart, and Winston.

Gickling E. E. (1977). Controlling academic and social performance using an instructional delivery model. *Programs for the emotionally handicapped: Administrative considerations.* Washington, DC: Coordinating Office of the Regional Resource Centers.

Gickling, E. E., & Havertape, J. F. (1981). Curriculum-based assessment. In J. A. Tucker (Ed.), *Non-test-based assessment: A training module.* Minneapolis: National School Psychologist Inservice Training Network, University of Minnesota.

———. (1987, October). *Curriculum-based assesssment: A task-success approach to instruction.* Workshop presented at the Kansas Council for Exceptional Children Annual Convention, Overland Park, KS.

Gickling, E. E., & Thompson, V. P. (1985). A personal view of curriculum-based assessment. *Exceptional Children, 52*(3), 205–218.

———. (1988, March). Optimizing instruction via curriculum-based assessment. Paper presented at the Sixty-sixth Annual Convention of the Council for Exceptional Children, Washington, DC.

Group for the Advancement of Psychiatry. (1966). *Psychopathological disorder in childhood: Theoretical considerations and a proposed classification.* GAP Report No. 62. Washington, DC.

Horvath, M. J. (1985). *Statistics for educators.* Seattle: Special Child.

Howe, C. E. (1981). *Administration of special education.* Denver: Love.

Kauffman, J. M. (1985). *Characteristics of children's behavior disorders* (3rd ed.). Columbus: C. E. Merrill.

Kohlberg, L. (1964). Development of work character and moral ideology. In M. Hoffman (Ed.), *Review of child development research* (Vol. 1). New York: Russell Sage.

Krathwohl, D., Bloom, B., & Masia, B. (1964). *Taxonomy of educational objectives: Affective domain.* New York: McKay.

Leles, S., & Bernabie, R. (1969). *Writing and using behavioral objectives.* Tuscaloosa, AL: Drake.

Lerner, J. (1985). *Learning disabilities: Theories, diagnosis, and teaching strategies* (4th ed.). Boston: Houghton Mifflin.

Long, N., Morse, W., & Newman, R. (Eds.). (1976). *Conflicts in the classroom: The education of emotionally disturbed children* (3rd ed.). Belmont, CA: Wadsworth.

Maher, C. A., & Bennett, R. E. (1984). *Planning and evaluating special education services.* Englewood Cliffs, NJ: Prentice-Hall.

Meyen, E. L. (1980). *Developing units of instruction: For the regular and special education teacher* (3rd ed.). Dubuque, IA: Wm. C. Brown.

Phelps, L. A., & Lutz, R. J. (1977). *Career exploration and preparation for the special needs learner.* Boston: Allyn & Bacon.

Rhodes, W. C., & Tracey, M. L. (Eds). (1974). *A study of child variance.* Ann Arbor: University of Michigan.

Salvia, J., & Ysseldyke, J. E. (1988). *Assessment in special and remedial education* (4th ed.). Boston: Houghton Mifflin.

Shea, T. M. (1978). *Teaching children and youth with behavioral disorders.* St. Louis: C. V. Mosby.

Smith, J. E., & Payne, J. S. (1980). *Teaching exceptional adolescents.* Columbus: C. E. Merrill.

Stephens, T. M., Blackhurst, A. E., & Magliocca, L. A. (1988). *Teaching mainstreamed students* (2nd ed.). Elmsford, NY: Pergamon.

Swanson, H. L. & Watons, B. L. (1982). *Educational and psychological assessment of exceptional children. Theories, strategies, and applications.* St. Louis: C. V. Mosby.

Taylor, R. L. (1989). *Assessment of exceptional students: Educational and psychological procedures* (2nd ed.) Englewood Cliffs, NJ: Prentice-Hall.

Thompson, D. G. (1977). *Writing long-term and short-term objectives: A painless approach.* Champaign, IL: Research Press.

APPENDIX 3.1. DIAGNOSTIC REPORT: SIDNEY JOHNSON

What follows is a typical report on a student in a special education class. There is a great deal of information in this report, and most of it would be useful in deciding on your curriculum for Sidney. Using some of the following questions, how would you use this report to establish a curriculum for Sidney?

1. What are Sidney's strengths and how would they apply to what he needs in school?
2. How will Sidney perform once he is ready to leave school? What should you be doing now to assist him for the future?
3. Is there any more information you need, and where can you get it?
4. When should another report on Sidney be developed?

Diagnostic/Prescriptive Assessment Report

Name:	Sidney Johnson	Parents:	George C. Johnson
Sex:	Male		Alma Mae Leonard Johnson
Date of Report:	10/27/89	Address:	417 East 10th Street
Grade:	8.2		Some City, ST 01234
Birthdate:	9/25/76	Phone:	634-5789
Current Age:	13-1	School:	Grace Middle School

PRESENTING PROBLEM

Mrs. Johnson reports continuing concern about Sidney's learning skills, reversals, and frustration with academics at home.

BACKGROUND INFORMATION

Sidney is the middle child of three in the Johnson family. He had a complete psychological and educational evaluation in 1985, which showed that Sidney qualified for placement in the learning-disability program. Difficulties in mathematics and written language were evidenced. It was determined that the most appropriate setting at that time was the regular class, based in part on Sidney's success in his regular classes. Sidney has not received any special services other than special reading since grade one. No medical problems other than normal childhood illnesses were reported. Mrs. Johnson had a normal pregnancy and delivery. Both parents agree that Sidney gets along well with his older brother and younger sister.

PRIOR TESTING

In 1985 test results were as follows:

WISC-R

Verbal IQ 103
Performance IQ 95
Full Scale IQ 100   (SEM of 3.14)

Sidney was above average in verbal reasoning, knowledge of how to react in social situations, sequencing, and attention to detail. He was weak in tasks involving verbal expression (vocabulary), problem solving, perceptual organization, work rate, and visual memory.

Woodcock-Johnson Psychoeducational Battery

Slightly below grade level in reading
Instructional level 3.9–5.5 grade levels
Math achievement was significantly below grade level at 4.0, with a range of 2.5–3.7
Writing performance, including spelling and grammar, was severely deficient, with a grade score of 2.9 and an instructional range of 2.6–3.4

Sidney was reported to have exhibited a low frustration tolerance with a high fear of failure.

PRESENT TESTING

Wechsler Intelligence Scale for Children—Revised (WISC-R)
Administered: 10/24/89

Results are similar to those obtained in 1985
Verbal IQ 105   Performance IQ 95
Full Scale IQ 100   (SEM of 3.14)
Sidney is in the normal range of intelligence.

My Self-Checklist

The My Self-Checklist was administered to give insight into how Sidney views himself. A positive self-concept means a person views himself as competent in a school setting and as accepted by classmates and adult school personnel within that setting. On this instrument, a score of 50 reflects a negative self-concept and a score of 100 indicates a very high self-concept. Sidney scored 91, listing more strengths than weaknesses. His response to a statement about self-regard was typical: "If I could change myself, I would . . ." "stay the same."

Peabody Individual Achievement Test (PIAT)
Administered 10/25/89

Grade Subtest	Percentile Equivalent	Standard Rank	Score

Math	7.0	39	96
Reading Recognition	3.9	5	75
Reading Compre-hension	5.3	17	86
Spelling	2.5	Below Norms	
General Information	10.1	67	107
Total Test	5.0	9	80

Sidney's scores on the PIAT indicate a wide range of abilities. Average ability was demonstrated in general knowledge and math, but significantly weaker ability was noted on spelling and reading recognition. His reading comprehension was barely in the average range. During this test, Sidney appeared very uncomfortable. He seemed anxious and frequently held his breath for several seconds when test items were difficult for him.

Jordan Left-Right Reversal Test
Administered: 10/22/89

This test measures number, letter, and word reversals and screens for neurologically caused reading problems. There are two levels. Level I presents letters and numbers, some of which are reversed. The student is required to cross out each letter or number that appears to be backward. Level II requires the student to select from a list of words (e.g., *good wor bab make cat*) the word(s) in which a letter is reversed and then to circle words presented backwards in sentences (e.g., *The dog ran no the grass*). This indicates a visual reversal problem. Sidney's developmental age score on this test is less than 7-0. On Level I, Sidney had two errors with the numeral 9. On Level II, he had five *b/d* reversals, four *p/q* reversals, and difficulty with the words *not/ton, tar/rat, tab/bat, wed/dew,* and *mad/dam.*

Slosson Oral Reading Test (SORT)
Administered: 10/22/89

The SORT is given individually and is based on the ability to pronounce words at different levels of difficulty. Sidney appeared to be very tense during this test. He scored a reading level of 4.0 on the SORT. There were no beginning errors, three medial errors, and three ending errors. Medial errors were: *went/want, beach/bench,* and *scissors/serious.* Ending errors were *happy/happen, heaven/heavy,* and *distance/distant.* Sidney would not attempt to sound out or attack unknown words and did not seem to employ any phonic strategies.

Basic Reading Inventory
Administered: 10/22/89

This is an individually administered informal reading test that includes a series of graded word lists and graded passages. Comprehension questions follow each passage. Form A word lists were used to determine Sidney's ability to read and pronounce words in isolation. Form A passages were used to assess Sidney's oral reading. As Sidney read, miscues such as mispronunciation of words, omitted words, repetitions, and substitutions were noted. Form B was used for silent reading, and form C was used to estimate Sidney's listening level.

Estimated Levels:

Independent	4.0
Instructional	5.0–6.0
Frustrational	7.0
Listening	9.0

Independent level: Sidney can read fluently with excellent comprehension. His accuracy in word recognition was 93 percent, and he scored 100 percent in answering comprehension questions.

Instructional level: This is the challenge level, and Sidney read with 96 percent accuracy in word recognition and scored 87 percent in comprehension.

Frustrational level: Sidney could not deal with the reading material, scoring less than 90 percent on word recognition. Comprehension was at the 70 percent level.

Listening level: This is the highest level that Sidney can comprehend when the material is read to him. At the 9.0 listening level, Sidney scored 75 percent comprehension.

Summary of Basic Reading Inventory results. Sidney uses context clues and his store of general knowledge to comprehend what he reads. He answered questions of recall, details, and inference. Sidney consistently scored higher on the comprehension checks than on word recognition. On stories about camping, Indians, and sunflowers, Sidney appeared to use previous knowledge to answer comprehension questions. On these three stories, comprehension scores were much higher than word-recognition scores.

In word recognition, Sidney had four beginning errors: *now/how, out/and, black/back*, and *frog/fog*. This may indicate a problem with consonant blends, particularly *r* and *l* blends. Sidney had only two medial errors: *witch/watch* and *odd/old*. There were six ending errors: *Bill/Billy, bird's/bird, an/any, fate/fat, light/lights*, and *cool/cood*. These errors suggest a weakness in the genitive *'s*, plural *s*, and *y* endings. Many of the substitutions Sidney made were consistent with the characteristics of a child reading material in a manner less grammatically sophisticated than his speech patterns. Examples of substitutions were: *long/log, And/The, to/in, for/from, that/the, the/these, the/their, the/to*. The majority of substitutions did not substantially alter the meanings of the passages.

INTERPRETATION

Sidney is a 13-year-old 8th grader who displays behavior that is similar to that found in learning-disabled students. He displayed a wide range of performance, showing above-average ability in areas involving verbal reasoning, knowledge of how to react in social situations, and attention to details. There was wide variation in his academic abilities, demonstrated by scatter on the PIAT, the informal reading inventory, and grades ranging from B's to F's.

During the testing sessions, Sidney appeared excessively shy and withdrawn. He initiated no spontaneous conversation and responded only to direct questions. Sidney rarely made eye contact during the testing and resisted all efforts to establish rapport. He appeared anxious and frequently held his breath for several seconds when test items were difficult for him.

He was weak on IQ tasks involving expression, problem solving, perceptual organization, work rate, and visual memory. On the PIAT, he did display average general information. Reading tests seemed to show that he was able to answer questions by relying on his store of general information. Listening skills appeared to be above average.

Sidney has been able to get by in school so far by drawing on his store of general information. Because of increasing curricular demands, this store of information will not be able to sustain him much longer.

Sidney needs help in building word-attack skills, especially consonant blends such as *r* and *l*. He frequently drops the endings from words. The *s* plural *'s* genitive, *ed* past tense, and *y* endings are areas of concern. Sidney exhibited weaknesses in distinguishing *a/i* vowels, the *ai/a*, and did not seem to grasp the generalization that a final *e* usually makes the preceding vowel long. Sidney had difficulty distinguishing between *l/d* in spelling and handwriting samples and in word-recognition tests.

Sidney has a low sight-word vocabulary. Combined with his lack of phonics skills, Sidney is forced to rely on context clues for understanding.

There is a discrepancy between Sidney's actions and his high self-concept test score. Observations gathered during assessment include: soft and hesitant speaking voice, failure to make eye contact, failure to make spontaneous conversation, test anxiety, fear of failure, and struggle with material to be learned. Sidney may be perceiving reality differently than those around him do.

DIAGNOSIS

Sidney appears to qualify for learning-disability services.

RECOMMENDATIONS

Sidney needs help in several areas.

Spelling. A modified form of the Fernald approach may help Sidney improve spelling and sight-word vocabulary. There are four steps:

1. Say the word while simultaneously tracing its cursive form with the index finger as long as necessary.
2. Cover the word and write the word as a whole. No erasing is permitted.
3. Uncover the word and check. If correct, go to step 4. If not, go back to step 1.
4. Cover the word again and write it again.

Sidney needs to capitalize on his memory skills. He can learn memory clues for particularly troublesome letters or words such as *saw/was*, *r*-controlled vowels (*ir, ar*), and *r*-consonant blends (*fr, br*). Rehearsals and mnemonics may help, for example, *ROY G. BIV* for remembering the colors of the spectrum in order.

Sidney may also benefit from a condensed spelling reference book, such as *Webster's New World Misspellers Dictionary, World's Most Misspelled Words* (Pocketbooks), or *The Bad Spellers Dictionary* (Random House). Repeated checking of commonly used or misspelled words may help commit these words to memory.

Reading

Sidney's ability to use comprehension and context clues should be capitalized upon to increase overall reading comprehension. A program such as Specific Skill Series (Boning, 1970) may be helpful. This series is designed to develop reading skills in following directions, getting the main idea, locating answers, working with sounds, drawing conclusions, getting facts, and detecting sequences. Building the skills will develop Sidney's weaker reading skills.

Special thanks to Karen Cutting, Carolyn Fuller, and Patricia Petz for their assistance in the preparation of this report.

Sidney needs to acquire a sight-word vocabulary. This will provide a foundation on which to teach word attack and other reading skills.

Self-Concept

Sidney needs to find some methods for academic success. This will help bring up the self-concept.

APPENDIX 3.2. PRESENT LEVEL OF FUNCTIONING: SIDNEY JOHNSON

Sidney scored in the normal range of intelligence on the WISC-R. His strengths lay in verbal reasoning, knowledge of how to react in social situations, sequencing, and attention to detail. He needs help in verbal expression (vocabulary), problem solving, perceptual organization, work rate, and visual memory.

Achievement Scores: Grade PIAT:	Equivalent	Percentile Rank	Standard Score
Math	7.0	39	96
Reading Rec	3.9	5	75
Reading Comp	5.3	17	86
Spelling	2.5	Below Norms	General
Info	10.1	67	107
Total	5.0	9	80

Informal Reading Inventory (IRI): Independent, 4.0; Instructional, 5.0-6.0; Frustrational, 7.0; Listening, 9.0.

In the area of language arts, Sidney earned low scores in spelling and reading recognition. His reading comprehension score was barely in the normal range. He exhibits reversal problems with b/d, p/q, not/ton, tar/rat, tab/bat, wed/dew, and mad/dam. In word identification, Sidney had no beginning errors; medial errors with went/want, beach/bench, and scissors/serious; and ending errors with happy/happen, heaven/heavy, and distance/distant. He has a poor sight vocabulary and poor phonics skills and exhibits mispronunciations, omissions, repetitions, and substitutions. Sidney has difficulty with consonant blends involving r and l. Problems occur with r-controlled vowels such as ir and ar. He frequently drops the endings from words. The s plural, 's genitive, ed past tense, and y endings are areas of concern. There is difficulty in distinguishing a/i vowels, the ai/a, and the generalization that a final e usually makes the l/d in spelling and handwriting samples and in word-recognition tests. His ability to use context clues, reliance on this general knowledge fund, and listening ability are strengths.

Sidney scored high on a self-concept test but demonstrates behavior indicative of a student with low self-concept.

CHAPTER 4

Models for Teaching as a Dynamic Problem-Solving Process

Teachers—like engineers, physicians, attorneys, plumbers, and contractors—often have paraprofessionals, technicians, assistants, aides, helpers, and laborers to support their efforts. Although direct contact with students is important, it comprises no more than half of the responsibilities involved in teaching, and paraprofessionals (teacher's aides) carry out a variety of tasks from delivering lessons to running off worksheets. What sets teachers apart from aides is the expectation that they will take responsibility for the *whole* teaching process—assessing student needs, determining curricula, applying methods, acquiring materials, adjusting interventions, and evaluating results. There may be support personnel, but they are directed by and receive instructions from their bosses, who are responsible for carrying out projects from start to finish.

The need to plan and coordinate requires that the teacher have a vision of what must be done to build skills and thus meet the needs of students. In this chapter, the basic responsibilities of teaching at the secondary level are examined. Presented are models through which these responsibilities can be carried out, systematically and yet thoughtfully. Teaching is an ongoing problem-solving process (Horvath, 1985), with selection of method at the heart of it. The next chapter shows strategies—including some that cross model lines—in action.

THE DIVERSITY OF STUDENT NEEDS

Teaching would be much easier if every student required the same curriculum, had common learning characteristics, and responded well to one or two methods of instruction. For years educators have labored to define a core curriculum for all students, often by working from a set of terminal behaviors to a set of entry-level expectations. No one curriculum has yet been devised that meets the needs of all learners. Examples of curricula used in teaching those with mild handicaps include enrichment, "watered down" approaches, several vocational versions, functional (useful) models, spiral (repetitious) varieties, and the remedial or basic approaches.

In addition to curricular needs, teachers know that students develop and acquire academic skills at different rates, or generally respond better to one approach over another. At any one time, there will be some students who are ahead of their peers in a given academic area and others who will be behind. To add a further complication, the same students who are behind in one area may actually be ahead in others. Some students learn better if a direct approach is used. Others prefer to discover the principles upon which their world operates. Some seem to learn faster if the learning is multisensory. Others seem to be confused by too much stimulation.

Challenges that stem from the normal diversity of educational needs are magnified for the mildly handicapped population. By individualizing instruction, teachers hope to meet the needs of all their students. Labeling a student as behavior disordered, educable mentally retarded, or learning disabled is only a start at meeting those needs. It is necessary to go beyond the labels to determine what will work with each student at any given time. Special education teachers have acquired the attitude that instruction must fit the needs of the student. They realize that no sector of education "owns" the methods of instruction and that good teachers share what is available. No teacher today has to reinvent the wheel.

Systematic instruction and strategies intervention are useful teaching models for secondary students. A distinct advantage of using models is efficiency. By *systematically* attending to the needs of learners, it is thought that optimal learning will take place. Good teaching practices are often incorporated into several different models. That is reflected in the feeling teachers now have that a common body of knowledge is emerging. Although not as developed as the knowledge of other disciplines, research is continually adding and validating practices to the art and science called pedagogy.

DIAGNOSTIC-PRESCRIPTIVE TEACHING

Within the dynamic, problem-solving process of teaching, several approaches are available, with the most successful of them characterized by decision-making processes based on the following principles:

- Systematic collection and examination of data
- The ability of the models to accommodate different theoretical approaches and subject areas
- Commitments to documentation so that information may be used in future educational planning.

Diagnostic-prescriptive teaching has evolved into a generic teaching approach that meets the criteria for success in a multistage format (Charles, 1980). After surveying the broad stages, we examine two models.

In the *first stage* a curriculum is selected. This starting point includes a series of goals and objectives arranged in a hierarchical sequence from easy to difficult, simple to complex, known to unknown, past to present to future, concrete to abstract, facts to generalizations, or practical to theoretical.

In the *second stage* the student is assessed to determine where he or she is in the curriculum. (Curriculum-Based Assessment, a natural application of Diagnostic-Prescriptive Teaching, was presented in Chapter 3.) Formal (summative) measures such as norm-referenced achievement tests give the teacher a general idea of where the student is functioning. These tests are generally followed by informal (formative) criterion-referenced tests to determine a student's mastery of specific objectives. Any other data relevant to the student's needs are gathered. These assessment data are used to prescribe educational intervention.

In the *third stage* goals and objectives are expressed, methods are determined, and materials are gathered. Intervention in the form of instruction takes place. With careful advance planning, instructional delivery becomes a more comfortable, smoother experience for both teacher and student. "What am I going to teach tomorrow?" is a cry that experienced teachers need not utter.

In the *fourth stage* intervention results are evaluated and the student advances to the next objective if mastery is achieved, continues to work on the objective if satisfactory progress toward mastery is being demonstrated, or has the program modified if necessary. The determining factor is the analysis of the evaluation results by the teacher.

Lerner (1985) used the term *clinical teaching* and wrote about the simplified "test-teach-test-teach" cycle. Wallace and Larsen (1978) wrote about a diagnostic teaching plan in which the teacher identifies a student's learning needs, evaluates those needs, develops a teaching plan, and implements that plan. Others have reported similar variations. In each of these general diagnostic-prescriptive models, an important assumption is that individualized instruction will replace the rote-based, competitive, lock-step, group-instruction orientation common to education. When learning is viewed in this way, goals, objectives, methods, and materials are selected for each student based on the needs of that student. Each student is provided with an equal opportunity to succeed, consistent with the democratic principles on which schools are operated.

At a less general level, several models have been proposed. Representative of them are the Systematic-Instruction Model (Affleck et al., 1980) and the Strategies-Intervention Model (Alley & Deshler, 1979). The first model offers a framework in which intervention may be provided. It is used to best advantage when the teacher is comfortable with an approach that does not have a high degree of structure. The more specific Strategies-Intervention Model (Schumaker et al., 1983) offers a high degree of structure plus content in the form of strategies that may be infused into subject-area curricula. Comprehensive models such as this are especially useful when secondary students exhibit deficiencies in their approaches to learning, their motivation, and their ability to demonstrate prerequisite skills.

The Systematic-Instruction Model

An important but often overlooked criterion for success in a model is its ease of use. The Systematic-Instruction Model meets that criterion. Although designed for elementary classrooms, it can easily be adapted for secondary students. Here are six steps in systematic instruction.

Systematic-Instruction Model*

1. Perform initial assessment.
2. Establish annual goals and short-term objectives.
3. Select instructional activities.
4. Select data-recording system for ongoing assessment.
5. Implement instructional plan.
6. Modify instructional plan.

The model offers a step-by-step sequence in which a teacher uses a systematic approach to determine educational needs for students based on an initial assessment, the setting of instructional goals and objectives based on the educational needs of the student, and the selection of instructional strategies based on what the teacher feels will meet the needs of a given student. Permeating the model is the need for a program of ongoing assessment so that the effectiveness of the instruction can be monitored continuously and fine tuned as needed.

The *first step* is for the teacher to gather information from which the current educational needs of the student can be determined. In terms of the Individualized Educational Program (IEP) demanded by Public Law 94-142, this step may be thought of as establishing the current level of educational performance. It is important to remember that this information must be educationally relevant and must go far beyond the mere listing of test scores. Zigmond, Vallecorsa, and Silverman (1983) discussed this type of information as assessment for instructional planning, viewing it as a bridge between assessment information and instruction. As such, it helps the teacher decide what to teach and how to teach it. Assessment for instructional planning, which was discussed in Chapter 3, is different from assessment for program eligibility and program evaluation. Instructional assessment should lead directly to the next step, establishing annual goals and short-term objectives.

In the *second step*, as we have seen, goals are written with a one-year time frame in mind in three broad domains: cognitive, affective, and psychomotor. In each of the domains, goals are written to meet the needs of each student. Three to eight objectives should be written for each goal area. They may encompass one-to-nine-week periods and may be thought of as units of instruction (Meyen, 1972). From this base, lesson plans should flow naturally.

The *third step* is to select instructional strategies based on the needs of each student as described by the data gathered in the initial assessment step. It is tempting to assume that the same methods and materials can be used with each student who is to meet a particular objective, but experienced teachers know this is not the case. Choosing instructional strategies is similar to a game of chance. Some days or weeks or periods, the selected strategy works. Other times the same formerly successful strategy is totally ineffective. This is normal and is addressed by the next step in the model.

---

*From J. Q. Affleck, S. Lowenbraun, & A. Archer. (1980). *Teaching the mildly handicapped in the regular classroom* (2nd ed.). Columbus: C. E. Merrill.

The *fourth step* involves record keeping. Because the selected instructional approach may or may not be effective, it is important to have a formative assessment plan in place to determine progress toward mastering a given objective. This type of assessment is ongoing and enables the teacher to check progress on at least a weekly if not a daily basis. Modification of instructional strategies can be carried out as appropriate.

The *fifth step* is instruction. When prospective teachers learn that approximately one-half of their time will be spent in activities other than providing direct instruction to students, they often are skeptical. It is true that planning occupies a major portion of a teacher's days, nights, weekends, and vacations. In this model, the implementation of the instructional plan occurs at the fifth step in the six-step process.

The *sixth and final step* in the model involves modifying the instruction based on the results of the data collected in the ongoing assessment. If the student is making satisfactory progress, no modifications are necessary. If the student has mastered the objective being assessed, it is important to move the student to the next objective in the sequence. If the student is bogged down in the task, modification of the objective or strategy is in order.

The Strategies-Intervention Model

Specifically designed for the secondary student, strategies intervention is a comprehensive model that includes components on teaching the student how to learn, how to solve problems, and how to complete tasks independently (Deshler & Schumaker, 1984; Schumaker et al., 1986). The learning-strategies curriculum comprises the core of the model and is an alternative to the basic-skills remedial model and the tutorial model often used in secondary programs. Those who use a basic-skills approach extend upward the curriculum found in elementary programs. An overemphasis on tools or basic skills to the detriment of content skill development is often the result. In practice, demanding that a 16-year-old memorize the arithmetic tables is futile. It is much better to supply the student with a calculator and get on with the functional mathematics necessary for better success in adult life. Tutorial approaches allow the adolescent learner to meet only the immediate demands of pass tests and completing homework assignments. Learning is fragmented and retention is minimal.

To meet lifelong learning needs, the strategies-intervention approach weans the secondary student from overdependence on the teacher. The greater independence in learning that results develops students who are more likely to remain motivated to continue using skills learned in secondary school well into adult life. Although based largely on the earlier work of Kass (1977), the model was developed by Alley and Deshler (1979) and is being continually refined (Deshler et al., 1983).

Learning-strategy interventions are based on pragmatic concerns (Deshler & Schumaker, 1984). Deshler and Schumaker (1986) identified the instructional principles underlying the approach as outlined and summarized below.

Instructional Principles Underlying Learning-Strategies Instruction*

I. Match Instruction with Curriculum Demands.

II. Use Structured Teaching Methodology.
  A. Organize learning strategies curriculum into three strands.
    1. Acquisition of information from written materials
      a. Word identification—decode multisyllable words.
      b. Reading comprehension
        i. Visual imagery
        ii. Self-questioning
        iii. Paraphrasing
      c. Interpreting visual aids
      d. Multipass
        i. Survey
        ii. Obtain key information
        iii. Study critical information
    2. Identification and storage of important information
      a. Listening and note taking
        i. Identify organizational cues in lectures.
        ii. Note key words.
        iii. Organize key words into outline form.
      b. First-letter mnemonics
      c. Paired associate learning
    3. Facilitating written expression and demonstration of competence
      a. Sentence-writing strategy
      b. Paragraph-writing strategy
      c. Theme-writing strategy
      d. Error-monitoring strategy
      e. Assignment-completion strategy
      f. Test-taking strategy
  B. Teach the seven-step acquisition methodology.
    1. Test to determine current learning habits.
    2. Describe the new strategy to the student.
    3. Model the new strategy.
    4. Rehearse verbally to learn the steps of the strategy.
    5. Practice with controlled materials.
    6. Practice with regular class materials.
    7. Posttest.

III. Deliberately Promote Generalization.
  A. Orientation
    1. Make student aware of when strategy should be used.

---

*From D. Deshler and J. Schumaker. (1986). Learning strategies: An instructional alternative for low-achieving adolescents. *Exceptional Children, 52*(6), 583–590. Copyright 1986 by The Council for Exceptional Children.

      2. Discuss adaptations of the strategy.

      3. Make student aware of cues for using strategy.

   B. Activation

      1. Program student use of strategy in variety of situations.

      2. Provide feedback.

   C. Maintenance

      1. Conduct periodic reviews.

      2. Test maintenance of strategy usage.

      3. Provide feedback.

IV. Apply Critical Teaching Behaviors.

V. Use Scope and Sequence in Teaching.

   A. Learn three to four learning strategies per year.

   B. Teach units.

VI. Insure That Teaching Decisions Are Governed by Outcome Goals.

VII. Maximize Student Involvement.

VIII. Maintain Realistic Point of View.

   A. Learning strategies

   B. Social skill strategies

   C. Motivation strategies

   D. Transition strategies

   E. Executive strategies

I. Match Instruction with Curriculum Demands: Educators are increasingly making the assumption that what occurs in special and regular classrooms should be related to curriculum demands. Direct instruction (Stephens, 1970) and Curriculum-Based Assessment (Gickling & Havertape, 1981) are examples of the movement to match instruction and curriculum. In the Strategies-Intervention Model, the teacher must identify curriculum demands that the student is failing to meet. Through analysis of daily lessons, the teacher determines why the student is not successful. Learning-strategy instruction then begins with those learning strategies that are most critical to each student. By providing task-specific activities that help the student succeed, the teacher is able to motivate students to acquire skills that are of use immediately and in the future.

II. Use Structured Teaching Methodology: The task-specific learning-strategies curriculum component is organized into three strands or components. Acquisition of information from written materials is the *first strand*. To gain meaning from the printed page, it is thought that four skills are essential.

1. The ability to identify words. Students are taught to decode multisyllable words.

2. The ability to comprehend what is read. Visual imagery helps students form mental pictures of events described in text. Self-questioning is helpful when the author has not provided enough information. The student learns to ask pertinent questions and answer them later in the passage. Paraphrasing allows students to restate in their own words the main idea and supporting details after a passage is read.

3. The ability to interpret visual aids. Students are taught to gain information from pictures, diagrams, charts, tables, and maps.
4. The ability to read for important concepts. A strategy called multipass is taught to help students read chapters in textbooks (Schumaker et al., 1982).

Multipass is an adaptation of the SQ3R (survey, question, read, recite and review) method. By using multipass, the student is able to determine main idea, organization, and specific information from textbook chapters without having to read each word in the chapter. In the first or survey pass, the student becomes familiar with main ideas and chapter organization by reading the title, reading the introductory paragraph, placing the chapter in context by reviewing the table of contents, reading the major subtitles, looking at the illustrations and captions, reading the summary paragraph, and paraphrasing all information gathered. The second or size-up pass is devoted to the acquisition of key information by having the student read the questions at the end of the chapter, determine which questions can be answered without further study, look for textual cues to help answer unknown questions, make a question out of each cue, and skim the surrounding text to find each answer. In the third or sort-out pass, the student performs a self-test by reading and answering questions at the end of the chapter and repeating earlier steps if immediate success is not achieved.

Identification and storage of important information is the *second strand*. Three skills are thought to be important in this strand:

1. *Listening* and *note taking* consist of teaching the student to identify organizational cues in lectures, note key words, and organize key words into outline form.
2. *First-Letter Mnemonics* is one of many memorization-enhancing techniques. Students are taught to use first letters of a series of words to trigger their memories. The use of the mnemonic HOMES to remember the names of the Great Lakes is an example.
3. *Paired associate learning* is just that: An unknown word or concept is linked to one that is familiar to the student. After practice, the association helps the student recall the meaning of the new word or concept.

Facilitating written expression and demonstration of competence is the *third strand*. Six strategies are taught in this area:

1. Sentence writing. Students are exposed to different types, their purposes, and when to use them appropriately. For some students, this is the first systematic instruction they have had in this area.
2. Paragraph writing. Organizing and writing a cohesive paragraph may look like an insurmountable task for a student experiencing difficulty in school. Instruction in this area often makes a noticeable difference.
3. Theme writing. Students are taught how to organize and write an integrated five-paragraph theme.
4. Error monitoring. Detecting and correcting errors in written products is taught.

5. Assignment completion. Students are taught scheduling and organizing techniques that will help them get their assignments in on time.
6. Test taking. Students who know the material but have difficulty demonstrating their knowledge on tests benefit from instruction on test taking.

To learn the various task-specific strategies, a seven-step *acquisition methodology* is suggested. The steps are based on teaching methodologies that are known to be effective, including task analysis, modeling, rehearsal, feedback, and direct instruction. The steps may be summarized as follows:

1. The student is tested to determine his or her current ability to perform a particular task. Results are shared with the student. During this time, the teacher stresses the importance of developing greater proficiency in performing this task. It is the job of the teacher to motivate the student to learn a strategy that will insure success. When the student makes a commitment to learn the strategy, he or she proceeds to the second step.
2. The teacher breaks the learning strategy into steps and describes each step to the student. To help the student accept responsibility, the teacher discusses why the strategy works, how and when it can be used, and what results can be expected. Students are encouraged to set goals for themselves regarding how fast they will master the strategy.
3. The new strategy is modeled by the teacher. During this time, the teacher performs and talks through the strategy from start to finish. After teacher modeling, the student participates in subsequent demonstrations of the strategy.
4. The student uses verbal rehearsal to learn the steps of the strategy. Although tedious, it is necessary for the student to internalize the strategy.
5. The student practices the strategy on controlled materials. Instead of overwhelming the student with regular class tasks, the teacher presents materials that are simpler, shorter, and easier to master. Reinforcement and corrective feedback are used to help the student concentrate solely on learning the strategy. When a specified criterion level is reached, the student moves to the sixth step.
6. The student practices the strategy on classroom materials. Criterion levels are set that reflect both the accuracy and speed expected in regular class environments. As in the prior step, reinforcement and corrective feedback assist the student's mastery of the material.
7. The student is posttested. Instruction is completed when the student demonstrates an ability to use the strategy successfully to cope with curriculum demands in the given area.

III. Deliberately Promote Generalization: Performance of a task in the resource room is an important step in the learning process. It is necessary to demonstrate that the task can be performed in different settings and over a period of time. To meet those ends, a three-phase procedure is used.

In the *first phase*, or orientation phase, students are taught when a strategy should be used, how the strategy can be adapted, and how to look for events that will cue the strategy. It is recommended that a series of problem-solving meetings be held in which events are simulated.

The *second phase* is activation, in which the student practices the given strategy in a variety of settings and with different materials. Feedback on the appropriateness of his or her use of the strategy is provided by the teacher.

Maintenance is the *third phase*. It consists of a series of teacher probes to determine the extent to which the student is having success with the strategy.

IV. Apply Critical Teaching Behaviors: Instructional quality is critical to success. The following behaviors are thought to be necessary:

> Providing appropriate positive and corrective feedback
> Using organizers throughout the instructional session
> Insuring high levels of active academic responding
> Programming youth involvement in discussions
> Providing regular reviews of key instructional points and checks of comprehension
> Monitoring student performance
> Requiring mastery learning
> Communicating high expectations to students
> Communicating rationales for instructional activities
> Facilitating independence.

Good teaching practices are independent of the model of teaching employed. When used with a good model, those practices make learning more efficient for the student.

V. Use Scope and Sequence in Teaching: It is recommended that three to four strategies be learned each year, beginning in the 7th grade and continuing through 12th grade. After students learn several strategies across the three strands (acquisition, identification and storage, and facilitating written expression and demonstration of competence) of the learning-strategies curriculum, they enjoy greater success in their regular education courses.

Seventh grade is thought of as the entry point for learning-strategies training. Students who are younger may not possess the metacognitive skills necessary for optimal success. Lerner (1985) defined *metacognition* as the awareness of one's systematic thinking strategies that are needed for learning. Younger students are thought to benefit more from a curriculum emphasizing tool-skill or basic-skill acquisition.

VI. Insure That Teaching Decisions Are Governed by Outcome Goals: Independence in learning and performance is the major focus of the strategies-intervention approach. Its originators used curricular demands and terminal behaviors expected of secondary students as their starting point.

They caution that those who teach must never lose sight of those exit-level skills. As a teacher, it is important to remember that the value of school is measured in adult life. Is the curriculum preparing each student to live a viable adult life?

VII. Maximize Student Involvement: In the literature on organizations, a great deal of space is devoted to the topic of policy development and enforcement. A number of theorists believe that it is good practice for those who will be affected by policy to have a voice in the setting of that policy. When people feel some degree of ownership, they are more motivated to comply with both the spirit and letter of the law or policy.

The developers of the Strategies-Intervention Model believe that learners should have a vested interest in their learning. In fact, they want students to assume control of their learning through participation that results in active goal setting. Internalization of student commitment to learning is regularly affirmed by encouraging student participation in the IEP process, self-evaluation, and acceptance of responsibility for learning.

VIII. Maintain Realistic Point of View: Learning how to cope with increasingly complex curricular demands is just one component of the adolescent-development process. Growth in other areas is also important. To provide a truly comprehensive intervention package, teachers must be prepared to offer adolescents training in strategies designed to help them cope in several other areas besides academics (Schumaker et al., 1986).

In social skills, adolescents often feel insecure or inadequate. They often need to know how to read the facial expressions, body language, and gestures of others. Sarcasm, irony, and hyperbole can be confusing to students with mild handicaps. Systematic instruction in resisting peer pressure, negotiating, and solving problems can help these students improve social behavior.

Because many students experience widespread failure in their school careers, motivation may be a problem. Students can be taught to set goals and monitor their progress in the attainment of those goals. By using the self-control techniques of behavior contracting, self-recording, self-monitoring, and self-reinforcement, students can be taught to overcome learned helplessness.

Young people must cope with a variety of environments. Although the transition to postschool life may be overwhelming, students can be taught how to face life on their own, make their own decisions, express their own thoughts and wishes, set and accomplish their own goals, be independent learners, and accept responsibility for their own mistakes.

Executive strategies enable adolescents to solve their problems independently. Developed from the executive component found in information-processing models, executive strategies mirror the idea that coordinating and sequencing specific control processes help overall personal organization. Analogous to metacognition, executive control processes include planning, reality testing, monitoring, predicting, and evaluating the level of one's understanding.

The Strategies-Intervention Model is divided into the components of curriculum, instruction, and organization. Constantly evolving, the model incorporates sound learning techniques into instructional practices in a systematic fashion.

Several models exist within the diagnostic-prescriptive framework. Systematic instruction and strategies intervention are just two examples of those available. After gaining familiarity with a specific model, the next step is to apply that model to a specific student in a specific curriculum with specific subject matter. This process is lesson planning and is left up to the individual teacher.

SUMMARY

Teaching is an ongoing, dynamic, problem-solving process in which instruction should be deliberately planned, systematically delivered, continually evaluated, and based on data. Several models are available, from basic outlines to comprehensive programs. The choice of which model to use is guided by the needs of students and the philosophy of the teacher(s). Two representative models include systematic instruction and learning strategies.

Systematic instruction is an easy-to-use model that takes the teacher through the steps from gathering information through delivery of lessons. The Strategies-Intervention model is comprehensive and teaches the student how to approach any learning task. It includes components on how to complete tasks independently.

It must be remembered that good teaching practices transcend models and are universally applied in instructional intervention. Those who teach students with mild handicaps at the secondary level must realize that curriculum, methods and materials specially designed for those with nontraditional needs are widely available. Meeting the needs of those students has evolved from relying almost exclusively on one's expertise to writing curricula, developing methods, and painstakingly collecting and constructing materials. In Chapter 5, interventions that have been shown to be effective are presented.

STUDY QUESTIONS

1. What is the difference between a teacher and a teacher's aide?
2. What is the process of teaching?
3. Are there advantages to using models to teach?
4. Why should teachers use the diagnostic-prescriptive approach?
5. What is the Systematic-Instruction Model, who should use it, and when should it be used?
6. Why should anyone bother to learn to use the Strategies-Intervention Model?
7. What is *multipass?*
8. Why is the learning-strategies-intervention approach thought to be more effective with secondary-aged students than with those who are younger?
9. Are models such as strategies intervention for the exclusive use of special educators?
10. What can special educators do to help bridge the perceived gap between regular and special education?

REFERENCES

Affleck, J. Q., Lowenbraun, S., & Archer A. (1980). *Teaching the mildly handicapped in the regular classroom* (2nd ed.). Columbus: C. E. Merrill.

Alley, G., & Deshler, D. (1979). *Teaching the learning disabled adolescent: Strategies and methods.* Denver: Love.

Charles, C. M. (1980). *Individualizing instruction* (2nd ed.). St. Louis: C. V. Mosby.

Deshler, D. D., & Schumaker, J. B. (1984). *Strategies instruction: A new way to teach.* Salt Lake City: Worldwide Media.

————. (1986). Learning strategies: An instructional alternative for low-achieving adolescents. *Exceptional Children 52*(6), 583–590.

Deshler, D. D., Warner, M. M., Schumaker, J. B., & Alley, G. R. (1983). The learning-straegies-intervention model: Key components and current status. In J. D. McKinney and L. Feagans (Eds.), *Current topics in learning disabilities* (Vol. 1). Norwood, NJ: Ablex.

Gickling, E. E., & Havertape, J. F. (1981). Curriculum-based assessment. In J. A. Tucker (Ed.), *Non-test-based assessment: A training module.* Minneapolis: National School Psychologist Inservice Training Network, University of Minnesota.

Horvath, M. J. (1985). *Statistics for educators.* Seattle: Special Child.

Kass, C. E. (1977). Identification of learning disability (dyssymbolia). *Journal of Learning Disabilities, 10*(7), 425–432.

Lerner, J. (1985). *Learning disabilities: Theories, diagnosis, and teaching strategies* (4th ed.). Boston: Houghton Mifflin.

Meyen, E. L. (1972). Special education curriculum development program (SECDC), Univeristy of Iowa. Des Moines: Department of Public Instruction of the State of Iowa.

————. (1980). *Developing units of instruction: For the regular and special education teacher* (3rd ed.). Dubuque, IA: Wm. C. Brown.

Schumaker, J. B., Deshler, D. D., Alley, G. R., & Denton, P. H. (1982). Multipass: A learning strategy for improving reading comprehension. *Learning Disability Quarterly, 5*(3), 295–304.

Schumaker, J. B., Deshler, D. D., Alley, G. R., & Warner, M. M. (1983). Toward the development of an intervention model for learning-disabled adolescents. *Exceptional Education Quarterly, 3*(4), 45–50.

Schumaker, J. B., Deshler, D. D., & Ellis, E. S. (1986). Intervention issues related to the education of LD adolescents. In J. K. Torgeson and B. Y. L. Wong (Eds.), *Learning disabilities: Some new perspectives.* New York: Academic Press.

Stephens, T. (1970). *Directive teaching of children with learning and behavioral handicaps.* Columbus: C. E. Merrill.

Wallace, G., & Larsen, S. C. (1978). *Educational assessment of learning problems: Testing for teaching.* Boston: Allyn & Bacon.

Zigmond, N., Vallecorsa, A., & Silverman, R. (1983). *Assessment for instructional planning in special education.* Englewood Cliffs, NJ: Prentice-Hall.

CHAPTER 5

The Process of Using What Works: Strategies for Implementation

In this chapter we explore strategies and discuss variables in developing and implementing academics in the special class. Techniques, devices, and activities are presented; a priority is increasing student motivation.

Practices that extend across different models include unit teaching, cooperative learning, and instructional modifications. It is not possible to include a discussion of all good teaching practices, but it is hoped that a representative sampling will give you an idea of the many possibilities available. When the teacher wisely picks and chooses to accomplish the needs of the students in his or her classroom, teaching becomes a process of using what works.

Academic instruction in special education is in a state of transition. The focus of both the content of instructional objectives and the methods of teaching are changing. Teachers through middle school have emphasized a catch-up remedial approach. Now, teachers are more concerned with terminal objectives and with the acquisition of skills students can use independently to learn. Special educators are trying to reverse the failures of the past. Although successful academic achievement, school completion, and successful transition to adult life have been illusive outcomes for students in special education, special educators are committed to making these outcomes common expectations.

Is it possible to change the failure rates and dropout patterns of these students? What is known about them that gives direction for possible approaches to the development and implementation of academic programs? What is known about the academic demands made of students in regular classes that could help define objectives for meaningful intervention? Answers to these questions are beginning to emerge, and it is evident that there are no quick fixes and trendy, cosmetic, band-aid approaches to eliminate the problems.

THE COMPONENTS OF MEANINGFUL INTERVENTION

The components of a meaningful intervention are the result of considering what will motivate the students being taught. Once the student who has been identified as having a special need understands the *meaning* or point of the material, intervention can begin. Another consideration is how the student can *use* the material in later life. Furthermore, that consideration includes the proximity in time of what is being taught to the use of the instruction in the world after school. Many students, especially those with learning problems, cannot plan for the future. For some of these students the future may be this afternoon. Use of material in the near and far future are important concepts to be taught.

When dealing with students with learning problems, whether they are in special education classes or regular classes, the educator must be aware of the special circumstances of each of the learning styles of the students in the class. Specific pedagogical techniques that are appropriate to the learning styles must be brought to bear on the situation. Less consideration of what is normally done in a classroom and more attention to the individual needs of students will help insure a more impactful learning experience.

A case can be made for the teaching of arithmetic facts to students who see little need for understanding basic facts. But what will give these facts relevance? For many of the students the only time they see math used is in stores, where numbers are automatically computed by a cash register or other mechanical device. Math facts need to be set into situations familiar to the student or into those he or she will experience. Since many students play cards, lottery, or other gambling games, important to them as a vehicle for getting rich quick, the game of Black Jack could provide motivation because it is a way of immediately and enjoyably applying newfound knowledge.

Once the educator has found the correct situation and motivators for the student, it is time to identify problem areas specifically and how the student is attacking these problem areas at present. There should be diagnosis of process rather than answers (Feuerstein, 1980). This is achieved by using tasks that allow a student to solve problems and the teacher to ask questions about the process employed. Then the teacher can develop an educational plan to address what is needed to improve process. This strategy encourages the educator to teach, guided not by what the student does not know but by what knowledge exists.

Identify Problems

The first step in eliminating or ameliorating problems of students is to identify the problems. Formal and informal assessments, grade reports, schedules, examples of student work, and anecdotal records will provide much of the information requisite in defining specific needs of students. Of particular concern is the ability of students to adjust socially and academically to regular class environments.

Much attention in programming is being given to preparation of students for mainstreaming and to the development of effective study skills. Both academic and behavioral expectations must be clarified before mainstreaming, and they must be used to identify and prepare students targeted for regular classes (Salend & Lutz, cited by Conway & Gow, 1988). An effective procedure for compiling this information and for identifying variables that impact student academic performance in regular classes is the use of a survey-type inventory. Appendix 5.1 at the end of this chapter is an example of a form that is used for this purpose. Teachers from each discipline are to complete the survey. When completed, the inventories provide information that can be translated into guidelines for modifications of regular classes as well as for intervention by special education services (Appendix 5.2).

Focus on School Survival Skills

After student profiles have been developed and regular class assignments have been made, the special education teacher can begin to project an instructional focus on skills students will need to survive in their regular classes. The primary focus of intervention for many mildly handicapped students can be categorized as school survival skills. These skills generally do not involve content specific to any particular discipline, but rather, they are skills students need if they are to profit adequately from any instructional environment.

Students may have poor organizational skills or deficiencies in study skills that make it impossible for them to meet the demands of regular classes. Students may not be actively involved in learning because they lack the necessary skills for active participation, and they may not have the social competence that allows them to interact appropriately with peers and teachers, thereby impairing positive gain from their educational experiences. Instruction involving learning strategies, study skills, and social skills can help students acquire competencies that will help them profit from regular classes as well as acquire skills valuable at the worksite and in lifelong learning needs.

Motivate

Regardless of how much one wants to change the academic performance of students, if students are not motivated to learn, change will be minimal if at all. All learning-theory experts emphasize the importance of motivation as a first step in academic success.

There are variables that can be manipulated by the special education team to motivate students. *Purpose, self-esteem*, and *choice* are significant variables. To convey purpose, show students that what they do in school is important for achieving other goals that extend beyond school, adopt a teaching style that is both task and human relations oriented, and apply appropriate schedules of reinforcement (Samuels, 1986). Self-esteem is developed when students feel included and respected. Educators should spend time talking and listening to their students, and when making programming decisions, the students should be involved.

The power of choice in motivating secondary students is great. It is the basis for developing trust, cooperation, and individuality. It is the foundation for developing authentic relationships with teachers, and it is the source for helping students recognize their strengths and weaknesses so that appropriate goals can be set. For example, a student is given the choice of taking a parallel course to be taught in a special education class or being enrolled in a regular class. The student opts for the special class because he knows that he needs more time to meet the demands of a vocational class that he wants to take. As a result, he may have made a commitment to specific outcomes. If the staff had made the decision without giving the student a choice, they could have inadvertently told the student that they lack confidence in him, thereby eroding elements of motivation. Expectations individuals hold about their ability to master certain tasks affect both the initiation and persistence of coping behavior. Moreover, the strength of these expectations predicts whether or not a person will even try to cope within given situations (Gresham, 1984). Best work is done when people believe in what they are doing and are committed to the goals.

Conditions necessary in developing and maintaining motivation include interest, knowledge of results, success, and relation of activity to reward (Hunter, 1967). Hunter explained the four conditions:

> *Interest*. The more interest we can generate, the greater the learning dividends.
> *Success*. Unsuccessful effort or tasks that are too difficult depress motivation. Success and the right degree of difficulty increase motivation.
> *Knowledge of results*. The more specific the feedback on performance, the more motivation should increase.
> *Relation of activity to reward*. When the activity itself is rewarding, it produces a situation where motivation is intrinsic, the activity will always achieve the goal, and motivation compounds. Extrinsic motivation is dependent on and changes with the specific environmental situation. (p. 37)

Children who have experienced early failure and disapproval have a tendency to develop extrinsically motivated orientation. The typical student with mild handicaps will at first require a more externally controlled approach in order to be appropriately engaged in the classroom activities (Switzky & Schultz, 1988). Extrinsically motivated students believe that factors outside of themselves, such as chance or luck, determine success or failure. When the locus of control is intrinsic, students believe performance is due to their own efforts. Developing intrinsic motivation requires that students are actively involved in instruction.

One of several programs to motivate students is the Teacher Expectations and Student Expectations (TESA) program developed by Kerman, Kimball, and Martin (1980). The model appears as Figure 5.1. The TESA was founded on the belief that students will do better if offered equal opportunities to perform, independent of curriculum goals. This is accomplished when teachers practice specific motivating and supportive interactions equally with all class members. The TESA identifies fifteen major interactions grouped in three strands (themes). Five interactions are found within each strand. In each of five months, teachers attend a seminar and then practice one interaction in each of the three strands in their classes. They work in five-person teams, and each teacher is confidentially coded by the other four once each month on the three interactions being targeted that month. Each teacher is responsible for taking the coding sheets and using the information as he or she chooses each month. At the end of the five-month period, each of the fifteen major interactions will have been practiced.

Figure 5.1. TESA Interaction Model

UNITS	STRAND A: RESPONSE OPPORTUNITIES	STRAND B: FEEDBACK	STRAND C: PERSONAL REGARD
1	Equitable distribution of response opportunities	Affirm or correct student's performance	Proximity
2	Individual helping	Praise of learning performance	Courtesy
3	Latency	Reasons for praise	Personal interest/Compliments
4	Delving	Listening	Touching
5	Higher level questioning	Accepting feelings	Desisting

Source: S. Kerman, T. Kimball, and M. Martin. (1980). *Teacher expectations and student achievement.* Bloomington, IN: Phi Delta Kappa.

The TESA has several advantages. The program is designed to be voluntary, and confidentiality is maintained. Self-improvement and not a summary evaluation of performance that results in salary, promotion, tenure, or retention decision is the goal. It is assumed that teachers possess the necessary expertise and are motivated to improve their performances. Each teacher has a unique style and is the best judge of how to incorporate competencies developed in the program into that style. It has been found that it is not necessary to have supervisory personnel monitor the program.

Research shows that when the TESA is implemented, three things occur. The first is that discipline problems diminish. The second is that achievement scores for all students increase. The third is that teacher and pupil absenteeism is reduced. In short, a more humane environment is created.

The TESA is one example of programs designed to motivate students and, in the process, enhance school climate. The positive benefits of these programs outweigh the cost of implementation. Supplemental activities include sending members of the teaching staff to conferences and holding meaningful retreats away from distractions that are a part of school buildings.

DEMONSTRATING RELEVANCE IN UNIT TEACHING

Students who see utility in skills they are asked to learn will strive to develop and improve these skills. Using relevant materials applied to the needs of students increases motivation and gets students ready to learn. Students who are ready to learn will also be more willing to deal with difficult components of their school work—reading, spelling, or math.

Meyen (1980) believes that one indicator of good teaching is the ability to challenge children without threatening them. Unit teaching is a methodology in which a series of objectives are organized around a central theme. Mildly handicapped students seem to feel more comfortable when they can relate to a theme or problem rather than study isolated facts.

Themes may be confined to a single subject area such as science or social studies. Examples of units in these areas might be plant reproduction or Native Americans of the Northwest. Units may also encompass several subject areas. Career education, lifelong physical fitness, nutrition and health, the monetary system, and the ecology of a small island are examples of integrated units. In an ecology unit, for example, objectives may be written in the areas of science, mathematics, reading, social studies, and writing. Many educators feel an integrated approach is more desirable for handicapped learners. A cooperative problem solving approach can be incorporated that may be even less threatening.

Good teaching skills are needed to deliver quality unit instruction. Meyen (1980) believes that the teacher must develop these traits:

Ability to ask meaningful questions
Sensitivity to the personal needs of students
Knowledge of the sequential aspects of curriculum
Familiarity with the necessary subject matter
Capability of modifying materials
Flexibility to change directions and timelines as needed

To construct units of instruction, the teacher follows a series of steps:

1. A rationale must be stated. Units are constructed to meet student needs. Just because the teacher feels good about a unit is insufficient reason to deliver that unit. It must fit into the sequence of instruction.
2. Specific topics that are related to the basic theme are stated. There should be at least six of these subunits.

3. A series of general objectives should be stated for each subunit.
4. Activities that will help a student master the objectives should be stated.
5. Resource materials should be collected.
6. Vocabulary should be stated.

After this preparation has been completed, lesson plans may be constructed.

Introducing a Unit of Study

The following procedures outline an effective way to motivate students; they enable students to feel they have a voice in what they will learn and how they will go about achieving their goals.

Step I: Enthusiastically give a brief introduction of the unit topic. Ask students to share what they know about the topic as they acquaint themselves with the chapter and resources to be covered.

Step II: Have students identify reasons that the topic is important. Use the blackboard or overhead projector to record responses. Be prepared to give situational examples that emphasize the use of competencies that are to be developed. Special educators are often discouraged by their students' inability to generate ideas. Examples from which the students can determine requested information, however, will help them formulate responses and contribute to the discussion. Summarize the results.

Step III: Have students brainstorm questions that they believe should be answered in the unit and identify skills that will be developed. Do this as a class or in small groups. Again, be sure that responses are recorded. Summarize and organize the results into a logical sequence. Unit goals can now be formulated.

Step IV: Have students identify ways that they can achieve the unit objectives—reading, films, computer programs, field trips, surveys, interviews, simulations, skits, guest speakers, self-appraisal, and so on.

Step V: Use exemplary activities or pretest procedures to identify specific needs of students. Formulate personal goals for the unit with each student.

Although you may have had most of the information outlined before introducing the unit, you will now have a better understanding of the students in relationship to the unit objectives, and the students will understand and accept the demands of instruction more readily since they helped design the unit. An interactive, cooperative approach has been initiated that can capitalize on a variety of learning strategies and experiences through which students can achieve their goals.

Delivering Lessons

Timelines are becoming an increasingly important part of teaching. In a climate of behaviorally based teaching in which data must be collected, it is important to incorporate planning, intervention, and evaluation into the teaching process. If the Individualized Education Program (IEP) is thought of as an integral part of the process of teaching, from two to eight objectives can be developed for each goal. These IEP objectives can be units of instruction that take from one to nine weeks to accomplish. In this way, the whole process is integrated and efficient. Daily lesson plans then flow as a natural part of the process of teaching.

Unit-based instruction varies according to the style of teaching employed. At the least creative or rote level, students sit at their desks while a teacher presents, in lecture form, the information they need to know to master the current objective in the unit. This approach requires limited and boring student participation. They are expected only to read necessary background information, which is probably redundant to the materials covered in class by the teacher, and take notes that are to be memorized later.

On the other end of the continuum, the teacher plans instruction so that students are involved. They may set up and run their own learning experiences, including experimenting, investigating, and presenting information to others in the class. In this type of unit approach, students are the ones who are active, and the teachers operate more as facilitators of learning than as presenters of facts.

Unit-based instruction can be used to introduce facts and concepts, to reinforce skills already learned, or to apply previously learned skills. Objectives may be expressed in behavioral or experiential terms. Special and regular education teachers have found success with unit teaching, often incorporating learning centers into units at any level of instruction. Mildly handicapped students stand a good chance of encountering unit-based teaching in their regular classes and should be prepared by special education to deal effectively with this methodology.

COOPERATIVE LEARNING

Johnson and Johnson (1986) offered an alternative to rote learning called cooperative learning. Lessons are structured so that students work together to accomplish shared goals. Rote teaching comprises much of the instructional day in many learning situations. In its most extreme form, rote teaching occurs when the teacher provides the question and specifies the answer, requiring the student to respond with the only acceptable correct answer on cue. Because this is a very efficient way to teach facts, a generalized feeling has developed that it should be applied to all instruction for handicapped learners. Acceptance of rote teaching is further reinforced by the pragmatic consideration that the teacher cannot afford to waste even a minute of precious time on what are perceived as nonproductive behaviors. Often, this kind of structure accompanies a competitive atmosphere in which students vie with each other to see who is best. Students may have to work against each other to achieve a goal that only one or a few can obtain. Curve grading forces students to work faster and more accurately than their peers or causes them to give up in frustration. The object in this kind of atmosphere is to get ahead by besting the others. Often mildly handicapped students do not do well in this kind of atmosphere. Some of the reasons for this include:

- Assignments that are too difficult
- Lack of important prerequisite skills
- Failure to understand what is required
- Instruction that is too fast paced and abstract.

Johnson and Johnson (1986) provided an outline of five major steps to promote their group-based method, which overcomes many of the problems encountered with rote learning.

1. Clearly specify objectives for the lesson for each student. Objectives should include both academic objectives and collaborative objectives for each student. Collaborative skills include leadership, decision making, trust building, communication, and conflict management. Mildly handicapped students benefit greatly academically, socially, and personally from mastering these skills.

2. The teacher must make decisions about group placement of students. Decisions to be made include:

    —Group size.   Two to six participants is the normal size. The less experience students have in group activities, the smaller the group size should be. The key is that groups should be small enough so that all members will have an opportunity to participate actively. At first, two to three members per group may be appropriate.

    —Group makeup.   This may be either homogeneous or heterogeneous, depending on need. Lower ability students must be readily accepted as active participants in the group. It is essential that the teacher promote a teamwork orientation.

    —Room arrangement.   Members of the groups must be able to talk with each other and share materials. Eye contact is important and may best be insured by having students sit in a circle.

    —Interdependence.   Materials should be distributed in such a way that interdependence is promoted. This is done by either giving only one copy of the needed materials or by giving each member a piece that needs to be put together with the material of other members in the group.

    —Roles.   It is important to assign roles to members in the groups to encourage cooperative learning. The roles assigned should reflect ability levels so that students may successfully carry out their assigned tasks. Examples of roles that may be assigned include a summarizer who restates the major findings of the group, a checker who insures that all members can explain an answer or a conclusion, and an accuracy coach who corrects any mistakes in another member's explanations or summaries.

3. Once the groups have been established, the teacher must clearly explain to the groups the task, the collaborative efforts required, and the learning activity. The task must be explained in such a way that the students understand the objective of the lesson and the assignment that is to be carried out. Lessons are structured so that students must work cooperatively. Normally,

the group must produce a single product, such as a report. Because all members in the group must learn the assigned material, individual accountability remains crucial. Success is dependent on all members of the group being able to demonstrate mastery of the terminal objective for the lesson. In this, each student in the group is held responsible for the learning of others in the group.

4. Once the groups begin operating, the teacher must monitor the performance of each group. The teacher should check to see that all members are actively engaged, fulfilling their assigned roles, and correctly completing their assignments. When necessary, the teacher should provide task assistance.

5. After the group has completed the assigned tasks, the teacher evaluates the overall performance of the group. Whereas one of the major components of this evaluation is to determine whether or not all members can demonstrate the desired behavior, it should also include an evaluation of how well the group carried out its collaborative efforts.

The use of cooperative learning strategies holds much promise for mildly handicapped students who must function in the regular classroom. When cooperative-learning strategies are used in the regular classroom, all students seem to benefit, both academically and socially. Additionally, intrapersonal gains such as greater persistence, higher motivation, improved self-concept, and greater overall psychological health have been reported.

BUILDING ORGANIZATIONAL SKILLS

Actively involved students listen, take notes, ask questions, answer questions, and contribute to discussions, whereas ineffective students do not attend to lectures or directions, rarely contribute, and do not answer or ask questions (Gleason et al., 1988). Furthermore, when given assignments, successful students tend to use time more efficiently, use their textbooks and resources to complete tasks effectively, and complete assignments in the time allotted. By focusing on characteristics of successful students, skills needed by students with handicaps become more evident. They fail because they lack basic skills and concepts necessary for responding to and using information. They are also inefficient in the use of study strategies that would help them make progress in spite of their deficiencies (Gleason et al., 1988).

Notebooks

Help students devise a transportable system for maintaining, retrieving, and storing necessary materials. Have students get a three-ring notebook equipped with pencil pouch, pocket dividers for each class, and notebook paper. If students cannot afford the notebooks, put the cost into your budget. Students may be motivated by your concern in helping them with organizational needs.

Hold students accountable by having regular notebook inspections. Provide positive or negative consequences for the way they are using the system.

Time-Management Strategies

Calendars: Provide students with monthly calendar pages to keep in their notebooks. They should have calendar pages for each subject and for each month that is involved in the grading period. Have students record all assignments and class activities. Use regular-size paper for the calendars so that students have adequate space to write needed information. Also leave a column at the right to use for special instructions. For some students, you may want teachers to initial the calendars each day until the student learns to record information correctly. Most students do not want to have this type of contact with their teachers. Inform students at the beginning of the school year that you require these records. Tell them why they are important and the consequences that will apply if they fail to keep their calendars current. Let them know that you will provide help in getting started.

Work Orders: Have students learn to budget their time. In many jobs a worker is issued a work order when checking in. The order is simply a listing of tasks that are to be completed that day. Demonstrate to students how to write a work order for themselves. First make a list of all tasks that will have to be completed that day. Assign a priority number to each item and an approximate amount of time that should be spent on the task. Identify times that can be used to complete the work. List the times and then the tasks to be completed in each time slot. Name materials that will be needed such as a pocket calculator, workbook, or dictionary. This procedure helps students to project their use of time, to be more adequately prepared for study sessions, and to recognize more accurately when there will be homework to do.

Time on Task: Under what conditions are students working most effectively? Provide carrels to block visual distractions. Arrange seating to avoid unnecessary socialization. Allow the use of headsets to listen to music, but stipulate that the sound is not to be heard by others.

Preparing for Lectures

Note Taking—Code Writing/Speed Writing: Y rnt u rit$_o$ /s ↓? (Why aren't you writing this down?) Students often have difficulty keeping up with lectures. Some students give up because spelling skills frustrate them. Speed writing can help both groups of students. There are several systems that are available in various study-skill programs. Helping students create their own system, however, is generally the most effective.

Vocabulary Lists: With the students, develop prelecture vocabulary lists so that the students are alert to important terms that may be used during the lecture. A spelling list is automatically provided. This process encourages more effective listening during lectures and promotes greater accuracy and ease in taking notes.

Study Groups: Determine the purpose of the reading assignment by having students survey the chapter looking at pictures, graphs, headings, and so on. Read any study questions provided in the text. Prepare an outline using the major headings and subheadings. List important vocabulary, people, and places. Practice pronouncing troublesome words. Read the assignment independently, as a team, or by listening to a tape recording. Initially, the teacher will model each step, supplying most of the information. With each session and as students improve their skills, she will contribute less information and the students will contribute more. Students should eventually use the lecture preparation strategy independently.

Listening Skills: Teach students to listen for advance organizers: There are *three* general . . . ; *Remember* this fact . . . ; *This* is *important* . . . ; *Because* . . .
    Model the strategy using a minilecture. At first, tell the students the cue words you will use. Have students orally identify the information that the words introduced. Gradually, move to longer lectures. Do not tell students cues you will use, and have students write down the expected information.

Assignments

Predictions: Teachers are creatures of habit when it comes to organizing their classes. Students can learn to predict events by observing their classes. Students can learn to predict events by observing patterns. Students may have a reading assignment, for example, but most often do not have written assignments due the day after a test. Current-events quizzes are on Friday. Study questions are usually due on Wednesday. Helping students recognize these patterns can help them to be better prepared for each class.

Appearance: Teach students to prepare attractive, properly identified assignment papers. Demonstrate how to identify papers, to use margins, to skip lines between topics, to use alternatives to scribbling out mistakes, to complete each question or problem in sequence instead of numbering down the page without consideration for the space that may be needed for each question or problem. Display models in the classroom for reference. Display students' work that demonstrates the appearance goals.

Writing Answers to Questions: Teach students how to change a question into a statement. Model the procedure. State the question and then have the student repeat the statement you modeled. Coach the student through the procedure. Rehearse statements and then have the students write the statement.

Test-Preparation Strategies

Test Preview: Using assignments that students have had to complete for a specific class, develop a minitest for the material. Include matching, multiple-choice, completion, true/false, and essay questions. Design the test so that it will take about one-third the time of the regular test. Have students follow procedures that should be followed when taking any test—write name on paper, listen for instructions not written on the test, survey the test, and so on. Evaluate results. Have students identify problem areas. After the first test of the year in a class, the students have model questions to help them with further study. Have the students develop minitests for their classmates to take.

Study Sheets: Using lists developed in prelecture preparation and notes from classes, have students develop study sheets using a computer word-processing program. Students in the group can work on the study sheets individually or in pairs. One title is used, however, so that information is not entered repeatedly. Vocabulary, important people, and events are some of the things that can be included. Entries that are made by one student can be improved or extended by another. When they are printed, each student has a precise study guide from which test preparation can begin.

Strategies for Acquiring Information

Problems: Most of us in the process of acquiring information from the written page underline or highlight important information. It is a standard method for focusing attention and increasing understanding of written material. The problem is that most schools will not allow students to highlight or underline in texts. Get permission to keep specific texts in your classroom. If necessary, use your budget to get the textbooks.

Locating Information: Develop units of study in which students learn how to use sources of information. From student-survey information, the types of skills most important should be prioritized. Test the students in their use of each type of resource, however. The following sources of information should be on your list: tables, indexes, readers' guides, dictionaries, thesauruses, encyclopedias, almanacs, libraries, catalogs.

On-line Computer-Generated Tests: Using a computer test-generating program, develop drill and practice tests that the students can take and retake. Instead of numbering or lettering multiple-choice questions, set these questions up so that students will have to respond to each question by typing the specific word or words. Use a program that will allow you to print out random questions and that requires students to study their mistakes. Have students chart their progress so that they recognize their progress.

Outlining: Teach outline procedures. Use topics of interest but mainly those from courses the students are taking. Begin with outlines that have only one word missing in each topic and subtopic. Have students locate the missing words in the material being studied. Identify ways of locating major topics and subtopics. Gradually, decrease the amount of information on the outlines provided as the students demonstrate their skill in using the strategies.

Reading Comprehension: Teach reading comprehension strategies such as SQ3R (Survey, Question, Read, Recite, and Review), REAP (Read, Encode, Annotate, and Ponder), or the 5R's of the Cornell Process (Record, Reduce, Recite, Reflect, and Review).

Students fail in regular classes because they frequently have not developed higher level thinking skills. Therefore, every opportunity should be taken to include in learning-strategy instruction components from this extensive list of reading comprehension skills: predicting outcomes, separating opinion from fact, recognizing devices used for effect, following directions, making up new titles, locating topic sentences, paraphrasing, locating main ideas, observing sequences, comparing and contrasting, making generalizations, and relating details to themes. Teachers should be sure to work with skills until they are used automatically by the students. Identify skills students will use the most, test students in their use of the skills. Do not assume that every student should be taught every component on this list.

Memory Devices: Use novel associations and mnemonic devices. Many people have learned the names of the lines of the treble clef in music with "Every Good Boy Does Fine." Teach students how to develop memory through association. Have contests each week for the best memory device developed. Recognize that memory difficulties may be the result of inadequate instruction such as too much material at one time, poor emphasis of important facts, or insufficient practice with material or skill. Work to change these conditions. All memorization relies on attention, interest, and repetition.

INSTRUCTIONAL MODIFICATIONS

Teachers have been modifying instruction to meet student needs as long as teaching has existed. Modifications in education have become institutionalized to the point that teachers are expected to function in an environment that both supports individualized instruction and is characterized by wide dissemination of the methods by which modification can occur. The ability to tap the successful experiences of teachers means that no teacher should be expected to "reinvent the wheel" in this area. Only a few of the popular modifications will be reviewed. More extensive discussions are found in the literature (e.g., Hammill & Bartel, 1986; Marsh & Price, 1980; Mercer et al., 1984). (See Chapter 7, Appendix 7.2.)

Alternative Texts

Teachers can provide alternative texts for students who exhibit low reading skills. These texts enable students to read about a topic at an easier reading level, which insures greater comprehension and less frustration. But the books must contain appropriate content and not appear "babyish" to the secondary student.

Taped Texts

Many school have used volunteers to read required texts onto tapes so that students with low reading skills can listen to a required reading at their own pace. With this modification, student headphones are a high priority.

Prepared Lecture Outline or Notes

A student who has poor writing skills may be able to take more accurate notes if he or she is provided a detailed outline that facilitates note taking. Other students may need to be furnished a complete set of notes that were prepared either by the teacher or a student who takes good notes. In the latter case the use of carbonless paper is helpful.

Oral Exams

Some students may not have an opportunity to demonstrate whether they have learned because their lack of reading and writing skills interferes with their test-taking ability. For these students, allowing them to take a test orally may provide a fair alternative. Regular and special educators work together to resolve scheduling and other conflicts that may arise.

SOCIAL SKILLS DEVELOPMENT

Behavior Contracts

Have a student identify a problem behavior that is interfering with adequate functioning in school. Have the student express why the behavior is a problem. Identify the costs of such behavior. Set up a standard of behavior that is wanted by the student to replace the behavior. Develop a self-monitoring chart for the student to record when the behavior occurs. Allow the behavior to be faded over time according to the schedule of costs and payoffs established. Behaviors may be as simple as negative statements about school work to complex problems that result in outbursts of aggression and profanity.

Group

Hold weekly problem-solving sessions that are concerned primarily with difficulties students have in dealing with people. Teach students to identify problems, devise plans to overcome the problem, to carry out the plans, and to evaluate the results. When direct action must be taken with another person, role play and rehearse what is to be done. Freedom of expression, search for alternatives, and short-term and long-term costs and payoffs should all be included as a part of these sessions. Social skills training is not needed by all students. Do not misuse a student's time just because you "think" it is important. Research has found that nearly two-thirds of the students identified as learning disabled do not manifest deficits in social skills (Baum et al., 1988).

Time Out

Some students have bad days. They generally come to school on these days in a poor frame of mind. Some students get aggressive, others get mouthy, and others become stubborn and obstinate. All of these behaviors spell disaster if they are not controlled by the students when in their regular classes. Respect a student's understanding of himself and allow him to check into a special area to cool off. Procedures for this action should be a part of the student's IEP, and all regular-class teachers with whom he is involved are to follow procedures.

The instructional applications that have been presented are but a few that can be used to prepare students for the mainstream. Appropriate behavior, organization, and study skills are all necessary for adequate academic functioning whether in regular classes or in special classes. Helping students learn how to learn is paying benefits. More and more, students with handicaps are experiencing success in higher education. Colleges and universities are developing support programs so that the potential of these students has a greater chance of being fulfilled.

Emphasis on regular class adjustment and related requirements does not replace the commitment of special education to the development of life skill needs of students. Decisions concerning the courses students should take require examination of the student's ability to carry on adult-life functions. These decisions must be made early in a student's high school program. For some students parallel courses will have to be substituted for regular courses. Parallel courses concentrate more on needed information than on what may be nice to know. Material used in these courses is selected for the level of functioning that suits the capabilities of the student.

For most of these students, educational intervention efforts should be shifted from a remedial to a more preventive approach by focusing on the demands inherent in postschool environments (Palloway et al., 1988). They claim that to be truly preventive, curricula should reflect considerations down from the goal of successful adjustment rather than up from the elementary curriculum focused on remediating basic skills. Chapter 10 emphasizes objectives that focus on the kinds of information that are needed to function adequately as an adult.

Curricular foci should include maximum participation in regular high school programs but must give attention to transitional needs of students moving into post-secondary settings (Palloway et al., 1989). There must be a commitment to both current and future needs of students. To insure that this occurs, there are several instructional guidelines that teachers should keep in mind.

1. Make all instruction relevant. Use content that is meaningful. Help students to understand why the information or skill is needed.
2. Do not waste students' time teaching something "new" just to be teaching or because the topic comes up next in the teacher's manual for the text. Pretest students so what is taught is needed by the student. Match evaluation information with instruction. Spend as much time as is needed to "plan" instruction. Be appropriately prepared.
3. Teach application of strategies while teaching reading, writing, and so on and by using the context and concepts from students' classes. Students who have assignments to complete for a regular class will resent time taken to develop study skills that do not apply to work that must be done.
4. Help students evaluate their work. Point out change and progress. Encourage

students to predict degree of success. Help them recognize the adult standard for completed tasks.

5. Apply behavior expectations of a worksite to the classroom. Use job placement as an incentive for improving attendance, behavior, and achievement.
6. In all subject areas, relate competencies to daily living and the world of work.
7. In all instructional situations, leave students with a sense of accomplishment and success.

As students move into the high school years, a shift in emphasis toward an adult outcomes model must be considered. We cannot assume that the effective transition to postsecondary situations will be satisfactory. The changes taking place in special education are an attempt to address the failures of the past. We must continue these efforts.

SUMMARY

Chapter 5 has given the reader some of the structure necessary to teach effectively regardless of the location of the educational setting. Identification of student strengths and weakness is emphasized along with the necessity of understanding the strengths and weakness of each student's learning processes in order to select appropriate modes of intervention. From the start, the student needs to see the relevance of instruction.

High priority should be given to motivating students through clear expectations, usefulness of education, and feedback on performance. The TESA Interaction Model is helpful in offering equal, consistent opportunity to students.

Specific skills and techniques that have been found to be effective extend across models. Varieties of strategies, such as time-management techniques, cooperative learning, unit methodology, reinforcement, and guidance on assignments and test taking have been explored in this chapter. Social skills development is an important complementary component. The chapter presented specific end products for the teacher, along with relevant questions that the teacher needs to ask as teaching progresses.

STUDY QUESTIONS

1. When evaluating a student, what are the initial steps of determining what the student needs to know?
2. How could you determine the means by which a student in your class tries to solve a problem? Develop some materials that you could use with students to determine their problem-solving techiniques.
3. What are some advantages of using the following methods of teaching?

   Unit method
   Cooperative Learning

   What are some of the disadvantages of these methods?

4. Skill development is an important aspect of teaching. Why is this so, and what are some of the skills that are necessary for students who are not college bound to have?
5. Take three of the skills you discussed in question 4 and indicate how you would motivate the students to learn them and then how you would teach and practice these skills.
6. How should accommodation strategies for students be determined?
7. Motivation is considered the first step in implementing instruction. Why is motivation important, and what are variables that should be considered?
8. What instructional guidelines can teachers use that will help them keep focus on both current and future needs of students?
9. Would you feel comfortable using cooperative learning as a teaching strategy?
10. How could you get regular education teachers to accept instructional modifications such as taped texts and oral exams?

REFERENCES

Baum, D. D., Duffelmeyer, F., & Geelan, M. (1988). Resource teacher perceptions of the prevalence of social dysfunction among students with learning disabilities. *Journal of Learning Disabilities, 21*(6), 380–381.

Conway, R. N. F., & Gow, L. (1988). Mainstreaming special class students with mild handicaps through group instruction. *Remedial and Special Education, 9*(5), 34–41.

Gleason, M. M., Herr, C. M., & Archer, A. L. (1988). Study skills: Special focus. *Teaching Exceptional Children, 20*(3), 52–57.

Gresham, F. M. (1984). Social skills and self-efficacy for exceptional children. *Exceptional Children, 51*(3), 253–260.

Feuerstein, R. (1980). *Learning potential assessment device.* University Park, MD: University of Maryland Press.

Hammill, D. D., & Bartel, N. R. (1986). *Teaching students with learning and behavior problems* (4th ed.). Boston: Allyn & Bacon.

Hunter, M. (1967). *Motivation theory for teachers.* El Segundo, CA: TIP Publications.

Johnson, D. W., & Johnson, R. T. (1986). *Learning Together and Alone* (2nd ed.). Englewood Cliffs, NJ: Prentice-Hall.

Kerman, S., Kimball, T., & Martin, M. (1980). *Teacher expectations and student achievement.* Bloomington, IN: Phi Delta Kappa.

Leon County Schools. (1988). Exceptional student education: Individual education plan. Leon County, FL: Board of Education. In J. J. Bugerty, L. W. Tindall, T. J. Heffron, and B. B. Dougherty (Eds.), *Profiles of success: Serving secondary special education students through Carl D. Perkins Vocational Act, 12 exemplary approaches.* Madison: University of Wisconsin, Vocational Studies Center.

Marsh, G. E., & Price, B. J. (1980). *Methods for teaching the mildly handicapped adolescent.* St. Louis: C. V. Mosby.

Mercer, C. D., Mercer, A. R., & Bott, D. A. (1984). *Self-correcting learning materials for the classroom.* Columbus: C. E. Merrill.

Meyen, E. L. (1980). *Developing units of instruction for the regular and special education teacher* (3rd ed.). Dubuque, IA: Wm. C. Brown.

Palloway, E. A., Patton, J. R., Epstein, M. H., & Smith, T. (1989). Comprehensive curriculum for students with mild handicaps. *Focus on Exceptional Children, 21*(8), 1–12.

Palloway, E. A., Smith, J. D. & Patton, J. R. (1988). Learning disabilities: An adult development perspective. *Learning Disabilities Quarterly, 11,* 265–272.

Salend, S. J. (1984). Factors contributing to the development of successful mainstreaming programs. *Exceptional Children, 50*(5), 409–416.

Samuels, S. J. (1986). Why children fail to learn and what to do about it. *Exceptional Children, 53*(1), 7–16.

Switzky, H. N., & Schultz, G. F. (1988). Intrinsic motivation and learning performance: Implications for individual educational programming for learners with mild handicaps. *Remedial and Special Education, 9*(4), 14.

APPENDIX 5.1. SECONDARY STUDENT INVENTORY
(Standard Diploma Goal Student)

Student _____   Exceptionality _____

DOB: _____   Student # _____

Conference Date: _____   ___ Promotion from grade ___ to grade ___

___ Transfer from (school) ___ to (school) ___

Woodcock-Johnson Assessment of Achievement
Date Administered _____

Subtest	Grade Equivalent	Standard Score
Reading		
Math		
Written Language		
Knowledge		

strengths +	weaknesses 0	cannot do—cross out item

INFORMATION INPUT INFORMATION SOURCES	INFORMATION OUTPUT TEST FORMAT	
___ Textbook	Short Answer	___
___ Worksheets	Essay	___
___ Lecture	Multiple Choice	___
___ Discussion	True-False	___
___ A-V Material	Matching	___
___ Audio Tape	Computation	___
___ Concrete Experience	Word Problems/Math	___
___ Observation		
Other:	ASSIGNMENTS	
	Worksheets	___
STRUCTURE	Short Papers	___
___ Directed	Term Papers	___
___ Independent	Demo/Lab Projects	___
___ Peer Tutor	Art, Media Projects	___
___ 1—1 Adult	Oral Reports	___
___ Small Group	Group Discussion	___
___ Large Group/Class	Computation	___
Other:	Word Problems/Math	___
	Maps, Charts, Graphs	___

• • • • • • •

CAPS   *Results*   Date _____

		Grade Equivalent	Percentile
	Reading	_____	_____
	Math	_____	_____
	Language	_____	_____

APPENDIX 5.1. (continued)

(check an item only if it is a confirmed and
repeated problem in the mainstream)

Learning Problems

___ Becoming interested
___ Getting started
___ Paying attention to spoken word
___ Paying attention to printed word
___ Following directions
___ Keeping track of materials, assignments
___ Staying on task
___ Completing tasks on time
___ Working in groups
___ Working independently
___ Learning by listening
___ Expressing self verbally
___ Reading textbooks
___ Reading study sheet or tests
___ Understanding what is read
___ Writing legibly
___ Expressing self in writing
___ Spelling
___ Seeing relationships
___ Understanding cause and effect; anticipating
      consequences
___ Drawing conclusions/making inferences
___ Remembering

Other Academic Skills Needed

___ Note taking
___ Outlining
___ Punctuation
___ Sentences
___ Paragraphs
___ Dictionary use
___ Independent research
___ Measuring (to _____)
___ Manual dexterity

Behavior Problems

Getting started   ___
Coming to class on time   ___
Coming to class prepared   ___
Following directions   ___
Staying in seat   ___
Staying on task   ___
Completing tasks on time   ___
Working in groups   ___
Working independently   ___
Demanding much help/attention   ___
Participating in class discussion   ___
Daydreaming   ___
Interrupting or talking in class   ___
Verbally disrespectful   ___
Using inappropriate language   ___
Harassing other students   ___
Abusing property   ___
Cheating   ___
Getting set up by other kids   ___

Other Behavior Skills Needed

Understands/follows safety rules   ___
Asks questions or requests help when
      needed   ___
Attendance Policy: _____
_____
_____

Student likes (interests and hobbies): _____

Student dislikes: _____

Comments and suggestions:

APPENDIX 5.2. COURSE MODIFICATION FOR REGULAR EDUCATION COURSES

Directions:
1. List only courses needing modifications.
2. Indicate course reference numbers for course modifications.
3. Obtain signatures of teacher(s) responsible.
4. Modifications of basic or vocational courses shall not include modifications to the curriculum frameworks or student standards.

Page _____ of IEB
Student _____
St # _____
Exceptionality _____ DOB _____
Teacher _____
Date: From _____ 19 ___ to ___ 19 ___
School _____ Grade _____

Reference Number	Course Number	Course Name
#1		
#2		
#3		
#4		
#5		

Modifications	Initiation Date	Person Responsible
I. Instructional Time Modifications.		
Additional time to complete assignments.		
Course outlines/requirements provided.		
II. Instructional Strategies.		
III. Special Communications Systems.		
Tape record lectures.		
Provide recorded text.		
IV. Classroom Test Modifications.		
Tests will be given orally.		
Verbal responses to questions recorded on tape or dictated.		
Time limits for test completion increased.		

Exceptional Ed. Teacher _____ Regular Ed. Teacher _____
Exceptional Ed. Teacher _____ Regular Ed. Teacher _____
Exceptional Ed. Teacher _____ Regular Ed. Teacher _____

White–cumulative/ESE folder   Pink–parent
Yellow–ESE office   Goldenrod–ESE teacher

110

APPENDIX 5.3. COOPERATIVE COURSE MODIFICATION PLAN

Course _____ Period _____ Student(s) _____

Teacher _____ ESE Teacher _____ Date _____

Problem Areas Identified (Learning Behavior)	Suggested Adaptations (Activity, Assignments)	Agreements	WHO	Time Line	Results

CHAPTER 6

What Teachers Do

When asked what teachers do, most people can easily list a number of activities that they observed when attending school—discussions and lectures, reading from the textbook, passing out worksheets, giving tests and grades, assigning homework, reading the newspaper. Regardless of the grade level, type of student, academic discipline or responsibilities, there are certain public activities of teaching. Charles Brown, principal of Pottstown High School, contended that the keys to success in teaching were controlling the behavior of one's students, having up-to-date plans for the substitute, and adhering to the policies and procedures of the school district and building. Although Brown was also concerned with a teacher's knowledge of the content area, he stressed that his "keys to success" were "public" activities.

More than Brown's "keys to success" or a teacher's public activities familiar to most people, teaching is a "complex problem solving activity, the goal of which is to facilitate student learning" (Gagne, 1985). This chapter first takes you to a number of classrooms to see some of the approaches, models, and strategies discussed in previous chapters in action. It then describes areas of activity especially important for teachers of special education: understanding the students and their particular community (Hallahan & Kauffman, 1988), formulating the curriculum that is to accomplish the expected outcomes (Harste & Stephens, 1986), and attaining and communicating knowledge of the outcomes of instruction (Lorber & Pierce, 1983). In addition, we see that today, special education teachers are more than instructors of specific content: they are managers and members of multidisciplinary teams.

THE EXPECTATIONS OF GOOD TEACHING: THREE CASE STUDIES

In recent years there has been much emphasis on improving the performance of classroom teachers. Good teaching is common to all levels, contents, and types of students encountered (Brophy, 1985; Emmer & Evertson, 1981). When you are observing a teacher, among the questions to be asked are:

1. Does the teacher employ a variety of instructional methods?
2. Does the teacher provide instruction in an organized manner with an established routine and smooth transitions?
3. Did students know what they were to learn?
4. How did questioning, assignments, and worksheets enable the teacher to know if students were learning?
5. What level of skills are being emphasized by the questioning, assignments, and so on?
6. Is instructional time maximized by the teacher?

The following cases show three teachers who are considered excellent by their district. Their approach reflects the qualities and skills thought to be effective. Information on the learning level of each class is given in the analysis of the teaching approaches.

CASE 6: ENGLISH CLASS

Mrs. Lambert asked the students to get their materials for that period's instruction. As she took attendance, she reminded several students about making up missed work and back assignments. All students were seated as the bell rang to begin the period.

Mrs. Lambert moved to a sideboard that listed the day's activities and future assignments. After identifying the objectives to be accomplished during this hour, she directed the students' attention to the board and briefly explained how that was to happen. Her explanation reviewed what they had done, how the day's work fit in, and where they would end up by Friday.

Mrs. Lambert directed the group to get out their journals. The students would write about something they had done or could do (i.e., winning the lottery). She probed different students with questions and wrote their ideas on the board. Then she asked if the students had any questions.

Soon the students were working individually. Mrs. Lambert walked about the room. She helped individuals read their paragraph and correct spelling and grammatical errors. She took aside three students who completed their assignment and had them correct one another's work.

Mrs. Lambert glanced around the room and noted which students had completed their project. She had each one come to her, and together, they corrected the students' journal entries. Then she announced that it was time to prepare for a vocabulary test. Students obtained their material and moved into their specific groups. They worked with each other or with a peer tutor, reviewing their vocabulary words for that week.

The students moved through the subsequent activity—reading. The transition between activities was smooth since the teacher gave cues to impending changes. She praised individuals who completed their assignments and praised appropriate behavior—social and work. As the period ended, the students were reminded of what they had done and what was coming up later that week.

CASE 7: GOVERNMENT CLASS

Mr. Slenz was teaching Basic Government for the first time. He returned papers to the students as they entered the room and took their seats. He reminded the group of an upcoming assignment (term paper) and asked for questions. Mr. Slenz responded to a question about getting sources as he took attendance. He cautioned students not to wait since other classes were using the same sources.

Mr. Slenz reviewed the previous day's lecture. From an overhead, he restated some key points of the lecture. Again he asked for questions from the class. Each student received an outline to be completed using notes and the textbook. The outline was to help students prepare for an upcoming test.

Mr. Slenz completed the lecture he had started the previous day. He highlighted specific terms that had been listed on the transparency. After calling for questions, he paused, but there was no response from the class—most were taking notes or trying to read the outline.

Mr. Slenz then explained the assignment and helped the students complete the first question. He directed the group to work on their own. He circulated among the students, giving assistance as needed.

As the period ended, Mr. Slenz collected the outlines from those who had completed them. The students were reminded of the next assignment and the term paper. The bell rang, ending the period.

CASE 8: ELECTRONICS

Mr. Catton has taught electricity and electronics for seventeen years. Unlike the other teachers, he works with each class two hours each day in both classroom and laboratory activities.

Mr. Catton's class began with a problem from the previous day. The class worked on the problem while Mr. Catton took attendance. A student was called upon to solve the problem. Mr. Catton reviewed the steps of the student's work and verbally reinforced him because he had correctly applied the procedure taught earlier in the week.

"Today, we're going to apply the process to . . ." Mr. Catton distributed a handout that outlined a more complicated application of the procedure. A filmstrip was shown to review the basic procedure and the new application. Information presented in the filmstrip corresponded to the handout.

Mr. Catton asked the class if there were questions on the filmstrip. He paused and asked the same question about the handout. After a lengthy pause, he asked a student to help with a demonstration of the procedure that students would do in the lab. As the student moved through the procedure, Mr. Catton asked a series of questions. What should the meter read? Is the pattern . . . ? How does it compare with . . . ? Although some took notes, most students focused their attention on the meters and scope pattern.

Mr. Catton reviewed the new procedure again. A handout for the lab was given to the class. After several minutes a student was asked how he would set up the first test. Again, the student was praised but corrected for missing one step.

At that point, most of the students moved to the lab. Some students met with Mr. Catton to get work they had missed or did not understand. They then worked individually on the lab's computers before beginning the day's exercise.

Mrs. Lambert's English class has only ten students. Each was classified as educable mentally retarded. Mr. Slenz teaches twenty students, five of whom were identified as learning disabled. None of the twenty-four students in Mr. Catton's electronics class was identified as disabled.

Each instructor was apparently in control, prepared to teach that day, and did it appropriately. Each employed the "Brown's Keys to Success," but were they effective? The following analysis uses the six checklist questions listed on page 113.

Choosing a Method of Instruction

At the secondary level the most common method of instruction is the *lecture,* particularly in English and social studies. This is true because of several factors: (a) time constraints due to the organization of high schools that requires instruction to be done within a specific time (forty, forty-five, or fifty minutes each day); (b) curricular demands that require the instructor to cover specific information or a large body of information in a short time, so "efficiency" is the key word; (c) increased control of the students since they are engaged in listening and note taking; and (d) instructors being most comfortable with lecturing because their own preparation for teaching emphasized that method.

In our cases, Mrs. Lambert and Mr. Catton relied heavily on the second most common method—*individual work* (reading, laboratory exercise, report preparation) under the direction of the instructor. It can also include seatwork or guided practice following a lecture, demonstration, or explanation.

Approximately one-half of the class time was spent with students working individually under the supervision of a teacher. The time followed the initial instruction to and guided practice with the group. Each instructor was *active* in this process—moving around the room, watching, and checking and correcting student work. Such activity may be beneficial in that students remain "on task" or engaged longer than if the teacher takes time to correct papers, reflect on their nonschool interests, and so on.

The characteristics of the mildly handicapped led both the English and government teachers to use more than one method of instruction. Of particular interest was the structure of the English class. The class had four segments that enabled the teacher to provide a variety of activities and further divide her students into working groups, not unlike an elementary class. The segments were based on her observation of the students' attention and behavior and the content she wanted to cover.

Although government did not offer the variety, Mr. Slenz's teaching strategies varied between whole-class and individual instruction. The first segment of large-group instruction was informational and review. Individual assignments and monitoring took place in the second segment. A lecture to the whole group followed by individual activities comprised the final two segments.

Although there were no special education students in electronics, the instructor recognized the different learning characteristics of his students (visual, auditory, mixed) in part due to their class and lab performance. In addition, the complexity of the subject matter led Mr. Catton to use a multimedia approach. The availability of a laboratory enabled students to apply most of the concepts they were taught that day.

Mrs. Lambert had three distinct advantages over her colleagues. First, she had access to case studies on each of her students, which provided information on learning and ability. Nothing similar exists for Mr. Slenz or Mr. Catton. Second, the class size (ten students) facilitated different instructional methods and enabled her to monitor students closely. Third, she had two peer tutors to provide more individualized assistance.

Of all instructional methods, the least frequently used is *cooperative learning*. In only two segments of the three classes represented in our cases did students work together. During the spelling segment of English and the lab portion of electronics, students worked together. This was unusual since many activities away from school require individuals to interact with others.

Class Organization

Each instructor developed routines or procedures for his or her classes. In the case of Mrs. Lambert and Mr. Slentz, their routine began as students entered the classroom. Materials were being distributed to or picked up by the students. Mr. Catton directed his students to complete a problem based on information presented the previous day.

All three teachers used the initial time to complete their administrative responsibilities such as attendance, check schedules, and distribute information to the students who were absent. In the case of Mrs. Lambert and Mr. Slentz, the preliminary activities took place before the start of class.

Mr. Catton and Mr. Slentz followed with a review based on the information presented during the previous class session. Their intent was to highlight and reinforce key concepts or procedures for the students.

Mrs. Lambert identified the activities that were to take place during the hour. She shared with the class how the material from the previous day related to the day's activities.

Two of the three instructors also identified the objectives to be accomplished by the students through the activities of the hour. Such a step was designed to give the instruction a specific focus or outcome that ultimately could be evaluated by the teacher.

Each instructor ended the hour with either a review of what was accomplished or what was to come the next day or later that week. The activity by the instructors "closed" off the hour by highlighting important information or directing the students' attention to a significant future activity.

As the instructors moved from each segment (review or preview, group presentation, individual activity) to a new segment, they clued the students to each change. Shifts can be clued in any number of ways with the most common being verbal.

All three instructors rely heavily on verbal clues to their classes to prepare them for an impending change. Students have the opportunity to complete work and get out assignments or material for the next segment after being given the cue by the instructor. Simply saying "Now" or "Okay, you have two minutes to . . ." prompted the students to expect the change that was about to take place.

Mr. Slentz cued his students by asking for questions, pausing and waiting for a response, and then turning off the overhead projector.

The instructors had their materials available for distribution to the students. Media were set up for immediate use during the next segment. The result was a minimum of disruption by the students and little loss of instructional time not only between segments but also for the entire hour.

The structure and organization of the classes permitted the instructors to make use of more than 95 percent of the available instructional time, or fifty-two of fifty-five minutes.

Evaluation of Outcomes

From the three cases, it cannot be determined if the students have learned what was expected or presented by the teachers. As the teachers observed the students working on individual assignments, responding to questions and correcting work completed in class, they could only determine a student's immediate retention. Even when a student performed in a laboratory setting such as electronics, the evaluation by the teacher was of newly presented information.

The teachers did examine the students' work on individual assignments as they walked around the room or, in the case of Mrs. Lambert, by reading journal entries. Individual students in electronics demonstrated their knowledge through board work and then in the lab.

All the instructors checked the students' understanding by asking questions that required them not only to recall information but also to apply or demonstrate their understanding of the information presented during class.

One advantage of teaching electronics or any laboratory course is that students have an opportunity to demonstrate their knowledge of a skill that was presented during a lecture or through another format. A student's performance on projects or experiments may count as much as their performance on tests and quizzes given in the classroom.

A home economics teacher from the same district as the three teachers presented in the case studies uses the project or demonstration approach to evaluate skills that cannot be easily "tested" in a written examination. Such an approach is an advantage to those students who have difficulty expressing themselves in writing or verbally recalling information.

Only when teaching at the graduate level does one ever have the resources and time to analyze test results, develop better questions, and revise items to reflect what was actually being taught. The drive in school is to evaluate better, but the resources will probably not be available to those in the average classroom.

Planning Revisited

The cement/adhesive to instruction is planning (Orlich et al., 1985; Woolfolk, 1987). It follows through from setting course objectives to evaluation. Without a doubt, planning facilitates teaching; it focuses one's direction and energy (Bluestein, 1989).

Gary Borich (1988) described *planning* as systematic, deciding form and content, and setting priorities on what is to be accomplished. It is planning that brings together outcomes, students, curriculum, instruction, organization, and evaluation. Yet it is underplayed in teaching.

For many teachers, *planning* is placing an entry in their planbook, which includes the pages in the textbook and a reference from the teacher's manual. The process continues with the selection of supplementary materials and probably the preparation of some type of evaluation, usually provided by the editor of the text or materials being used in the class.

The process presented above is not the process used by the teachers in the case studies. They spend considerable time matching materials with objectives, observing students and their behavior, preparing activities to accomplish objectives, using a variety of instructional methods to present their material, and devising multiple ways of evaluating their students.

What appears in their planbook is an objective, activities to accomplish the objective, closing activities, and key questions. The written effort does not reflect the time in devising that plan or the preparation of materials and/or media preview and so on.

As a special education teacher, Mrs. Lambert has access to information on each of her students that is not available on regular students. Thus she is able to consider the learning style and achievement levels as she prepares to teach. Mr. Catton and Mr. Slentz must gather their information on the students as they proceed each day.

THE IMPORTANCE OF KNOWING YOUR STUDENTS AND THEIR COMMUNITY

During the period of development known as "adolescence," the transition from childhood to adulthood, individuals experience significant physical, personal, and emotional changes. The difficulty of assessing social skills for this age group has been discussed in earlier chapters. In this tumultuous period, adolescents are characterized by the following traits (Mercer, 1983).

1. Experience physical growth—height and weight
2. Operate independently and with great mobility
3. Seek to establish a personal identity
4. Are influenced by their peer group, conforming to many of its norms
5. Mature sexually
6. Interact with their environment
7. Develop formal and abstract thinking ability
8. Want to be secure, yet independent
9. Can have a long attention span but be easily bored
10. Become self-motivating

The major tasks have been summarized by Smith, Price, and Marsh (1986) and are listed below.

Major Tasks of Adolescents

Creation of a sense of sexuality as part of a personal identity
Development of confidence in social interactions

Infusion of social values into a personal code of behavior
Acceptance of biological changes
Attainment of a sense of emotional independence
Contemplation of vocational interests
Identification of personal talents and interests
Awareness of personal weaknesses and strengths
Development of sexual interests with nonfamily members
Development of peer relationships
Completion of formal educational activities
Preparation for marriage, parenting, and adult relationships

Note that among the tasks related to education are contemplation of vocational interests, identifying personal talents and interests, and completion of formal education.

Although adolescents undergo many changes, they do not all become monsters as reported by parents and teachers. Unfortunately, some adolescents are faced with difficulties created by economic and family situations that may not make them monsters but do create new burdens and responsibilities for schools (Boyer, 1983).

Local statistics mirror what has been reported nationally. At United Township High School, East Moline, Illinois, more than 25 percent of the students are classified as economically disadvantaged. More than one-fifth of the students live with one parent, and more than half work to meet their personal needs. In this country one of five or six students has an alcoholic or drug-addicted parent. One-third of the graduating seniors reported a heavy consumption of alcohol. These trends, according to Halpern (1987), make learning more difficult for students.

It is not unusual for faculty members to complain about students. The teachers comment on how different students are more (unmotivated, preoccupied) than when they (the teachers) were first hired. When one considers what may be going on in a student's personal life, other than the traditional problems of adolescence, one can be more sympathetic to student concerns.

Some students not only deal with adolescence; they must also struggle with unique learning needs, so unique that they have been classified as *mildly learning disabled, mentally disabled*, or *emotionally disabled* and require some type of special education intervention.

Although each category exists separately for legal and administrative purposes, educators have combined the three groups for instructional purposes in multiclasses or cross-categorical classes. (Edgar, 1988; Miller & Davis, 1982; Smith & Payne, 1980). Patton and associates (1987) identified five common characteristics among the three categories:

1. Low achievement in mathematics, reading, and/or written expression
2. General low performance in other academic areas (science, social studies, reference skill)
3. Deficiencies in study-skill areas
4. Plateau in basic skill development
5. Difficulty in producing and implementing strategies for problem solving

The following cases describe students who are considered mildly disabled. The questions to be raised as one reads the abbreviated profiles might include:

1. Are the characteristics and needs similar?
2. What type of curriculum or program would be beneficial to each student?
3. What might be expected of the students after they leave high school?

CASE 9: EDUCABLE MENTALLY DISABLED (PAUL)

Paul was always on time to class. His assignments were complete except for questions in which he was required to analyze or contrast elements. Although prepared for class, Paul's written assignments were filled with spelling and punctuation errors. In mathematics, Paul was unable to set up problems using fractions or decimals or with more than one operation.

Paul's oral responses were monosyllabic, unless pressed to give a more extensive answer, and then it was a repeat of something said by the teacher or another student. His thinking was concrete—when asked about buying tires for his car, he said he would always buy the cheapest because it would save him money. When faced with a difficult problem Paul would wait, hoping someone would do it for him or take it away.

Paul scored between 50 and 55 on the Wescher Intelligence Scale for Children—Revised (WISC-R). His adaptive behavior placed him in the mildly retarded range when compared to individuals his own age. He had a relatively flat achievement profile below the 2nd percentile in reading, math, general knowledge, and language.

During his junior year, Paul was placed at a local pharmacy as a clerk trainee as part of this vocational training program. He had difficulty, however, remembering where to put stock, maintaining a steady work pace, and waiting on customers. As a senior, Paul was enrolled in vocational auto-body training through the area vocational center. He expressed an interest in working, but he did not believe he could be employed in the area of auto-body repair. Although he had not applied for any jobs, he did not want assistance from the school staff or community agencies. Since Paul had not taken any steps toward employment, he was referred to the Department of Rehabilitation for an extensive vocational evaluation.

CASE 10: BEHAVIORAL DISABILITY (JOHN)

John had difficulty relating to his peers and had no friends. He was unkempt, wore the same clothes for several days at a time, and had a strong body odor. He teased female students and the younger, smaller students.

John bragged that he was an outstanding welder. After graduation he was leaving the area for Michigan to train as a welder. Later, he informed students he was going to college and become an underwater welder.

In class, John constantly sought the attention of the teacher. He asked questions that were not appropriate to the discussion or activity in progress. His frequent interruptions caused negative comments from his peers.

John was reported to have had a violent temper, although it had not been observed by the staff. For more than three years he had received professional help from the local mental health agency and the school social worker.

Intellectually, John was within the lower average range. His individual and group-achievement test scores ranged from the 25th percentile in reading, spelling, reference skills, and mathematics application to the 50th percentile in mathematics computation. John did score above the 10th percentile on written language and related tests.

CASE 11: LEARNING DISABILITY (JODI).

Jodi had difficulty listening to lectures and then taking notes. She read slowly but was able to comprehend more than 85 percent of what she read. Her written expression was simple with few spelling or grammatical errors. Jodi preferred to discuss or present information orally.

Intellectually, Jodi was within the low-average range. There was evidence of auditory processing deficits and expressive language difficulties. Her performance on individual achievement tests placed her at the 12th percentile in reading decoding and comprehension and at the 20th percentile in spelling and mathematics computation.

Jodi was interested in becoming a nurse after high school. In preparation, she enrolled in a health-occupation course for her final two years of high school. After graduation, Jodi, with the help of her counselor, wrote to the area community colleges requesting information about nursing and programs for special needs students.

By the time these three students reached high school they had experienced several years of difficulties academically, personally, or socially or cognitively. Their difficulties were primarily within a school setting, although certain problems may have impacted on their ability to be successful in other areas of their environment.

Each student had been in special education since late elementary school, with the exception of Paul who was placed into special education in the 2nd grade. They had been reevaluated at least twice since their initial placement. Although each was classified differently, they exhibited one or more of the five characteristics described by Patton and associates (1987).

1. Low achievement in mathematics, reading, and written expression—Jodi and Paul had scores that placed them below the 12th and 2nd percentile, respectively, when compared to students in the same grade. John's overall profile was near the 30th percentile. John reached the 50th percentile in mathematics computation. When material was presented orally or John could respond orally, his scores increased to within an average range.
2. General low performance in other academic areas (science, social studies, reference skills, and so on)—John and Jodi showed achievement scores that were depressed when compared to students of similar ability and grade level. Paul's achievement scores placed him at the 1st percentile in the same areas. (Both John and Jodi were given individual intelligence tests and the results placed them within an "average" range of ability. Paul's profile placed him within the mildly mentally retarded range.)
3. Deficiencies in study skill areas—Unlike John and Paul, Jodi had developed compensatory skills to enable her to be successful in standard classes.
4. Plateau in basic skill development—Paul's overall profile was flat, but whether he or the other two students had plateaued is open to question.

5. Problems in producing and implementing strategies for problem solving—Both Paul and John experienced difficulties in this area. They were unable to generate alternative strategies, particularly when faced with social problems such as failure to accept criticism or handling stress.

For students such as Paul, Jodi, John, and even those not in special education who graduated from the school system, what opportunities awaited them?

FORMULATING APPROPRIATE CURRICULUM: HOW THE POTTSTOWN TEACHERS TACKLED THE PROBLEM

When we introduced Paul, John, and Jodi we asked what kind of curriculum might address their needs. Curriculum can be described in many ways. It may be:

The total content of instruction (Bigge, 1988)
A formal plan with directed activities, experiences, and a specific setting (Smith & Payne, 1980)
All of the experiences that individual learners have in a program of education whose purpose is to achieve broad goals and related specific objectives (Hass, 1987).

In the summer of 1969, six teachers from the Pottstown school sat together discussing the task at hand—to write guides for the entire special education program. The discussion ranged from what was done at each grade level—primary, junior high, and senior high—to what kind of students were in each class. It was finally suggested that the group first decide what it wanted special education students to know when they left school since they would now be graduating with diplomas (1970). From high school, the group then backed down through each level identifying essential skills and where they would be taught.

When asked about students who appeared to be above the level of instruction, one high school teacher said that students were placed into regular classes with permission of the instructor and the parent. Students had the option of being graded either on the basis of their individual ability, which was lower than their peers, or compared to the standard of the class.

At the end of two weeks, each teacher knew what was to be taught. The actual method of instruction, materials, course structure, and grading system were left up to each instructor. Each teacher had an idea of what information might have been taught to students in previous academic years.

It was decided that the high school program would present their information through courses of study similar to the course in the standard high school, with textbooks, regulation examinations, and grades. Any student who wanted out or had the ability to participate in standard classes would have the option of participating in the regular class. Furthermore, the dual grading system was retained and a diploma given only if a student met all requirements of the district.

The Pottstown writers had taken a major step by developing a curriculum for their program. They attempted to identify skills needed by students for success at the next grade. It was also an effort to communicate to other teachers what was being taught. Although the staff addressed only one element, special education, of a total program, the curriculum is as Grant (1982) noted, "a central component."

Availability and design of curriculum are not the major questions confronting a teacher today. Too much time and energy are spent creating a curriculum, and in this case, the writers had three possible alternatives to creating their own curriculum. They could have:

1. Selected an existing curriculum and adopted it for the district. Guides were available that identified goals or purposes, methods of presentation, material, philosophy and the characteristics of the population that was to benefit from the guide. Even today, programs can obtain "curriculum" from any number of sources and after purchasing the materials plus some inservice begin teaching (Kokaska & Brolin, 1985; Radabaugh & Yukish, 1982).

2. Selected one or more guides that contained skills, materials, and instructional strategies and adapted them to local use based on the types of students in the program, existing resources and materials, and expected outcomes of the instruction. Such an approach enables a teacher to enhance or complement existing instruction.

3. Used an approach that combined identified goals and actual skills being presented in the classroom during the year. Using texts, instructional material, and daily presentations, teachers identify the objectives being taught or reviewed and then classify the objectives under established goals (Glassford, 1981).

Throughout the years, special education has had many curricula offered or outlined (Brolin, 1983; D'Alonzo, 1983; Kokaska & Brolin, 1985; Kolstoe, 1976; Smith, 1974). Districts continue to devise comprehensive guides for specific areas such as reading and vocational and social skills, each identifying the needs of the population, skills, goals and objectives, materials, and methods in addition to presenting resources for technical support and information.

The Pottstownians wrote their guides, and many districts have taken similar steps, only to have their guides "gather dust" on a shelf. No approach to writing can overcome the problem of viewing the curriculum as static and not having the document or guide updated on a regular basis, such as a three-to-five-year cycle of development, evaluation, and revision.

Chapter 1 included a curriculum developed by the Special Education Staff of the North Fayette School District (Iowa). Although drawing on many sources, it emphasizes local needs and outcomes. A key feature in the North Fayette guide is that it has been revised and updated since being initially implemented years ago.

COMMUNICATING INSTRUCTIONAL OUTCOMES

Having a curriculum in place is only the beginning, for now the effective teacher must continually make adjustments to meet the all-important goal, highest-level functioning and success in later life, that is possible for a student. Here are two teachers at work fine-tuning objectives and communicating goals.

CASE STUDY 12 (MR. SEGURA)

By 12:28 P.M., several students had gotten out their assignment from the previous day. Others sharpened pencils or searched for calculators. Two students feverishly worked to complete the day's assignment of calculating the cost of a car.

Mr. Segura gave each student a copy of a quiz. The students were to determine the down payment, total monthly payment, and total cost of buying a car. He moved about the room, answering questions and providing assistance to students who had been absent. He suggested that students compare their problems to examples presented earlier in the book.

The class exchanged papers and, with the teacher's help, corrected the quiz. The teacher asked the class about the exercise they had just completed. Students summarized the procedure for calculating a down payment as well as determining the total cost of a car. The students were informed that for the next activity they would be using the same skills, but now they were to "buy" a new car based on advertisements in the newspaper. Before beginning the new activity, the teacher reviewed key vocabulary (*down payment, interest,* and so on) using the calculator to determine the down payment and steps for buying a car. He told the class that they would be making decisions to buy a car or make a major purchase in the next two years, and they needed to be able to determine if they could afford the car or item they wanted.

As the bell sounded, the teacher considered the next unit on consumer buying, as many of the students were saving for clothing, stereos, and personal items. At the same time, he considered information from other teachers on the students for next year's class. Their ability was considerably lower than the present group.

If the students had less ability, what would the curriculum need to be? What materials would be appropriate for next year's class? Were supplementary materials available? Was there a way to be more practical in teaching the skills? These questions would have to be answered within the next sixty days to select materials for the next school year.

Many of Mr. Segura's students were about to enter employment and become active consumers. As a result, he stressed activities that require students to apply learned skills to immediate or future situations (buying personal items, paying for a car and its maintenance, and so on).

With his knowledge of the incoming students, Mr. Segura was aware that the outcomes of the course would probably change due to their lower ability. The degree of change would not be evident until he obtained additional information *and* worked with the students in class.

There are even occasions when teachers must explain the purpose of their courses and identify the expected outcomes to a parent, as in the following situation.

CASE 13 (MR. FELLER)

At a parent conference, Mr. Feller was asked why students were required to study world history. The obvious answer was to meet the district's requirements for graduation and the state mandate in social studies. But Mr. Feller explained that his students came from various ethnic and racial backgrounds, they should have some knowledge of other kinds of people since contact would continue at school and in the community and workplace. He indicated that for some students study now was providing a base for future study after high school since more students were going on to community colleges. Furthermore, it provided an opportunity for students to apply a range of communication, problem solving, and reference skills that were taught in English as the social studies course required students to write reports, work in groups, and use sources other than the textbook.

At the secondary level, it is easier to identify these purposes than at any other level. Unfortunately, such purposes are not always clearly communicated to students and concerned others (Good & Brophy, 1984). In the case of Mr. Feller, however, a clear focus for a course was presented to both a student and her parent. Mr. Segura specifically identified for his students where and how they would apply the skills taught in his class.

Both cases demonstrate the need for teachers to look beyond their class to prepare students for the community. Through the latest mandate in special education, students are to be "transitioned" to the community through a coordinated effort involving them, agencies, and the school. Schools and agencies work to address not only students' vocational needs but also their academic, social, personal, and independent living needs in order to prepare them better for their adult responsibilities.

CASE MANAGEMENT: A SPECIAL RESPONSIBILITY

Secondary special education teachers are expected to carry out the same basic responsibilities and roles other teachers have, as well as the additional set that comes from working with students with handicaps. Because each area of special education has been identified, teachers are required to have an individual educational plan (IEP) and someone to monitor the plan. The individual is known as a primary implementer or case manager, and we will now see Mr. Segura in that role. It is useful to note, though, that even with the best of management, we cannot guarantee improvement in student learning. Nor can we guarantee that less time will be needed in teaching. It may be quite the contrary, in fact. But in the long run, students may benefit. That possibility is the justification.

CASE STUDY 14

During his conference period Mr. Segura prepared a written summary of a student's performance in class. The report (or Current Level of Functioning) included the student's needs, a recommended goal, and objectives for the class based on the curriculum and

Figure 6.1. *Current Level of Functioning*

Student's name _____ Week of _____

Period _____ Teacher _____ Goal _____ Objective

                             Mon   Tues   Wed   Thurs   Fri

Prepared
for class

....

Assignment

....

Participation

....

Attitude & behavior

....

Rate the student from 0 (F) to 4 (A) compared to other students in the class.
Comments: _____

....
....

                                                        Mr. Segura

                                                        Date ____

individual needs. The teacher was concerned because the student missed two days of school each week, did not attempt an assignment, and was in jeopardy of failing the class that was required for graduation.

Mr. Segura's next two periods were taken up by annual reviews (IEPs). In each conference the teacher served as case manager. He presented a summary of the student's current level of functioning based on information from other teachers. Goals were reviewed and revised by the conference participants. He helped complete the conference forms and received his own copy of the conference report.

Figure 6.2. *IEP*

Student's name _____ Class _____

Period _____ Date(s) _____

Please take a few minutes and rate the above-named student.

Attendance_____ 95 percent of scheduled day

On time_____ 97 percent of scheduled day

Prepared_____ Has pencil, pens, paper, assignments daily

Assignment_____ 60 percent or better on each

Attitude_____ Meets expectation of the class

Academics_____ Goal:

Mr. Segura was responsible for monitoring the students' progress. He prepared two short forms that were sent to each student's teacher either weekly or monthly (Figures 6.1 and 6.2). If difficulties arose, Mr. Segura could meet with the student, counselor, or parent if necessary. He also observed each student in his caseload as well as interviewed them as part of the three-year reevaluation.

Mr. Segura worked in a departmentalized program where each special education teacher was the case manager or primary implementer for up to twenty students. Most special educators have case-management responsibilities, but the demands vary from district to district. An example of the differences is shown in Figure 6.3, where United Township High School is a departmentalized program with 200 students and twelve teachers. Riverdale High School operates a combined resource and self-contained classroom for approximately 30 students under the supervision of two teachers.

The larger district has designed its case-management system so that teachers have limited responsibilities. Others are responsible for testing students, scheduling and conducting conferences, maintaining records, disciplining, and counseling. Unfortunately, case managers in larger systems do not always have contact with a student and, therefore, must rely on the information from other sources.

In the rural district, by comparison, two teachers are responsible for thirty to forty mildly and moderately handicapped students. The teachers have considerably more responsibility for the program. Not only do they teach six periods each day, they also evaluate students and serve administrative functions, including scheduling conferences and chairing the meetings. Such arrangements are not uncommon in smaller districts.

Figure 6.3. Case Management

United Township High School	Riverdale Community
1. Maintain and monitor current IEP.	1. Same.
2. Observe each student.	2. Observe—three-year reevaluation.
3. Interview each student.	3. Interview—three-year reevaluation.
4. Consult with counselors and standard teachers every four and one-half weeks.	4. Consult with counselor and standard teachers as needed.
5. Collect current level of functioning information from each teacher. Summarize information at annual reviews and reevaluation.	5. Arrange and schedule IEPs, MDCs.
	6. Disseminate current level of functioning forms. Prepare forms for IEPs and MDCs.
	7. Test achievement levels of students for MDCs.
	8. Chair and conduct IEPs and MDCs.

Min-competency Test

THE COMPLEXITY OF TEACHING

The four major elements of teaching—knowledge of curriculum, learner, instruction, and outcome—appear to be simple. They can be used to illustrate a lack of experience or failure to recognize how complex teaching actually is in relationship to what most people know as "teaching." One needs to combine educational psychology, methods courses, characteristics, and introductory courses in special education practice with practical experience to understand the complexity of teaching. Teaching is difficult not only because of the complexity of the elements highlighted in this chapter but also because of those that were not discussed (content knowledge, questioning, counseling, and so on). Very few people, in fact, can actually do a good job of teaching over a long period.

Although teaching becomes easier with experience (Armstrong & Savage, 1983), the complexity of the elements does not. The school population is expected to be diverse in its characteristics and needs. The community and its employers will demand more from individuals, particularly as the world continues to be competitive.

For special educators, success may not be measured by the placement of students into regular classes or even improved test scores. The success of programs could be determined or measured by the number of students employed, the length of their employment, and the type of jobs. It may be concluded from such quantifiable measures that the typical curriculum for a three-or-four-year program is not sufficient to prepare students for a complex world, one even more complex than teaching.

SUMMARY

This chapter looked at some of the responsibilities, issues, and approaches outlined in this book from the teacher's point of view.

Teaching is a complex activity that, if done well, may help students gain and use knowledge. Three classrooms were visited so that we could see teachers in action and analyze their effectiveness in terms such as variety of methods, organization, clarity of expectations, and effectiveness of assessment.

Teaching involves having a knowledge of what is to be presented through a written guide that is revised with regularity; the formulation of curriculum by one district, in response to a student's real needs, was detailed. The process involves having clear knowledge of outcomes, either short term (to attain specific skills at the end of a semester) or those evident only years after the student has left school. We studied how teachers evaluate outcomes and establish goals relevant to the student and community.

Teaching involves planning in order for instruction to have a specific focus and then, in an organized way, uses a variety of techniques to present skills and still other methods to ascertain acquisition of skills.

Teaching, in other words, is a complicated process, one that is both grounded in certain theories and proven approaches and is quite personalized. It will not get any easier in the future, only more complex.

STUDY QUESTIONS

1. What other methods could be used to construct a curriculum?
2. Is a written curriculum necessary?
3. What elements were considered in developing this district's curriculum?
4. Should the teacher rely on the individual needs of the student as the basis for instruction?
5. What student information would be of value in the process of teaching?

REFERENCES

Armstrong, D. G., & Savage, T. V. (1983). *Secondary education: An introduction.* New York: Macmillan.

Biehler, R. J., & Snowman, J. (1986). *Psychology applied to teaching* (5th ed.). Boston: Houghton Mifflin.

Bigge, J. (1988). *Curriculum based instruction for special education.* Mountain View, CA: Mayfield.

Bluestein, J. E. (1989). *Being a successful teacher: A practical guide to instruction.* Belmont, CA: David Lake.

Borich, G. D. (1988). *Effective teaching methods.* Columbus, OH: C. E. Merrill.

Boyer, E. L. (1983). *High school.* New York: Harper & Row.

Brolin, D. (1983). *Life centered career education: A competency based approach* (rev. ed.). Reston, VA: Council for Exceptional Children.

Brophy, J. (1985). Classroom management as instruction: Socializing self-guidance in students. *Theory into Practice, 24*, 233–240.

Brophy, J. (1985). Classroom management as instruction: Socializing self-guidance in students. *Theory into Practice, 24* 233–240.

Callahan, J. R., & Clark, L. H. (1977). *Introduction to American education.* New York: Macmillan.

D'Alonzo, B. J. (1983). *Educating adolescents with learning and behavior problems.* Rockville, MD: Aspen Systems.

Davis, W. E. (1983). *The special educator: Strategies for succeeding in today's schools.* Austin: Pro-Ed.

Edgar, E. (1988). Employment as an outcome for mildly handicapped students: Current status and future directions. *Focus on Exceptional Children 21*(1), 1–8.

Emmer, E. T., & Evertson, C. M. (1981). Synthesis of research on classroom management. *Educational Leadership, 38*, 342–345.

Gage, N. L., & Berliner, D. C. (1984). *Educational psychology* (3rd ed.). Boston: Houghton Mifflin.

Gagne, E. D. (1985). *The cognitive psychology of school learning.* Boston: Little, Brown.

Glassford, J. (1981). "Project SUCCESS." Secondary Special Needs Conference, Champaign, IL.

Good, T. L., & Brophy, J. E. (1984). *Looking in classrooms* (3rd ed.). New York: Harper & Row.

Grant, C. A. (1982). *Bringing teaching to life: An introduction to education.* Boston, MA: Allyn & Bacon.

Hallahan, D. P., & Kauffman, J. M. (1988). *Exceptional children: Introduction to special education* (4th ed.). Englewood Cliffs, NJ: Prentice-Hall.

Halpern, R. (1987). Major social and demographic trends affecting young families: Implications for early childhood care and education. *Young Children, 42*(6), 34–40.

Harste, J., & Stephens, D. (1986). Literacy in the secondary special education classroom. *Theory into Practice, 25*(2), 128–133.

Hass, G. (1987). *Curriculum planning: A new approach* (5th ed.). Needham Heights, MA: Allyn.

Havighurst, R. J. (1972). *Developmental tasks and education* (3rd ed.). New York: McKay.

Jorde, P. (1982). *Avoiding burnout*. Washington, DC: Acropolis.

Kokaska, C. J., & Brolin, D. E. (1985). *Career education for handicapped individuals* (2nd ed.). Columbus: C. E. Merrill.

Kolstoe, D. P. (1976). *Teaching educable mentally retarded children (2nd ed.)*. New York: Holt, Rinehart & Winston.

Langone, J. (1986). *Teaching retarded learners*. Boston: Allyn & Bacon.

FURTHER READING

Gearheart, B., DeRuiter J. & Sileo T. (1986). *Teaching mildly and moderately handicapped students*. Englewood Cliffs, NJ: Prentice-Hall.

Lorber, M. A., & Pierce, W. D. (1983) *Objectives methods and evaluation for secondary teaching* (2nd ed). Englewood Cliffs, NJ: Prentice-Hall.

MacMillan, D. L., Keogh, B. K., & Jones, R. L. (1986). Special education research on mentally handicapped learners. In M. C. Wittrock, *Handbook of research on teaching* (3rd ed.). New York: Macmillan.

Mastropieri, M. A., & Scruggs, T. C. (1987). *Effective instruction for special educators*. Boston: Little, Brown, College Hill Pub.

Mercer, C. D. (1983). *Students with learning disabilities* (2nd ed.). Columbus: C. E. Merrill.

Mercer, C. E. (1983). *Students with learning disabilities* (2nd ed.). Columbus: C. E. Merrill.

Miller, T. L., & Davis, E. E. (Eds.). (1982). *The mildly handicapped student*. New York: Grune & Stratton.

Orlich, D. C., Harder, R. J., Callahan, R. C., Kravas, C. H., Kauchak, D. P., Pendergrass, R. A., & Keogh, A. J. (1985). *Teaching strategies: A guide to better instruction* (2nd ed.). Lexington, MA: D. C. Heath.

Patton, J. R., Payne, J. S., Kauffman, J. M., Brown, G. B., & Payne, R. A. (1987). *Exceptional children in focus* (4th ed.). Columbus: C. E. Merrill.

Polloway, E. A., Payne, J. S., Patton, J. R., & Payne, R. A. (1985). *Strategies for teaching retarded and special needs learners* (3rd ed.). Columbus: C. E. Merrill.

Radabaugh, M. T., & Yukish, J. F. (1982). *Curriculum and methods for the mildly handicapped*. Boston: Allyn & Bacon.

Ryan, K., & Cooper, J. M. (1984). *Those who can teach* (4th ed.). Boston: Houghton Mifflin.

Saphier, J. (1982). The knowledge base on teaching: It's here, now! In T. M. Amabile & M. L. Stubbs (Eds.), *Psychological research in the classroom*. New York: Pergamon.

Smith, J. E. & Payne, J. S. (1980). *Teaching exceptional adolescents*. Columbus: C. E. Merrill.

Smith, R. M. (1974). *Clinical teaching: Methods of instruction for the retarded*. New York: McGraw-Hill.

Smith, T. E. C., Price, B. J., & Marsh, G. E. (1986). *Mildly handicapped children and adults.* St. Paul: West.

VanderZanden, J. W., & Pace, A. J. (1984). *Educational psychology in theory and practice* (2nd ed.) New York: Random House.

Westling, D. L., & Koorland, M. A. (1988). *The special educator's handbook.* Boston: Allyn & Bacon.

Wilkins, G., & Miller, S. (1983). *Strategies for success: An effective guide for teachers of secondary-level slow learners.* New York: Teachers College, Columbia University.

Williams, F. (1977). *Teachers without fear.* Buffalo: DOK Publisher.

Woolfolk, A. E. (1987). *Educational psychology* (3rd ed .). Englewood Cliffs, NJ: Prentice-Hall.

CHAPTER 7

Academics in Special Education: Issues and Goals

The focus of this chapter is programming for academic competence. Efforts to implement the academic component in secondary special education programs parallel the task of providing vocational preparation (described in Chapter 8) in terms of the need to develop the competencies needed by students for effective adjustment to adult roles. But decisions made by special educators concerning the academic components of students' programs do not come easy. There are many problems that must be resolved.

At the secondary level, a prescribed number of core subjects and electives are combined to establish minimum requirements for graduation. If students with learning problems are to be graduated from their high schools, it seems then that they should have to meet the standards set for regular education students. This is not always the case, however. Policies for graduation and program completion vary from state to state, from school to school. Even within one school district there are inconsistencies. There may be board-approved policies that recognize the need for modification of regular education standards in favor of more functional and developmental requirements for students in self-contained classes—but often students classified as resource students may be excluded from these modifications.

Nationally, disagreements in philosophies have reached unprecedented proportions, and there are good reasons—the failure to develop successful students and the failure to prepare competent adults—to reexamine the quality of special education. As the search for increased effectiveness continues, trends are emerging that focus on four significant questions:

1. Where should special education students be taught—the mainstream, special class or a combination of the two?
2. What standards for graduation should be met?
3. What accommodations can be provided for special education students to promote academic achievement?

4. What is the role of the special educator in implementing the academic curriculum—tutor, strategist, teacher?

Resolution of the above questions can help translate philosophies and provide sensitive direction for academic programming decisions. Preceding chapters have made it apparent that political, educational, and legal issues affect identification, eligibility, and placement, as well as what and how students with mild handicaps will be taught. At the secondary level these issues have reached the apex of concern as government officials and researchers analyze with chagrin the dismal statistics that define the transition status of students who have been in special education programs. Maintaining the status quo will not be acceptable. Special educators at all levels are being asked to analyze their philosophies and determine how they are being translated into delivery of programming for students. The discussion that follows will address each of the above questions to provide a comprehensive awareness of variables affecting academic programming.

WHERE SHOULD STUDENTS WITH LEARNING PROBLEMS BE TAUGHT?

Special education literature abounds with discussions concerning the inappropriateness of maintaining a duel system of education—regular education and special education. Will (1984) claimed that regular education and special education have evolved into somewhat artificially compartmentalized service-delivery systems. More and more handicapped children are receiving their education outside the regular class, and many of our traditional models create instructional hurdles for students and place more distance between the child and the regular curriculum. The House Select Education Subcommittee found that the practice of assigning students to special education reinforced programmatic separation and eliminated demands on general education programs for increased flexibility and inclusiveness (Will, 1984).

Remember, PL 94-142 mandates that students should have the benefit of the least restrictive environment. All or nothing policies do not take into consideration individual needs, talents, interests, or abilities. Policies affecting programs need to be flexible, reflect compliance with mandated legislation, and maximize the use of available resources. The trend is definitely toward a more cooperative and unified delivery of services and programs. The special educator must be willing to relinquish ownership of students, become more cognizant of the benefits possible in the mainstream, and work for the best possible solutions in cooperation with general education.

Some students in special education will be mainstreamed entirely, others part of the time, and a very limited number only for social considerations such as physical education and lunch. If you are a first-year teacher, policies and traditions at the building level will dictate much of what you can do. Will you agree to subscribed practice? If you do not, how will you effect change? How will you maximize student achievement within the current delivery system?

WHAT STANDARDS FOR GRADUATION MUST BE MET?

Each time our country perceives a threat to its national security, our educational leaders respond by increasing standards in our schools. The most recent call for excellence in education has caused many schools to increase the number of units required for graduation and also to require passing minimal competency tests. These conditions impose barriers for students with special needs in achieving the expected outcome of a high school education—graduation.

Units required for graduation reflect mandated requirements established at the state level as well as any additional requirements set by local boards of education. Appendix 7.1, the diploma options set forth by the school board of Leon County, Florida, illustrates the strong academic demands of a typical, four-year comprehensive high school. To keep pace with their class, students must take no less than six courses each semester, and for three years, four of the six courses are required academic core subjects. The standards set by this school district are not unusual. They represent a response to what is perceived by the state and community as comprising a basic education.

Not only have school districts increased the number of academic credits required, but teachers have increased the standards of their classes, making it even more difficult for students with handicaps to experience success. Furthermore, students may also be required to pass minimum competency tests (MCTs) to receive their diplomas. Approximately forty states have passed legislation requiring MCTs. Students are spending more time trying to meet academic demands, and as a result, electives are rapidly diminishing in these high schools due to lack of demand (MacMillan, 1988).

There are alternative ways by means of which students can prepare for MCTs and graduation requirements: parallel courses, alternative grading systems, more time for completing units through an additional year or more in high school, summer school, independent study, and school-board policies that recognize alternative programs specifically designed for special populations. See Appendix 7.3 for alternatives in grading procedures.

Requiring higher academic standards for receipt of a high school diploma will force special educators to spend even more energy on getting students with mild handicaps through the required academic courses and less time on career and vocational experiences (Edgar, 1987). Edgar considered the transition process incomplete because few handicapped students move from school to independent living, secondary special education programs appear to have little impact on students' adjustment to community life, more than 30 percent of the students enrolled in secondary special education programs drop out, and neither graduates nor dropouts find adequate employment opportunities.

How can policies, programs, and resources at the secondary level be used to impact favorably the eventual adjustment of special education students to community life? Are students frustrated with their high school programs because they have never been taught how to learn?

WHAT ACCOMMODATIONS CAN BE PROVIDED FOR SPECIAL EDUCATION STUDENTS TO PROMOTE THEIR ACADEMIC ACHIEVEMENT?

There are three categories of accommodations that focus on improving the academic performance and success of students with special needs:

1. Accommodation strategies, which comprise modifications in methodology, curriculum, or environment within the regular class
2. School survival skills, which include learning strategies, study skills, and classroom behavioral expectations
3. Parallel courses, which supplant regular core classes with similar classes taught in the special class.

Accommodations should be or are designed to help students become responsible, motivated, actively involved participants in the learning process to improve chances for their academic success and to increase involvement with the school mainstream. Focus on academic accommodations has been brought to the forefront of concern in part because the population of students being served in secondary special education programs is changing, and this change appears to be closely related to the excellence in education movement.

An educator who started teaching in secondary special education nearly twenty years ago related her experience with the changing population.

CASE STUDY 15

All of the students in my self-contained classes had been certified educable mentally handicapped. Adaptive behaviors and achievement levels clearly separated these young people from their agemates in regular classes. Without exception, these students had been placed in special education before they had reached the 4th grade, and the majority of the students had been removed from regular classes while in the 1st or 2nd grade.

During this time, students in special programs were separated for almost everything, expectations for achievement were minimal, and curriculum was poorly defined and rarely considered what was being taught in regular classes. Furthermore, materials were extremely deficient in content and format of presentation. Fortunately, these conditions have improved dramatically. Although there are still students entering high school who need a specialized curriculum and modified graduation requirements, this group of students comprises a very small part of the population in our secondary special education programs today.

The population of our school district is considerably less than it was twenty years ago, but the special education population has nearly tripled. In examining the records of students in our secondary special education classes, characteristics surfaced that are common to the majority of students who populate our program. These students in most cases are not that much different from nonhandicapped, low-achieving students in regular education. Furthermore, nearly 70 percent of the students had been identified for special education placement while in junior high school, and a few had been identified for special education while in high school. Failure to achieve in academic areas and problem behaviors were standard descriptors of these students. The handicaps of these students are considered very mild as indicated by the fact that two-thirds of the students have been assigned to multicategorical resource programs.

These students need help, and they are getting it as special education students. But should they have had to be labeled in order to get that help? Shepard (1987) suggested that 90 percent of special education students are very mildly handicapped if at all, and Reynolds and associates (1987) considered the identification of three-fourths of mildly handicapped students to be questionable. The students described by this teacher may not match these statistics, but they are not that much out of line.

Why are so many adolescents identified as being in need of special education? Are students opting for special education status because regular education is less tolerant of interstudent differences? Have course offerings become less relevant to students in general? Have schools created barriers to accessing the regular curriculum by increasing course demands? As the responsibility for the education of all students is sorted out, special educators will be dedicating much time to accommodating the needs of students that will facilitate reentry and successful involvement in general education.

General education teachers have learned to believe that they do not have the time, support, or training necessary for working effectively with handicapped students in their classrooms (Hudson et al., 1979) and that accommodation is unreasonable (Fagan et al., 1984). Special educators can change these attitudes by introducing accommodations that general educators can use but then must provide support in helping teachers implement the strategies. Most accommodations simply emphasize good teaching practice, and by using these strategies general educators will be helping not only students from special education but all students in their classes.

An Iowa project (Owens, 1986) set out to identify as many general education program modifications and accommodations as possible that would be appropriate for secondary-level learning-disabled students. Nine accommodations were listed under classroom environment; 110 under instruction, materials, and aides; and 26 under evaluation. Findings were used to survey general educators as to the reasonableness of these modifications and accommodations. The results of the survey are shown in Appendix 7.2. The letters on the left of each item indicate teacher ratings according to the following scales.

H = *High Reasonableness* = accommodations that require little extra time, little change in usual teaching practices, and little additional help.
M = *Moderate Reasonableness* = accommodations that require some extra time, some change in usual teaching practices, and some additional help.
L = *Low Reasonableness* = accommodations that require much extra time, much change in usual teaching practices, and much additional help.

The numbers provide a rank order of acceptance within each of the three degrees of reasonableness.

The survey results suggest that many of the things that are needed by special students are considered to be of low reasonableness—learning partners, peer tutors, taped material to listen to rather than read, taping of answers rather than writing them, adjustment of course expectations, modifications of tests, or simply allowing tests to be taken orally. Perhaps more important is the fact that the survey identifies a wealth of things general educators perceive as being highly reasonable accommodations.

Modifications and accommodations can be the bridge for assuring general educators that they can work with special students. Special educators can then begin to introduce modifications of moderate and low reasonableness needed by mainstreamed students; however, at the same time, the special educator must be willing to provide support to general educators in developing and implementing the accommodations. The survey components also serve as a reminder to special educators of teaching practices that should be evident in their own classes. Making the environment of a special class more like a class in general education can help to enhance student adjustment to the mainstream.

Regular and special education settings often differ in instructional format, curriculum demands, teaching style, behavioral expectations, physical design, and student-socialization patterns (Hundert, 1982). The handicapped learner also differs from successful regular students. While successful students are taking notes, participating in questioning, and contributing to discussions, special needs students display passivity, dependency, inability to use time constructively, disorganization, and inappropriate social interaction. These students are *inactive learners*, adopting a posture of learned helplessness, lacking in intrinsic motivation, and exhibiting motivational deficiencies (Zigmond et al., 1988). The demands of regular education programs and inadequacies of special education students in dealing with these demands are the focus of school survival skills. Adequate study skills, learning strategies, and social skills are viewed as essential for academic success.

To achieve the goal of transforming students from passive into active learners, teachers will need to work systematically to establish the behaviors needed for success in the regular classroom (Gleason et al., 1988). Research has indicated that most academic failures can be attributed to surmountable strategy difficulties rather than limitations in capacity (Baron, 1978) and that students who are taught learning strategies can greatly improve their overall academic performance (Scruggs et al., 1985). Tutorial intervention is perhaps the most common service provided by special educators at the secondary level. It has to be considered a strategy that helps students in the short term but is of limited value in the long term (Patton & Palloway, 1988). Skills should be taught that generalize to regular classroom settings. There is little doubt that teaching school survival skills will accommodate the needs of a great number of mildly handicapped students in meeting the academic demands of their classes. If students are to be motivated to learn, they must be taught how to learn so that they can experience academic success. (The components of school survival skills were introduced in previous chapters.)

For some students, instructional accommodations made in regular classes together with survival skills knowledge are not enough for them to experience academic success. Furthermore, the time used to get these students through regular classes cannot be justified if the development of vocational and life-skill competencies is sacrificed. For these students, parallel courses should be considered an alternative to supplant requirements of regular academics.

A combination of factors should be considered in determining how accommodations are to be used in making programming decisions. Most importantly in making these decisions the needs of students are to be considered on an individual basis, and the programs developed should be sensitive to the development of appropriate skills for transition to the community. (Review the components of a mental disabilities curriculum framework, Chapter 10.)

How will you accommodate the academic needs of your students? Will you continue to remediate and tutor? Will your students develop skills needed to be competent adults?

WHAT IS THE ROLE OF THE SPECIAL EDUCATOR IN IMPLEMENTING THE ACADEMIC CURRICULUM—TUTOR, STRATEGIST, TEACHER?

As special educators seek to identify ways to improve the success rates of students, attention is being given to special education delivery systems. Educators are discussing changes that would involve many of the traditional responsibilities of teachers, differentiated staffing within special education departments, as well as changes in what and how to teach. Policy makers are looking for a new approach that offers an alternative to expensive pullout programs. Will (1986) has suggested that special education programs establish a partnership with regular education to assess cooperatively the educational needs of students with learning problems and to develop cooperatively the effective educational strategies for meeting those needs.

Teachers who have been assigned to resource rooms may by tradition or choice spend a major portion of their time serving as tutors. The tutorial approach as the primary responsibility of special educators (which may be needed in all programs some of the time) is criticized because (1) there is not sufficient concern for whether the content being presented is relevant to the present and future needs of students, (2) duties performed by tutors do not require specialized training and in many cases could be performed by paraprofessionals, and (3) it promotes learned helplessness (Patton & Palloway, 1988).

The consulting teacher model for delivering services to special education students is getting increased attention. Special education services are geared primarily to students and teachers in the mainstream, with the intent of reducing the need for pullout special education services. It offers possibilities for improving educational services in the mainstream to mildly handicapped children and other children at risk and is consistent with reform strategies urging creation of master teachers (Huefner, 1988).

Team teaching with general educators and teaching in integrated classrooms are innovative ways that special educators are being used to provide more effective instruction and provide for the least restrictive environment. Traditional teaching roles will still be needed in the special education delivery system; however, special educators can expect to become *facilitators of change*, serving as tutors, strategists, and teachers not only to special education students but to teachers in the mainstream.

How will you perceive your role as a special educator? Will students be better equipped for transition as a result of changes in the delivery of services and in instructional focus?

Reflect on the variables related to each of the four questions discussed and the controversies and solutions. Then consider yourself in each of the following teaching situations.

CASE STUDY 16

Dave arrives to his assignment as a multicategorical resource teacher in a suburban high school. There are twenty-two students on his class roll: fifteen boys and seven girls, ten sophomores, eight juniors, and four senior girls. Categorically, the students include sixteen learning disabled (LD), four mentally disabled (MD), and two behaviorally disordered (BD). Students have been scheduled, and no student is scheduled for the resource room more than one hour each day. Math and reading test scores range from 5th- to 10th-grade equivalents.

CASE STUDY 17

Jeanette is to be a special education team member assigned to instruction in language arts four periods each day. She will have two classes of 10th-grade language arts and two classes in 11th-grade practical English. She also has four seniors assigned for independent study. Classes range in size from eight to ten students. Reading grade equivalents tend to fall between the 3rd and 5th grade. Anytown High School is in a community of approximately 30,000 population.

CASE STUDY 18

Kevin has signed a contract to teach in a rural high school of 300 students. His assignment is a multicategorical, self-contained class serving 12 students distributed evenly in grades 9 through 12. Categorically, the students include 7 learning disabled and 5 mentally disabled. Grade equivalents in reading range from mid-2nd grade to the 8th grade. Math levels are between the 3rd and 11th grade. No schedules have been built. School begins in three days.

What would you do first? What would influence your decisions? Would you work alone, or would you seek help? What would you plan for your first day of classes?

SUMMARY

The population, the curriculum, and the delivery of special education services are changing. These changes are the result of the excellence-in-education movement and of reports implying that special education is not doing a very good job.

The excellence-in-education movement has had these direct results: standards for graduation are being upgraded, standards within courses are becoming more demanding, and states are adopting minimal competency tests. These changes have become barriers to graduation for students with handicaps.

Considerable emphasis in many special education programs, especially in resource rooms, is currently being placed on "getting students through school." A tutorial emphasis in instruction dominates these programs, and little attention is given to the application of skills needed for adjustment to work and adult living. The desired program should instead teach students how to learn as well as the value and utility of what is being taught.

In these programs, learning strategies and study skills are included in instruction to eliminate learned dependence, which is highly associated with the tutorial model. Accommodation strategies are also emphasized in these programs together with a high degree of cooperation between general education and special education.

Some students will need a more functional emphasis in their programs. Special educators cannot sacrifice the development of daily living competencies for skills such as theme writing and other higher level skills. Instructional time management must consider the final outcomes.

Special educators would like to see dropout rates decrease, and they would like to see employment rates increase for students who have graduated. Such statistics would indicate that special education is addressing the comprehensive needs of students. Meeting the academic needs of students is a complex process. Whatever the emphasis, whether regular classes or parallel courses, we must not lose focus of what it will take for each student to become a successful adult. Special educators must be ready for change and be willing to work for changes that improve outcomes for their students.

STUDY QUESTIONS

1. How is the population of students with mild handicaps changing? What effect is this having on special education programs?
2. How has the excellence-in-education movement affected requirements for graduation? How do these requirements affect special education students?
3. Define *accommodation strategies*. Why are they needed?
4. What is the current trend concerning mainstreaming?
5. What are parallel courses? Why are they used?
6. Identify five accommodation strategies in each category that general educators consider to be of high reasonableness, moderate reasonableness, and low reasonableness.

REFERENCES

Baron, J. (1978). Intelligence and general strategies. In E. Underwood (Ed.), *Strategies of information processing*. London: Academic Press, 9, 403–450.

Edgar, E. (1987). Secondary programs in special education: Are many of them justifiable? *Exceptional Children, 53,* 555–561.

Fagan, S. A. et al. (1984). Promoting successful mainstreaming: Reasonable classroom accomodations for learning disabled students. In R. N. Ianacoma and R. A. Stodden (Eds.), (1987). *Transition issues and directions*. Reston, VA: Council for Exceptional Children, Division of Mental Retardation.

Gleason, M. M., Herr, C. M., & Archer, A. L. (1988). Study skills: Special focus. *Teaching Exceptional Children, 20*(3), 52–57.

Hudson, F., Graham, S., & Warner, M. (1979). Mainstreaming: An examination of the attitudes and needs of regular classroom teachers. *Learning Disabilities Quarterly, 2*(3), 58–62.

Huefner, D. S. (1988). The consulting teacher model: Risks and opportunities. *Exceptional Children, 54*(5), 403–414.

Hundert, J. (1982). Some considerations of planning the integration of handicapped children into the mainstream. *Journal of Learning Disabilities, 15,* 73–80.

Iowa Department of Public Instruction. (1984). *Mental Disabilities Curriculum Framework*. Des Moines, IA: Special Education Division.

Leon County Schools. (1988). Exceptional student education: Individual Education Plan. Leon County, FL: Board of Education. In J. J. Gugerty, L. W. Tindall, T. J. Heffron, and B. B. Dougherty (Eds.), *Profiles of success: Serving secondary special education students through Carl D. Perkins Vocational Act, 12 exemplary approaches*. Madison: University of Wisconsin, Vocational Studies Center.

MacMillan, D. L. (1988). "New" EMRs. In G. A. Robinson, J. R. Patton, E. A. Palloway, & L. R. Sargent (Eds.), *Best practices in mental disabilities* (Vol. 2). Des Moines: State of Iowa, Department of Education.

Owens, R. Project Coordinator. (1986). *Project report: General education modifications for students with learning disabilities, grades 7–12*. Des Moines: State of Iowa, Department of Education, Bureau of Special Education.

Palloway, E. A., Patton, J. R., Epstein, M. H., & Smith, T. (1989). Comprehensive curriculum for students with mild handicaps. *Focus on Exceptional Children, 21* (8), 1–12.

Patton, J. R., & Palloway, E. A. (1988). Curricular orientations. In G. A. Robinson, J. R. Patton, E. A. Palloway, & L. R. Sargent, (Eds.), *Best Practices in Mental Disabilities* (Vol. 2).

Reynolds, M. C., Wang, M. C., & Walberg, H. J. (1987). The necessary restructuring of special and regular education. *Exceptional Children, 53,* 391–398.

Scruggs, T. E., Mastroperi, M. A., Monson, J., & Jorgensen, C. (1985). Maximizing what gifted students can learn: Recent findings of learning strategy research. *Gifted Child Quarterly, 29,* 181–185.

Shepard, L. A. (1987). The new push for excellence: Widening the schism between regular and special education. *Exceptional Children, 53,* 391–398.

Will, M. C. (1984). Let us pause and reflect—but not too long. *Exceptional Children. 51*(1), 11–16.

———. (1986). Educating children with learning problems: A shared responsibility. *Exceptional Children, 52,* 411–415.

Ysseldyke, J. E., & Algozzine, B. (1982). *Critical issues in special and remedial education.* Palo Alto, CA: Houghton Mifflin.

Zigmond, N., Kerr, M. M., & Schaeffer, A. (1988). Behavior patterns of learning-disabled adolescents in high school academic classes. *Remedial and Special Education, 9,* 6–11.

APPENDIX 7.1. HIGH SCHOOL DIPLOMA OPTIONS: THE SCHOOL BOARD OF LEON COUNTY, FLORIDA, EXCEPTIONAL STUDENT EDUCATION GRADUATION REQUIREMENTS*

DIPLOMAS

Standard Diploma		*Special Diploma*	
Language Arts (English)	4	Language Arts (English)	3
Mathematics	3	Mathematics	3
Science	3	Science	1
Social Studies	3	Social Studies	1
Physical Education	1	Physical Education	1
Life Management Skills	1/2	Life Management Skills	1
Fine Arts	1/2	LITE/Vocational, to include:	
Practical Arts	1/2	1. Occupational Training	
Electives	as needed	2. Employability Skills	
		3. On-the-Job Training	
		Electives	as needed
Total Credits	24	*Total Credits*	24

Standard Diploma: will be awarded to those students who meet the standard diploma credit requirements and demonstrate mastery of the minimum performance standards on the State Student Assessment Test (Parts I and II).

Special Diploma: (SLD, EMH, HI, PI, EH, SED, TMH, PMH) will be awarded to those students who meet the special diploma credit requirements and demonstrate mastery of the minimum performance standards for their exceptionality. For graduating classes of 1987 and 1988 twenty (20) credits must be earned in grades 9 through 12. Beginning with the graduating class of 1989, twenty-four (24) credits must be earned in grades 9 through 12.

CERTIFICATE OF COMPLETION

A student who has successfully completed the district requirements for Standard Diploma, including the required number of credits for graduation but has failed to pass 100 percent of the standards tested on the state student-assessment test—Part I (SSAT-I) or failed to pass the state student-assessment test—Part II (SSAT-II) shall be offered a Certificate of Completion.

*Courtesy of the School Board of Leon County, Florida.

SPECIAL CERTIFICATE OF COMPLETION

A Special Certificate of Completion shall be issued to those students who have successfully completed the Leon County District requirements for a Special Diploma, including the required number of credits for graduation, but fail to pass 100 percent of the special state minimum performance standards for his or her exceptionality.

APPENDIX 7.2. GENERAL EDUCATION MODIFICATIONS FOR STUDENTS WITH LEARNING DISABILITIES, GRADES 7–12. RICHARD OWENS, PROJECT COORDINATOR. STATE OF IOWA DEPARTMENT OF EDUCATION, BUREAU OF SPECIAL EDUCATION, AUGUST 1986.

I. Accommodations in Classroom Environment

H1 Provide for preferential seating.

H2 Reduce visual distractions (unusual/unnecessary clutter, gaudiness).

H3 Post assignments in same place.

M4 Reduce auditory distractions (unusual/unnecessary noise factors).

L5 Assign learning partners (two people).

L6 Use listening center.

L7 Use peer tutors.

L8 Use volunteers (if available).

L9 Assign to cooperative learning groups (three to six in group).

II. Accommodations in Instruction, Materials, and Aides

H1 Use diagrams and other visual aides.

H2 Provide clear copy (worksheets/handouts, etc.).

H3 Explain the textbook format at beginning of course.

H4 Write key points on board or overhead.

H5 Complement lecture of materials with added explanations.

H6 Provide vertically lined paper (graph paper).

H7 Allow using a calculator and other appropriate aids.

H8 Use samples of finished product as model.

H9 Provide uncluttered worksheet format.

H10 Encourage use of a notebook with dividers for subject organization (student purchases).

H11 Provide a list of materials needed.

H12 Teach abbreviations germane to the specific course.

H13 Clarify the criteria and format when giving written assignments.

H14 Ask students to skip lines in draft when doing written assignment.

H15 Use a consistent format for worksheets.

H16 Use a multisensory presentation (e.g., written, oral, lab work)

H17 Use "hands-on" activities.

H18 Teach in small, sequential steps.

H19	Have frequent review.
H20	Have structure (concrete developmental procedures).
H21	Use clues/hints.
H22	Summarize key points.
H23	Use concise directions (both written and oral).
H24	Introduce new vocabulary.
H25	State purpose for reading when giving reading assignment.
H26	Teach use of context clues.
H27	Verbalize steps necessary to complete assignment.
H28	Orally emphasize key words.
H29	Distinguish operations in math.
H30	Summarize and allow for questions.
H31	Give oral and written directions together.
H32	Emphasize where directions are located.
H33	Talk slower.
H34	Vary voice, tone, and pitch.
H35	Circulate and assist (teacher).
H36	Teach cues and other listening skills.
H37	Establish daily routine.
H38	Explain change in routine.
H39	Work from factual to abstract questions (concrete to abstract).
H40	List steps necessary to complete assignment.
H41	Provide time frame for long-term assignments.
H42	Provide direction when student has several options.
H43	Work from easy to hard problems.
H44	Allow explanation time—provide teacher instruction before giving assignment.
H45	Use short answers.
H46	Stress accuracy.
H47	Provide work time during class.
H48	Provide specific feedback on completed work.
H49	Provide immediate feedback when possible.
H50	Allow notes with oral report.
H51	Allow visual aides with oral report.
H52	Provide option to read silently or orally.
H53	Adjust time limit on oral reports.
H54	Teach techniques to aid in generalization.
H55	Organize lectures following an outline form.
H56	Reduce copying activities.
H57	Teach outlining/provide a model.
H58	Teach the needed structure for reports (model).
H59	Assist student with spelling requests.
H60	Provide feedback during lectures.
H61	Provide careful structuring to teach writing skills.
M62	Provide activity worksheets.
M63	Have student maintain notebook for misspelled words.
M64	Use tangible teaching aids.
M65	Use peer student to take notes and share and/or compare with notes of learning-disabled student.
M66	Provide examples on worksheets.
M67	Use audiovisual to introduce and/or summarize.
M68	Modify map/chart work.
M70	Provide a list of all assignments given—syllabus.
M71	Provide a study guide.
M72	Teach divided-page note taking.
M73	Discuss the individual's written response.
M74	Use small groups to discuss main ideas.
M75	Brainstorm words (both when introducing or practicing).
M76	Have student repeat directions.

M77 Give additional time for student to organize.

M78 Provide cues to comprehension of inferential thinking.

M79 Allow some written assignments to be done as a group project.

M80 Allow more time to complete (pacing).

M81 Modify original task to meet needs of handicapped students.

M82 Proofread the student's draft.

L83 Select material relevant to student.

L84 Provide taped material to listen to, rather than read.

L85 Allow correction of notes by using a model.

L86 Provide highlighted texts for student use.

L87 Divide multisyllable words.

L88 Visually illustrate new vocabulary.

L89 Use log or personal journal.

L90 Coordinate spelling needs with reading vocabulary.

L91 Give student a copy of teacher's notes.

L92 Give student a written outline of lecture.

L93 Use problem-solving sequence chart.

L94 Use worksheet guide with film.

L95 Allow use of marker when reading.

L96 Supply page number that answer is on.

L97 Use a story starter approach (e.g., give first paragraph and have student complete story).

L98 Allow student to preview lecture notes.

L99 Use instructional games.

L100 Accept multimodel response (e.g., if can't write, do orally).

L101 Allow students to tape answers rather than write out.

L102 Allow student to tape oral reports rather than present to group.

L103 Substitute comparable projects in exchange for written assignments.

L104 Match pupil's reading ability to text used or use companion text.

L105 Provide large print materials.

L106 Use reading pairs (two students read assignment together).

L107 Have discussions with the individual to insure comprehension.

L108 Adjust expectations—minimizing amount students must do to pass course.

L109 Teach SQ3R process (Survey, Question, Read, Recite, Review).

L110 Use team teaching (when feasible).

III. Accommodations in Evaluation

H1 Vary test format (written, oral, short answer, essay, multiple choice, true–false, matching, computation, yes–no, demonstration testing).

H2 Provide feedback to parents re: progress via phone, letter, or parent conference.

H3 Provide feedback to learners re: progress via teacher/student conference or written report.

H4 Underline important words in directions or test items.

H5 Read the directions to the student.

H6 Vary grading system—homework, tests, class discussion, special projects.

H7 Provide clear test copy.

H8 Provide review time in or outside of the class (emphasizing key points to study).

H10 Allow to recheck work on calculator.

H11	Have grading system reflect varied activities (homework, tests, projects, presentation).	**L19**	Allow student to tape answers on recorder (essay).
M12	Emphasize higher use of objective test in contrast to subjective tests.	**L20**	Take test orally (with teacher after school or with special teacher in resource room).
M13	Increase allowable time for completion.	**L21**	Assist by reading the test questions to the student.
M14	Block matching question into smaller groups (e.g., five/five/five rather than group of fifteen).	**L22**	Take exam in classroom during regular time; take exam again orally in resource room; average two scores.
M15	Review orally and individually to insure comprehension of essay questions.	**L23**	Change fill-in-the-blank to multiple-choice format.
M16	Provide examples of test content and format.	**L24**	Eliminate one of the choices in multiple choice (choose three answers instead of four).
M17	Chart grade progress for student use.	**L25**	Reduce weight of test importance.
L18	Teacher records test on cassette tape.	**L26**	Allow self-checking.

Source: Dr. Richard Owens, Project Coordinator. State of Iowa Department of Education, Bureau of Special Education, August, 1986. *General education modifications for students with learning disabilities, grades 7–12.*

APPENDIX 7.3. ALTERNATIVE GRADING PROCEDURES

One of the major areas of concern for regular education teachers involves grading and assessing the mainstreamed handicapped student. Specific issues include maintaining the course standards, dealing with reactions from other students when adjustments are made, and establishing appropriate methods of modification and accommodation for the handicapped student.

The following information is take from *Alternative Procedures for Grading Handicapped Students in the Secondary Schools* by Stanley F. Vasa (Lincoln: University of Nebraska, 1980). The full contents are:

Introduction
Issues in Grading
Alternative Grading Practices
Alternative Evaluation Practices
Conclusion
Additional Comments

I. INTRODUCTION

Public Law 94-142 has led the way in advocating the development of individualized instructional systems for the mildly handicapped student. Traditional grading and reporting systems do not adequately reflect this philosophy or intent. The traditional system of comparing the individual with the rest of the class is no longer appropriate. In the case of the identified mildly handicapped student, there is little merit in verifying that the student does not perform as well as the other students on traditional tests or in traditional classrooms. New systems of grading need to incorporate a recognition of individual differences in intellectual ability and learning strength. Grades must begin to provide more descriptive information by showing individual student gains and identifying specific needs for improvement.

In order to be more adequate, grades should provide a reporting method which is of a descriptive nature about the student's relative achievement. Some of the ideal functions to be addressed by grading and reporting systems are:

- the student's current level of performance;
- the student's readiness for future units of instruction;
- the quality of the student's performance compared to others;
- the effort put forth by the student;
- the student's ability to relate and work with others; and
- the relative improvement of the student's performance compared to past records.

When compared to this standard, traditional systems are often found wanting. This article will explore current grading practices, purposes of grading, issues concerning grades, alternative systems, and suggestions for implementing those alternatives. It is hoped that as educators objectively view traditional grading systems informed changes will occur.

If the purpose is to give the school administrative office a convenient way to sort out those students who should receive promotions, honors, scholarships and valedictories—grading works well

If the purpose is to decide who should go to college and to help college admission officers select candidates for their freshmen classes—grading also works well

If the purpose is to communicate with the parent, giving information about the child's progress and asking for help in overcoming problems—grading could stand improvement

If the purpose is to motivate the student toward intensive learning—grading often doesn't work well at all.

Teachers face the problem each reporting period of what would be a fair and equitable way to mark the performance of a student who seems to try but just doesn't perform as well as is expected. The problem for the vocational teacher or content-area teacher is magnified by the concern about standards and providing an accurate picture of the student's performance in the "work world." All conscientious secondary teachers who have been involved in the grading process have spent countless hours trying to determine whether a student should be passed or failed on a specific assignment or course. Their concerns range from:

upholding the standards of the school;
maintaining their integrity with their fellow teachers;
being honest with the student;
justifying the grades with other students;
motivating the student for better performance in the future;
communicating accurately to the next teachers; and
avoiding the reputation of being an easy teacher.

The dilemma of grading is complicated by expectations placed on teachers by others.

Administrators, parents, special educators, college admission personnel, and employers all send mixed mesaages about the purposes of grades. The purposes provided in Table 2 represent only a sample of the possible reasons for the use of grades in the public schools. Some of the reasons may seem to be "tongue in cheek"; however, they need to be considered. The dilemma cannot be resolved without considerable evaluation of:

1. Why am I grading and reporting student progress?
2. Who cares about the relative performance of the student?
3. How will others use the grades?

Current Practices

Presently, there are many different types of grading practices employed in the secondary schools. In an information survey, thirty different grading practices or variations of grading practices were found to be employed at the junior-senior high school level (Vasa, 1979). The practices ranged from the traditional letter grades to written letters to parents and "gentlemen" agreements between the resource teacher and the classroom teachers. The number of variations in grading practices point out the difficulty in providing specific direction on the best grading and reporting procedure to utilize. Six of the most common grading and reporting practices used in the secondary school are given in Table 1.

Table 1: Six Common Grading Practices in the Secondary Schools

Grading Practice	Description
Letter or Numerical	traditional system of giving the student a mark of A, B, C, D, and F or 1, 2, 3, 4, and 5 to demonstrate relative level of performance on unit or course of study
Pass/Fail Credit/No Credit	criterion-based measurement system which permits the individual teacher to indicate that the student has either met or not met previously determined standards
Checklists	criterion-based measurement system which has the instructor check student's progress against a predetermined list of needed skills or completion of specific tasks
Contracts	student and teacher agree to assign a mark based on predetermined goals and objectives which the student will reach during the instructional period. The goals may be written in conjunction with the special education teacher/consultant
Letters to Parents	a written report provided to the student or parents to give narrative information about the student's performance
Blanket Grades	all students receive a predetermined grade at the end of the marking period

Purposes of Grading

Some of the controversy surrounding current grading practices is summarized in the statement from the National Association of School Public Relations Association:

Purposes for Grading and Marking: Table 2

Administrative Functions
    to indicate whether a student has passed or failed
    to indicate whether a student should be promoted or not

to indicate whether a student should graduate or not
to be used by employers in evaluating prospective employees
to transmit information from one school district to another
to consolidate records of students' learning and work done so far
to enable a course to be evaluated
to give schools public accountability
to provide the public with a guarantee of competence
to provide college admission departments with patterns of student performance

Student Functions
to give students a reward and sense of achievement
to give students feedback on progress
to motivate students
to give students experience of competition
to test ability to stand up to stress and pressure
to have students experience real-life situations
to prepare students for a stratified society
to test performance in real life

Teacher Functions
to evaluate students' progress during the course
to assess amount of effort put in by the student
to give feedback on teaching
to grade in relation to other students
to grade in relation to criteria of excellence
to maintain standards
to maintain staff authority over students

Guidance Functions
to assist personal development of student
to predict future performance
to provide for screening of candidates for occupations and schools
to stimulate students to greater efforts
to determine the number of courses in which a student should enroll
to decide on the advisability for enrolling in other courses
to permit participation in school activities, play on teams, and win scholarships
to preserve the existing structure of society

Parent Functions
to give parents feedback on student progress
to provide parents with information about appropriateness of course placement
to provide parents with a means of evaluating the success of the IEP
to provide parents with information to report to their friends on the student's performance

The only agencies which regularly ask schools about the class rank of program graduates are colleges and vocational/technical schools. Generally, other agencies only want to know if the student has completed a program. They are more concerned about the student's ability to relate to others and to work in a cooperative environment. Graduation from a school program does not necessarily mean a certain level of competence is guaranteed by the public schools. If we accept the contention that the most concerned about students' comparative performance is the schools, we may be able to avoid the over concern associated with the marking of handicapped students enrolled in the regular classroom.

II. ISSUES IN GRADING

Determining Grades

One of the problems commonly cited in the use of traditional grading procedures is how the marks are determined. In many of the academic courses of study in the secondary schools, a majority of the grade or rank in the class is determined on written tests and written work. The mildly handicapped student may often have extreme difficulty in completing written tasks. Written tests and written work may not, therefore, adequately reflect that student's knowledge level. Teachers need to examine very carefully what procedures should be used to determine the appropriate grade or mark. Alternative or supplementary ways of evaluating and reporting student progress could include the use of other measurement devices. For example the teacher might use some or all of the methods listed below:

> class interaction and discussion;
> class projects;
> papers;
> verbal reports;
> student interviews;
> anecdotal records of student performance;
> daily logs of student activities;
> files maintained on the student;
> modified tests—verbal, performance
> shortened; and
> checklists.

By the utilization of some of the above techniques, the teacher may not need to make modifications in the grade reporting system for the mildly handicapped student. Instead, the strategy might be to employ alternative ways of assessing the student's progress toward the course objectives. For example, a student who has a severe reading problem but is capable might be evaluated by oral tests. Other students may need to be evaluated on daily tasks and performance to provide a clearer picture of their progress in the course. In these cases, the classroom teacher would modify the evaluation procedures and not the progress reporting system.

Teacher Attitudes and Student Reactions

When a modified grading system is adopted for one or more handicapped students in a classroom it may be expected that other students will react negatively: there may be resentment that the handicapped student is getting an unfair "break," by lowered expectations for his/her performance; or the modified grading may draw attention to the handicapped student' as inferior and unable to compete without special considerations; or non-handicapped students, but those who are still struggling for grades in school, may feel they are being discriminated against, by receiving no special help with their own school problems; and, in an adolescent society, anyone "different" is somehow considered bad, and to be avoided, leading to isolation of the student so perceived. These and other possible reactions are concerns to teachers when a modified grading system is to be installed. However, it should be pointed out that the key to the success of the installation of a modified system is the attitude portrayed by the classroom teacher, who should model the attitude of acceptance toward individual differences. If the teacher models a contemptuous attitude toward the adjustments or makes negative comments about the system, students will soon pick up this discontent on the part of the teacher and probably react accordingly. From the experience of the author, the teacher is advised to never discuss one student's performance with another student. The precedent for this opinion is contained in he code of ethics for teachers (National Education Association, 1963). It states that the professional should not discuss one student with another individual unless it serves the purpose of benefiting the student in question. The best response the teacher can make when a student questions the procedures or grading practices employed with another student is to state, "I do not discuss your grades or performance with other students, and I will not discuss the performance of other students with you. If you have questions or concerns about the methods being used to evaluate your performance, I would be pleased to discuss them with you." Students commonly seek to improve their status in classes by making unfair comparisons with other students.

The "Watered Down" Curriculum

Vocational teachers have often expressed a concern that they cannot vary the competencies for their respective courses for the mildly handicapped student. They argue that adjusting grading criteria provides an inaccurate representation of student skills. Further, that industry and business maintain standards which they expect of program graduates; therefore, allowing a student differential criteria for competencies would bring discredit to the institution's training program. This is a legitimate concern if the school's vocational program chooses to provide only a letter grade or a dichotomous grade and does not provide the potential employer with a list of skills or competencies completed by the student. The question should not be one of standards but rather reporting what skills the student has mastered. This problem can be resolved by using a competency checklist for each goal in the curriculum. For example, if the goal were to teach bookkeeping skills, a checklist could be developed that listed the skills, in a developmental sequence, that the student would need to master to reach that goal. If requested by the employer and approved by the student or his/her parents, a form containing information on the student's performance, perhaps even the checklist itself, could be forwarded at the time of employment.

The curriculum of the vocational programs or the content areas do not necessarily have to be "watered down" because mildly handicapped students are enrolled. Instead, the instructional and evaluation procedures may need to be redesigned to more accurately reflect the needs and knowledge of participating students.

Comparison Grading

One concern which has caused controversy is the comparison of mildly handicapped students' performance with the performance of other students in the class. John Holt (1970) states very eloquently that grades should be abolished because of their detrimental effect on learning. They foster unhealthy competitive attitudes in students, and they hurt self-esteem and create misleading expectancies about students' future school performance. These statements were not directed at the mildly handicapped but pertain to grading in general. Competition for grades benefits the small minority of students who end up as "winners." The vast majority of the students are confronted by frustration and humiliation. Millman (1970) suggests that criterion-reference grading and the use of the mastery report card would alleviate some of the inequities of current grading practices. All in all, there is a great concern about how performance of handicapped and non-handicapped students in the classroom should be evaluated and reported.

III.   ALTERNATIVE GRADING PRACTICES

In this section, four alternative or adjusted grading practices are presented: 1) contracts; 2) pass/fail systems; 3) letter or numerical grades; and 4) checklists. Each of these grading systems will be discussed in terms of their advantages, disadvantages, and suggestions for the implementation of the system.

Contracts

Contracting between the student and the teacher has been a common practice in many elective courses in the secondary school. The contract is merely an agreement between the classroom teacher and the student about the level of performance to be maintained in order to obtain a specific grade. The contract with mildly handicapped secondary students is frequently based upon the Individual Education Plan (IEP) written for the student. A good contract would include the following:

types of work to be completed by the student;
the quantity of work to be completed by the student;
an agreement as to how the grade for the student will be determined;
a statement of how the quality of the work will be determined;
the signature of the involved parties, e.g., teacher, student, special education resource consultant, parent; and
timelines for the completion of the work, when appropriate.

Advantages. **Advantages to the utilization of the student contract form are summarized as follows:**

clearly identifies for the student what is expected;
subjectivity on the part of the teacher is reduced because quality and quantity requirements are stated in advance;
diversity of tasks and assignments is encouraged for students;
competitive grades are discouraged because the criteria for grades are determined for the individual student;
recognizes the ability of the student to participate in goal setting; and
promotes better mental health in the classroom.

Disadvantages. **Disadvantages commonly cited for the utilization of student contracts are:**

creates additional record keeping for the teacher;
quantity of work rather than quality of work can be overemphasized;
difficulty in finding creative ways to measure the student's performance; and
differences may arise between student and teacher on agreement of assignments.

Implementation

The two most important criteria for a contract are that it should be written in simple, easy-to-understand language, and it should provide for commitment among participants. The teacher employing the contract as an alternative grading practice must be organized, goal directed, accountable, and capable of task-analyzing objectives. In addition, the contracting process requires skills in communicating and interpreting students' interests. The process of contracting involves a modified problem-solving approach on the part of the teacher and student.

In using the problem-solving model, the teacher needs to be clearly aware of the options which are acceptable for the student to demonstrate knowledge or competence in the classroom. In reviewing the student's strengths and weaknesses, the resulting contract could provide alternative strategies for the student mastering information in the course and alternative methods of evaluating the student's progress towards the stated objectives. The contract is one of the most widely used methods of accommodating the mildly handicapped student in the general education classroom. In some cases, the contract can be a "gentlemen's agreement" between the special education resource teacher and the classroom teacher on modifications needed for the course.

The major point to remember is that the contract should be written and agreed upon in advance of the instruction.

Pass/Fail System

The pass/fail system of grading is one of the simplest to operate. In this model only the minimum competencies for the course or for individuals need to be determined. The successful completion of the minimum level or exceeding the minimum level permits the student to receive a grade of pass or "P". Students not reaching the minimum criteria fail or receive an "F". The pass/fail grading system can be reviewed as a part of the blanket grading system where all students receive a "P" or fail. The pass/fail system can also be viewed as a contract system in which the student meets the established criteria and receives a passing grade.

Advantages. Advantages of the pass/fail system are:

less pressure placed on students for competition;
less anxiety on the part of the students;
cheating and "buttering up" the teacher are not needed;
student knows what is expected and works towards a goal;
student's achievement level can be increased or levels of aspiration can be increased;
careful examination of the student's relative abilities and disabilities; and
relieves the teacher of the responsibility of comparative evaluation of students' work.

Disadvantages. The following disadvantages for the utilization of the pass/fail system are noted by teachers:

teacher may not provide corrective feedback in weak areas;
passing grade is meaningless in distinguishing between students with differing abilities;
some students do less work when freed of pressures for traditional grades;
presents same pressures on students close to failing as the traditional grades; and
minimum standards may be arbitrary and difficult to define.

Implementation

The pass/fail system does not require many modifications to present procedures on the part of the classroom teacher. The key is to establish the competencies for the course and to determine what each student should complete for a passing grade. The major concern is whether the student reaches the designated competencies or skill level rather than how has the student performed in comparison with other students. In adopting this system, the instructor still needs to utilize a number of different types of evaluation techniques to measure the student's progress towards the competencies.

In utilizing the pass/fail procedure, teachers more commonly rely on observational data about students rather than formal tests. The observational data would include: student performance on daily tasks, completion of assigned tasks, interviews with the student; and anecdotal records of student performance. The contract form in Figure 1 could be easily adapted to allow for its use with the pass/fail system of grading.

Letter or Numerical Grades

Letter or numerical grades in one form or another are the most widely employed reporting systems in use. These traditional grades have been utilized because they have relayed comparative information about student's performance to parents, other interested parties, and students. Often, the information provided by this system may be inaccurate and distorted. By some school's policies, teachers are locked into a grading system which requires them to utilize a range of grades from A to F or 1 through 5. When the teacher does not have the option of developing grade reporting procedures, he will need to adapt to the situation by modifying the measurement techniques used in determining the grades.

> *Advantages*. **Below are listed some of the advantages of the letter or numerical grade system:**

> easy and convenient for use by the classroom teacher;
> readily accepted by most parents of high achieving students;
> fairly good predictor of future grades; and
> can be numerically converted single score (GPA).

> *Disadvantages*. **Disadvantages of the letter or numerical grade system are:**

> meaning may vary between schools and individual classes;
> unusual combination of motivation, performance, and achievement;
> provides for unfair competition for students;
> produces anxiety for students;
> probably does not relate to any future performance in the work world;
> teachers have a tendency not to use the whole scale.

Implementation

From a philosophical viewpoint, traditional numerical and letter grades are more harmful than helpful to the mildly handicapped student. In many secondary schools, however, teachers do not have the option to employ other methods of reporting student progress. In these schools, teachers need decide what ways of modifying the measuring system exist for these students. Teachers may need to adjust the testing procedures and allow for greater use of other techniques of measurement, such as, daily assignments, progress checklists, student interviews, and class projects.

The essential ingredient in accommodating the mildly handicapped secondary student will be to establish criteria for the completion of work at relative standards (A, B, C, D, F), rather than basing the grades on a comparison. Again, the student contract form would be helpful in this area.

Checklists

Competency checklists have been widely used in skill-oriented courses and in developmentally sequenced academic courses, such as mathematics. The checklist provides for a guide to the individual student's progress towards goals stated in the instructional plan or IEP. For example, in the vocational auto mechanics course, the teacher could break the learning units into small modules to permit easy assessment of skill acquisition.

Advantages. The checklist offers the following advantages:

more value than a grade alone and helpful to the student;
more meaningful to parents and future employers;
gives more detailed information about the student's performance;
can pinpoint weaknesses in the school instructional program; and
skills may be prioritized

Disadvantages. Disadvantages cited for the checklists are given below:

may be time consuming for the teacher;
increases the amount of paper work for the teacher;
tasks and objectives may not be understood by the parents;
changes in instructional objectives can necessitate changing the reporting form; and
written evaluation allows the teacher to be more subjective and checklists tend to focus on
    weaknesses.

Implications

The checklist is an excellent way for the teacher to indicate the progress a student has made during the course of instruction. The competencies for the checklist are derived from the course goals and/or objectives. They could also be derived from the goals and/or objectives on the student's IEP. The checklist is written in competency form with an accompanying means of determining student mastery of each step in the attainment of the necessary skills. There needs to be a balance between detail and ease in use of the checklists. Generally, the more difficulty the student is having the more detailed the checklist needs to be.

Source: Stanley F. Vasa. *Alternative procedures for grading handicapped students in the secondary schools.* Lincoln, NE: University of Nebraska, 1980.

CHAPTER 8

Vocational Education: Development and Implementation of Programming

Parents send their children to school with the inherent faith that the quality of their children's lives will be enhanced by their school experiences. School personnel are doing a good job in a number of areas. In fact, it is often easy to forget how much is being accomplished, especially in the face of constantly rising expectations. School as an institution has never really been seen as just a place where basic academic skills are taught, and now parental and societal demands dictate that elementary and secondary teachers assume roles once reserved for postsecondary educators.

All students enrolled in secondary special education programs are to be offered an opportunity to fulfill their vocational potential. If students' successes are to be optimized, appropriate and efficient programming should be provided for each pupil. Therefore in this chapter, you will be given the information needed to develop, implement, and manage the vocational component of a special education program. This includes the following areas:

1. Essential goals and objectives of the curriculum that outline a developmental vocational sequence appropriate for students with special needs
2. Assessment instruments for students' current levels and for evaluation on an ongoing basis—with an explanation of how resulting information is to be applied to programming
3. Strategies, activities, and instructional methods for implementing program objectives; use of full scope of community and school resources
4. Training agreements and plans together with procedures and instruments needed in coordinating vocational placements
5. An outline of the teacher's responsibilities in managing a vocational progam and an explanation of the advocacy role that is an integral part of these responsibilities.

Through a combination of effectively sequenced experiences defined by program goals and objectives and matched with evaluation data, students can be guided, trained, and prepared to use their aptitudes, skills, and knowledge in making success-ful transitions into the world of work.

GENERAL CONSIDERATIONS

Students coming into a secondary special education program will bring with them a wide range of experiences. Career-education concepts introduced in elementary school, exploratory courses in junior high school, and activities of daily living are examples of experiences that should have exposed students to the reality that people are needed to work at many kinds of jobs involving many different skills. Few students, however, will understand how to use these experiences to make career decisions and vocational choices. They will need considerable assistance from support personnel, as well as the classroom teacher, in making decisions that will be meaning-ful and challenging to their potential as workers.

In considering instruction for students, keep in mind that the learning characteris-tics of these students vary widely in rate of learning, adaptive behavior, ability to generalize, and learning styles. Students with special needs generally learn more efficiently when they actively participate in learning tasks. Therefore, the teacher should provide realistic experiences in a variety of settings through which students can develop useful knowledge and practice in needed vocational skills. Vocational litera-ture and paper-pencil activities are valuable and for some objectives essential. Teach-ers are obligated to work toward generalization of skills, however. This is best accomplished when training takes place in settings most like that in which the behav-ior is expected to be used. Using only reading activities as the way to learn about the world of work is not adequate in most situations.

Students in special education programs experience failure much too frequently. Fear or avoidance of failure is evidenced recurrently by the way students approach new experiences. Insufficient involvement with procedures and processes related to job skills may limit vocational options a student may consider. Choices students will make in the future can be broadened by planned exposure to success. When students are expected to perform new tasks, the teacher should provide sufficient opportunity for the student to realize success or at least to develop a sense of accomplishment. If teachers would practice this policy, their students would not be as threatened by new experiences and would be more willing to give new activities a chance. Students soon learn that they can approach challenges with positive anticipation rather than the threat of failure.

It is essential that teachers involved with work-experience programs become knowledgeable of the child labor laws. These regulations will affect planning and placement of students at worksites. Failure to follow these federal regulations could seriously jeopardize employers who are working with students provided by your consultation. Employers count on school representatives to be knowledgeable of regu-lations that apply to students being placed. A copy of current child labor laws can be obtained from the United States Department of Labor, Wage and Hour Division.

Providing for the many aspects of a vocational program requires the combined skills of professionals from several disciplines. The expertise of the facilitating team is used to develop, implement, monitor, evaluate, support, and manage student programs. It is essential that a member of this team becomes an advocate for each student (Weisenstein & Elrod, 1987). This assignment should not be avoided by the classroom teacher but should be recognized as an opportunity to provide direction and coherence to individual programs. There is a good reason for teachers to shoulder this responsibility. Teachers meet with their students daily while other team members may not have this opportunity. Teachers are also in the best position to monitor the comprehensive development of students, to recognize the need for intervention by special service personnel, and to serve as the person to promote the needs of special students in regular vocational classes.

Readers will find that consideration of these issues as they develop their programs will help them to understand better the purpose of program components, to consider the best possible delivery system for accomplishing goals and objectives, and to plan for effective use of support personnel as well as school and community resources.

VOCATIONAL PHASES

Vocational programming for special education students is a dominant component of the comprehensive curriculum. It provides students with meaningful vocational assessments, planned exploration, and specific job/life preparation (Robinson & Polloway, 1987), which follows a logical, developmental sequence characterized by four distinct but greatly dependent phases.

Phase I: Readiness and self-awareness
Phase II: Exploration
Phase III: Preparation/training
Phase IV: Employment/transition

Phase I: Readiness and Self-Awareness

The goal of the readiness and self-awareness phase is to prepare students for active participation in realistic vocational experiences that have been identified as being appropriate for their aptitudes, skills, interests, values, and personality. The goal is not for students to identify the jobs they plan to have for the remainder of their lives but rather to identify a cluster or family of jobs with which a student will feel comfortable. Students must be made aware of vocational options and must have extensive knowledge about themselves to match their traits to appropriate career choices. For students to benefit from opportunities to experience job choices, they must exhibit appropriate attitudes and be willing to work.

Developing student readiness for the world of work is a preparatory component of the curriculum. Instructional objectives will help students to

Develop appropriate attitudes about work and the place that work will have in their lives

Evaluate reasons that people work

Develop knowledge about jobs

Define goals for independent living in relationship to vocational interests

Working conditions, environments of jobs, and skills needed by workers will be identified and related to career clusters. Life-styles common to workers should also be examined. Preparation for training and employment in a variety of vocational areas will have to be outlined. Students will also learn to identify behaviors and jobsmanship skills appropriate to the worksite and to evaluate themselves in relationship to worker responsibilities. (Refer to Appendix 8.1, at the end of this chapter, for examples of curriculum components.)

Self-awareness is an evaluation process that includes forms of self-appraisal. Instruction involves students with varied experiences and activities through which they can learn to identify factors of their personality, as well as the multifaceted composition of traits that makes each student a unique individual. Formal vocational evaluation procedures are to be included in this process. As students develop their knowledge of jobs and of themselves, they should be given sufficient opportunity to match their traits to jobs in order for them to understand the relationship between making appropriate vocational choices and eventual job satisfaction and success.

Guidance and counseling by the professional staff are to be provided throughout all of the vocational phases to assist students in making decisions. Students need to be encouraged to freely express choices and preferences, however, so that they will acquire an attitude of ownership of their vocational decisions rather than a feeling that others will make or should be making their decisions for them. Demonstrated readiness to work together with carefully chosen jobs to explore prepares students for involvement with the exploration phase.

Phase II: Exploration

The goal of the exploration phase is to verify training and work-adjustment needs of students. Areas that will be involved include vocational choices, related instruction, and work adjustment. The activities of Phase I should have provided a profile of each student's general vocational aptitudes and interests. These results are now used to initiate a continuum of exploratory experiences through which the presence or absence of a student's interest in identified job families can be confirmed. The more accurately a student is matched with a career cluster, the more precisely appropriate future programming objectives can be defined.

Mainstreaming students into regular vocational classes should be encouraged during this phase. Although students may have been involved in exploratory vocational classes in junior high school, training in specific vocational areas requires that students become involved with a designated *sequence* of courses that may require at least two or more years for completion. Usually, the vocational education teacher teaches specific skills related to jobs, and the special education teacher teaches more general skills. Finally, it will be necessary to assess how students will interact with regular employees and supervisors and how they will respond to the demands of the worksite so that work adjustment needs can be addressed directly with each student. Attention to these needs, as they are identified, encourages efficient continuation of the developmental process.

Instruction during this phase involves the development of job knowledge through the use of vocational literature and media, vocational classes in cluster areas, job-analysis procedures, development of plans for job exploration, preplacement orientation, visitations to job sites, and, most importantly, through actual worksite involvement. Emphasis should be placed on skills needed by workers to perform their jobs. The student would learn to relate not only academic skills to jobs, for example, but also physical and social skills. Students learn to analyze jobs through their personal experiences, to define tasks by skill requirements and procedures, to describe work environments, and to relate jobs to potential income and benefits. Students will be more realistic about their abilities to perform specific jobs if they have experienced the related tasks in a realistic setting. Students should be assisted by the vocational team in rating their potential as workers in areas of exploration, in clarifying vocational decisions, and in determining preparation that will be necessary for entry-level employment.

Information about each student's ability to adjust to real work environments, to use needed skills, and to apply job knowledge is obtained through ongoing worksite monitoring and evaluation. The reports generated help determine instructional needs of students. Individualized instruction to improve jobsmanship skills and to correct problems that are interfering with work adjustment comprises a major part of the teacher's work during this phase. Students exiting this phase should demonstrate appropriate work habits and the ability to adjust to various worksites and should have in place a definite plan for ongoing training and preparation for improvement of job knowledge and related skill areas.

Phase III: Preparation and Training

The goal of the preparation and training phase is to help students acquire specific marketable skills. Regular vocational classes, academic skills, individualized instruction, and on-the-job training are brought together for this common purpose. Vocational development during this phase is concerned with the student's ability to learn and perform tasks normally found in selected job families. Accumulated assessment information must be used to select community-based training sites and to develop training plans. The scope of preparation should be designed to give students exposure and opportunity to develop essential skills for employment within a specific job cluster. Effective use of available resources, interagency participation, and cooperation among vocational team members will maximize the appropriateness of experiences selected to achieve program goals.

Instruction during this phase will take place in three environments: the vocational class, the special class, and the community. Students should be enrolled in vocational classes that teach specialized skills and occupational concepts whenever appropriate. It will be necessary for the special class teacher to work with vocational teachers to determine objectives for individual student programs, to assist in identification of strategies for accommodating needs of students enrolled, and to provide support for teachers and students as needed.

Instruction in the special classroom will continue to develop the scope of understanding of work-related topics such as job-keeping skills, job-seeking skills, economic relationships, and knowledge and competencies involving job/life areas. Individualized instruction will continue to address specific needs of students in job training and in vocational classes. Teacher reports, on-site evaluations, and training-plan schedules will provide information for determining these needs.

Occupational guidance will continue during this phase, but it will be more concerned with the ability of each student to adjust to work in a designated family of jobs than in the identification of an appropriate job cluster. Instead of a student being a utility stock person in a grocery store, for example, he specializes in produce preparation and display. Selected training sites in the community should involve work in job families identified by matching job descriptions to accumulated assessment information.

Placement in community-based job sites will provide student workers with planned training under the direct supervision of a site employer or trainer. This resource person serves as the student's vocational teacher while the student is in the community and instructs the student about performance of specific work tasks as well as the general requirements and specific expectations of a particular job (Robinson & Palloway, 1987). Management of community-based training and the on-campus components of student programs involves coordination procedures for monitoring students at the worksite and for determining related instruction needed to maximize student progress. Students completing this phase should be ready for supervised employment in Phase IV.

Phase IV: Employment and Transition

The primary goal of the employment and transition phase is for each student to learn to become a competitive employee in a specific work environment. At the conclusion of this phase students should be able to satisfy the basic requirements and job expectations of most employers (Robinson & Palloway, 1987) (see Chapter 2). This does not mean that all students will be expected to seek employment upon being graduated from high school. Postsecondary training and education should be encouraged for qualified students. Supported employment, adult services, and jobs in sheltered workshops are other alternatives that may have to be considered as appropriate in transition plans for some students. A critical function of the vocational team will be to assist students in planning for transition from school to society.

Instruction during this phase becomes highly individualized and continues to involve the community as well as the school. Later in this chapter training plans are introduced. These plans help identify the specific skills a student will need to perform a job. Some of these skills will be taught in vocational classes, some on the job, and others through related instruction in the special class. Support for students in regular vocational classes should be provided, and specific needs of students on the job must be addressed. Students will need to be given an increasing opportunity to work with support staff and community agencies. Guidance services should be considered an integral component of programming. Remember, *all* components of the comprehensive curriculum should focus on skills needed for transition so that students develop a holistic understanding and confident acceptance of job/life transition.

Recent federal attention has been focused on the problems that handicapped youth encounter in making the transition from school to adult life. The Education of the Handicapped Act Amendments of 1983 (P.L. 98-199, Section 626) designates funds and support for secondary vocational preparation and the transition from school to work. Transition, as defined by Will (1984), includes the following points:

1. A period of time that includes high school, the point of graduation, additional postsecondary education or adult services, and the initial years of employment.
2. A process that requires sound preparation in the secondary school, adequate support at the point of school leaving.
3. An effort that emphasizes shared responsibility of all involved parties for transition success. (p. 2)

In 1984 Congress backed up their commitment to transition improvement with the passage of The Carl D. Perkins Vocational Education Act (P.L. 98-524). For the first time, a mandate has been handed down requiring that appropriate vocational assessment be provided to handicapped students and that the results be used by professionals with respect to successful completion of vocational education programs by these students.

The Carl Perkins Vocational Education Act was reauthorized in 1989, through fiscal year 1995, as the Applied Technology Education Amendments (H.R.7). Amendments include the strongest language yet seen aimed at guaranteeing the participation of students with handicaps in vocational education programs.

Major provisions relating to students with handicaps are:

1. Students with handicaps who have a vocational education component contained in their individualized education program (IEP) will be afforded, with respect to vocational education, all of the rights and protections of P.L. 94-142 (Part B of the Education of all Handicapped Children's Act of 1975 [EHA]). In effect, appropriate vocational education programming will be made available to such students. Furthermore, the other rights and protections of Part B of the EHA will also be guaranteed, such as due process procedures and instruction in the least restrictive environment.
2. Students with handicaps who do not have IEPs (not in special education) will be afforded all the rights and protections of Section 504 of the Rehabilitation Act of 1973, that is, equal access to vocational education programs.
3. Because the rights and protections of Part B of the EHA and Section 504 are now clearly made applicable to vocational education programs, provision is made for joint monitoring of these programs by the special educa-

tion unit of the state education agency and the state board for vocational education.

4. The 10 percent of funds set aside to support participation of students with handicaps in vocational education is removed, as are all other "setasides" (e.g., for economically disadvantaged students) except for retention of a setaside that combines support for promotion of sex equity and for displaced homemakers.

5. The House amendments drop use of the term *vocational education* and substitute the term *applied technology education*.

6. Eighty percent of funds going to each state will be allocated to the local school districts (LEAs) with the remainder retained by the state agency. Distribution to LEAs will be based on the following formula:

   —70 percent based upon the LEA's relative allocation under Chapter One
   ᶜederal education program for economically disadvantaged children)

   ⁾0 percent based upon the LEA's relative count of children with handi-
   served in special education

   ᵉrcent based upon the LEA's relative overall school enrollment

   of federal funds under the act, there is a stipulation to serve first
   ing the highest concentration of students with handicaps, as well
   ᵗ concentrations of students who are economically disadvan-
   ᶰts of limited English proficiency, and to approve for federal
   ᵉ programs that assist students with handicaps, as well as
   ᶜonomically disadvantaged and of limited English profi-
   ᵒortive services such as counseling, English-language
   and special aids.

   ᶠor funds by an LEA and other eligible institutions
   ᵗo programs of good quality will be provided to
   ᵒw the LEA and other eligible institutions will
   ᵗational education to students with handicaps,
   ᶦons will facilitate and promote the effective
   ᶜaps to employment and additional training

   ᵒr students with handicaps that enlarge
   ᶦuding:
   will be coordinated between appro-
   ᵈucation, special education, and

   ᶦces, including adaptation of
   ᶦes to achieve full participa-
   ᵈucation.
   , and career-development
   ᶰselors.
   ᵉnts with handicaps and their
   ᵈents are eligible for vocational

education, and in no event later than the ninth grade, information concerning opportunities available in vocational education, including specific courses that are available and special services that are available.

10. The U.S. secretary of education is required to maintain detailed information through scientific sampling on the participation of students with handicaps in vocational education, including types of programs available and enrollment of students with handicaps by type of program, type of instructional setting, and type of handicap. Essentially the same provision is included in current law.

11. The General Accounting Office (GAO), an arm of the Congress, is ordered to do a three-year study on the participation of students with handicaps in vocational education aimed at seeking answers to a number of key questions, such as:

—Has the number of students participating increased?

—How many are participating in programs that will lead to an occupational skill or job placement?

—What types of disability and severity of disability are represented?

—How many students have vocational courses included in their IEP's, and how many do not?

—To what extent do special education and vocational rehabilitation personnel participate in the selection and provision of vocational education cours for students with handicaps?

There is a need to view transition as a process that enables us to inte effectively life-development activities into the developmental curriculum for al dents. The intent is not only to provide life-development activities but also to bu previous interests and experiences, involve appropriate service providers, and in aspects of home/school/community life in a manner that lessens the transitiona between home, preschool, elementary school, middle school, high school, school services, and employment (Ianacone & Stodden, 1987, p. 4).

Transition preparation actually begins when students enter the secor gram. The phases of vocational programming provide a developmental pl which students can effectively acquire needed skills and understandings fe tion of their job/life success. Preparation of the final draft of a studen plan requires that a strong spirit of trust and cooperation exists among t staff, the student, and his or her parents or guardian if the plan is to be followed by the student and supported by his or her family. The e vocational programs can and should be evaluated according to the succ of its students into society and the world of work.

TIME FRAME OF THE VOCATIONAL CURRICULUM

We have purposely left any comment concerning a time frame vocational sequence out of the preceding discussion because reader to conclude that each phase was to be completed within programs will offer the phases as year-long or semester courses. Setting up the vocational sequence in this way may be necessary if the courses are offered as a part of a departmentalized program. This is appropriate if within the scheduled course structure students can be "recycled" as is necessary to meet the goals of each phase. Moving students in a lock-step manner through the four phases, however, because the students are identified on class roles as sophomores, juniors, or seniors, may be programming students for failure. A student may need to spend three or four semesters in exploratory positions to find that job family that best complements his or her vocational profile. Persistent social and work-adjustment problems or a slow rate of skill acquisition may require that the student have a longer period for training and adjustment. Some students may demonstrate the inverse of these problems. These students may express very appropriate vocational goals and demonstrate satisfactory work adjustment skills, and therefore, they may need only to have the opportunity to become acquainted with specific vocational environments and to get related work experience.

There are several other factors that can affect the time frame of the secondary vocational program. If students have experienced a strong career-education program in middle school or junior high school, much less time may be needed to develop readiness and self-awareness. Consideration may have to be made for students who enter a program late in their high school careers and have not had the benefit of a comprehensive vocational program. Flexibility of scheduling may also be necessary to meet the needs of students that have been targeted as potential dropouts. Programs should be designed primarily to satisfy students' needs, not for administrative convenience. The special class teacher must be ready to serve as an advocate for students to insure that schedules are developed appropriately.

EVALUATION AND ASSESSMENT

The evaluation process used with the vocational component in special education is a comprehensive process including evaluation and reevaluation over a considerable period. It is carried out at varying levels of intensity as a shared responsibility of teachers, work-experience staff, special services, and community-resource people. The object of the evaluation is to create a vocational profile for each student that will increasingly improve the accuracy of projected career options and instructional needs.

Although a student's current level of functioning should be determined before programming can be designed, this does not mean that a formal vocational assessment and identification of appropriate jobs should precede a student's entry into a high school program. Research indicates that students who are referred for vocational assessment services are not always at a point to have sufficient motivation or to focus on career decision making (Ianacone & Leconte, 1986); this could make test results unreliable.

Initially then, assessment in career development is not as concerned with testing as it is with discovering and describing the multifaceted characteristics of students. Building student profiles becomes an integral part of the instructional activities through which students learn to define their aptitudes, interests, values, strengths, and weaknesses. To optimize the accuracy of the information, it is important that students believe that what they say and do are valuable in mapping out the way to their career success. This will require that students receive timely feedback on classwork as well as the opportunity to discuss the implications it may have on future career decisions.

Through the four developmental phases, the reader should plan to use traditional methods of evaluation to test for concept development but should also use experiences through which the student can demonstrate application of these concepts. Standardized tests and criterion-referenced tests, such as the *Brigance Tests of Essential Skills*, may also be helpful.

Information from these sources, however, will be insufficient in developing student profiles. Much of the information that is important in describing a student deals with affective behavior. Evaluating affective behavior requires that behaviors of concern are identified, observed, and rated. Anecdotal records and rating scales are methods used to help define the affective nature of students. Work maturity, need for supervision, learning styles, ability to apply skills, reaction to work assignments, concern for quality, and many other subjective characteristics that relate to worksite adjustment will have to be monitored. A student profile will include evaluation data that should be considered cumulative, evolving, and developing. Eventually, the profiles will be used to make recommendations for formal evaluation and for selecting and designing exploratory experiences and training programs.

As students become more involved with community-based experiences, situational assessment and competency-based evaluations become increasingly more important. Also, it becomes necessary for other members of the vocational team to assume more of the responsibility for making reports and collecting data. Situational assessment relies exclusively on observation of the workers as they work, giving information about behaviors under realistic conditions (Glascoe & Levy, 1985). Competency-based evaluations measure a student's ability to complete specific tasks or to demonstrate acquisition of knowledge required for designated jobs. Teachers and work-experience coordinators must be able to provide employers with accurate information concerning the assets and liabilities of students being placed. Through situational assessment and competency-based evaluations, placement information is more accurately defined.

The special class teacher should be prepared to implement the evaluation process and to assume responsibility for collection of reports from other sources. Some techniques, strategies, and instruments to assist in carrying out these responsibilities are included in the next sections of this chapter.

ORGANIZATION: DETERMINING INSTRUCTIONAL OBJECTIVES

The teacher should now be able to set up a general outline of program goals and objectives together with a rudimentary framework of resources that will be needed for the program's implementation. Preparation of the outline is essential in determining the instructional objectives that will be needed to continue each student's program.

Planning the vocational component of student programs requires that involved personnel identify as closely as possible the placement of students within the schema of the four developmental phases of the vocational program.

Using the program outline as a checklist, the teacher can identify from student records exposure to and documented achievement of objectives. As the records are reviewed, an analysis of behaviors, knowledge, and vocational experiences should be summarized. A format for processing this information is presented in Appendix 8.2. The questions on the form come directly from the program goals and emphasize readiness for the type of vocational experience and instruction that should be pursued. Completion of this analysis determines the vocational placement of students, which in turn identifies objectives that should be emphasized.

The teacher should not be alarmed if some questions cannot be answered with the records on file. Additional information can be obtained from instructional staff and resource personnel. Contact with these people can be used not only to get or to clarify information about students but also to help determine perceptions and attitudes that have developed. The teacher can also schedule interviews with students that will give the teacher an opportunity to observe affective and communication skills and to gather information concerning work attitudes, job knowledge, and vocational interests. Regardless of how complete the analysis of a student's development may seem, plan to confirm student abilities through contact with the student in the classroom.

Evaluation and reevaluation are integral components of vocational programs. Keep in mind the concept of development rather than mastery when it comes to attainment of vocational goals. Evaluation of affective behavior and knowledge is a subjective process, and there is no point in people's lives at which they will know everything about themselves, have all knowledge about work that is appropriate, or deal perfectly with social, economic, and psychological issues related to the world of work. The vocational team must use knowledge of the developmental process, comprehensive student profiles, and sound judgment to make decisions affecting student programs.

DESIGNING CLASSROOM INSTRUCTION

Special class teachers should not feel that they have as many programs to develop as they have students enrolled in their classes. The goals and objectives that are adopted for the vocational component of a special education program are the guidelines of instruction and development for all students to be served by the program. When combined with appropriate information about the students to be served, objectives selected from the sequence comprising the vocational component work to formulate individual programs. Mild learning difficulties do not significantly change what should be learned. The learning problems, however, require that special instructional accommodations be made.

Students' special needs can be accommodated in a number of ways. Individualized instruction, as well as instruction in small groups and classes, should be employed to meet these needs. A variety of instructional environments and personnel will be needed, and the goals and objectives can be organized and presented in different ways. Review Chapters 4 and 5 for models, instructional strategies, and processes that can be incorporated into the instructional process.

Group instruction should be considered not only an appropriate but an essential instructional approach. Effective application of teaching strategies within organized classes can accommodate for most individual differences in learning styles, modality preferences, and knowledge needs of students. Special needs can also be met within a class structure through diversity of presentations, carefully planned experiences, assignment variations, and appropriately selected materials. Most importantly, a class or small group provides a setting through which clusters of objectives that emphasize particular content or skills can be efficiently presented while encouraging an interactive and experiential approach to learning.

Individualized instruction requiring one-to-one interactions will be needed by some students and should be provided as is necessary. As students progress into the training and employment phases, an increasing amount of their time is spent at the worksite and in vocational classes in the mainstream. These students may have skills and concepts to learn that relate only to their particular jobs or classes. Providing specific instruction to meet the special needs of these students should·be recognized as a critical responsibility of the special class teacher.

The special class teacher is not the only person responsible for the vocational development of special education students. Preparing adolescents for the world of work is an integral component of the comprehensive curriculum; therefore, many of the competencies needed are taught in regular classes. Students will also develop skills through work activity coordinated and supervised by support personnel. Therapists, counselors, and other specialists may have instructional responsibilities as well. Each student's IEP should identify and define instructional assignments for all personnel.

Instruction should always be as efficient as possible. Efficiency of instruction is greatly improved when related objectives are organized into units. Units of instruction should be considered essential components of the vocational curriculum as they can provide a logical, efficient, and thorough schedule for development of competencies.

Organizing and preparing instruction is difficult and time-consuming if basic resources are not readily available. It is recommended that a vocational text or series of specific topic booklets be adopted for the program. (See Chapter 9, "Resources.") A good text together with a companion activity workbook will provide organized units of instruction as a variety of activities from which to choose. Special topic booklets can be obtained that cover most of the program objectives. These booklets are particularly valuable for independent study, accommodating reading deficits, supplementing the primary text, and as resources for studying occupations and job clusters.

The text selected for a program will provide the foundation material needed to develop most units. A tentative schedule of units to be presented throughout the school year should be organized. As units are planned, a preliminary outline of learning outcomes together with strategies, activities, and resources that could be included throughout the unit should be developed. Keep in mind that vocational instruction will need to consider all aspects of a student's development—attitudes, values, behaviors, personality, skills, aptitudes, and knowledge. Educators will have to provide practice in using information in a variety of ways and over time.

The time allotted to accomplish specific objectives of a unit will depend on the levels of achievement to be attained and the individual needs of students. Many objectives can be developed through ongoing activities once the basic concepts have been developed. Planning in this way helps accommodate for individual needs and makes it possible for instruction to move to the next unit scheduled in a reasonable time. The interrelationship of program objectives is also emphasized by the process.

As you organize your program and review resources, you will need to consider projects, experiences, and activities that will work to accomplish goals and at the same time keep students motivated and actively involved. The next part of this chapter will provide suggestions and ideas that will help you get started.

USING THE CLASSROOM AS A WORKSITE

An effective way to develop appropriate work habits and related attitudes is to get students to think of the school setting as a worksite. The rules, regulations, and expectations of the classroom should be developed by the students to reflect behaviors that are commonly practiced by responsible workers, such as punctuality, keeping materials organized, consideration for others, respect for authority, working without supervision, effective use of time, concern for quality, seeking help when needed, cooperation, proper use of equipment and materials, and concern for safety. Have students interact with parents and friends who are working to identify important jobsmanship skills. Make posters to emphasize the rules established. Set up ways to recognize and reward students for being good workers. Do not concentrate on penalties for breaking the rules. Relate good work habits and effort to "earned" rewards such as good grades, job opportunities, special activities and privileges, advancement, wages, friends, and freedom to make decisions. The cost of poor work habits will become evident to the students very quickly.

Surveys

Surveys can be conducted for a variety of purposes and in a variety of ways. They are a valuable teaching tool since they get students to determine information that they need to interact with a variety of people, to process information, and to summarize results or draw conclusions. Example surveys could have students ask workers to identify the three most important reasons that they work or to identify two rules that they consider to be the most important rules of their workplace. After information is gathered, class discussion should be used to organize results, clarify the differences in responses as they relate to different jobs and workers, and formulate conclusions.

Interviews

Have students brainstorm information that is valuable in learning about jobs. Develop an interview questionnaire using the most important points. Practice conducting interviews in the classroom using teachers or other school personnel before students schedule interviews with workers of their choice. Students can videotape or audiotape their interviews to simplify recording of information and also to make it easier to share interviews with classmates.

Computers

Computer activities can provide valuable involvement with important vocational content. Consider these uses of the computer in assisting instruction.

Vocabulary Development: Using a teacher utility program, develop simple quizzes of vocational terms to be learned. Use multiple-choice answers requiring the input of the correct word rather than a number or letter. Students will not only learn definitions but also improve their spelling of important words. Word lists can be personalized to help with specialized vocabulary needed for specific courses or jobs. Students should keep track of their scores to help them realize improvement.

Puzzles and Word Find: Have students work in teams to develop word lists and clues for making crossword puzzles and to make word-find activities to be used by the rest of the class.

Resumes and Data Sheets: Provide each student with a data disk for a word processing program on which you have entered a resume-data-sheet outline. Have students complete the outline using their personal data. If programs are saved using the names of students, the original program can be recalled unchanged in case of problems, and students can retrieve their programs to make corrections and update information as needed. A current fact sheet and personal resume will always be ready.

Letters of Application: Basic letters of application can be developed by students using a computer-word processing program and saved as a text file. When a student needs to write a letter of application, necessary changes and additions can be made very quickly and a neat businesslike copy can be presented.

Job Bank: Prepare a job-analysis questionnaire as a computer text file. Make copies of the questionnaire and use them when on field trips to job sites. Later, have students enter responses to the questionnaire on the computer and save the programs by job title. Individual students, teams, or the entire class may complete assignments.

Problem Solving: Each week put three-to-five job or social skills problems into a word processing text file. Describe the problem providing relevant situational conditions. Provide students with their own data disks. Have students enter their solutions and make a hard copy of their responses. At a specified time each week present the solutions to the class. Discuss and compare responses.

Job Matching: Use programs such as Career Information Systems of Iowa to help students develop the relationship of their interests and preferences to job titles and clusters. State vocational and guidance divisions develop these programs so that there is access to area-specific job information. Check with the guidance department of your school.

Recognition and Public Relations: There are many computer graphics and desktop publishing programs available to teach students to make posters and banners and to use their skills to plan honors for fellow students for accomplishments, birth dates, and so on. Use these programs to make announcements, newsletters to parents, bulletins to employers, and monthly calendars.

Videotapes

When planning a field trip, arrange to videotape the visitation. Be sure to get permission from the business establishment. Some firms will not allow filming of any kind. Most businesses, however, will give permission for filming for educational purposes. The tapes provide a medium for emphasizing important characteristics of specific jobs. Safety equipment and clothing, specific procedures used for task completion, and environmental conditions are some of the factors of job analysis that can be reidentified and reviewed when back in the classroom.

Another very valuable use of videotaping is for filming students at their worksites. The tapes can be used privately in evaluation to assist students in identifying problems they may have on the job and also to help them recognize work done well. The tapes can be used to increase job knowledge and awareness of other students. Student workers exhibit a great deal of enthusiasm when asked to present their tapes to the class. The tape presentations give class members the opportunity to see fellow students in actual on-the-job activity and to ask questions of the worker. Tapes of student workers can also be used for placement purposes since they visually demonstrate what the student can do.

Simulation

It is impossible to provide students with experiences in the actual environments in which skills will be required all of the time; however, it is possible to simulate conditions that will make tasks more realistic. Three simple and inexpensive simulations have been selected to help get your creative thoughts stimulated.

Restaurant.   Help students create a restaurant. Develop a menu or collect menus from different types of restaurants. If dishes and flatware are not available in the classroom, purchase disposable materials. Have students assume various roles—set-up person, waiter/waitress, host/hostess, cashier, bus person, customer. Job skills can be experienced and social skills can be developed.

Job Samples.   In job-analysis procedures, terminology is used that defines characteristics and demands of jobs. Students need experiences that relate to these terms to understand job requirements and also to evaluate themselves in relationship to these demands. Students can have a lot of fun and learn a great deal from simple and inexpensive activities. For example, consider this project used to acquaint students with fine motor dexterity.

Obtain apothecary containers from a pharmacy to use as the packaging unit. Purchase rice, corn, and beans and place each grain in a separate container at the workbench. Provide a work order defining the number of each grain to be placed in a package. Students are then instructed to sit at the workstation and to use only a tweezer to place the grain on a grid (for grain-count accuracy) and then to transfer it to the apothecary container. Have students do the tasks right-handed, left-handed, and with both hands. Time the students when they start and after an opportunity to practice. Upon completion of the project, students should be given an opportunity to express their feelings and impressions. The teacher should observe behavior during the process. How did each student approach the task. Was there frustration? Could students talk to other workers and stay on task? Could they identify actual jobs that require fine motor dexterity?

Assembly. Have students design a simple widget (useless contraption) out of toy construction components or varied nuts, bolts, and metal plates so that a very defined assembly process is created. Prepare an illustrated schema for the assembly and place it at the workbench. Have students organize the workstation—bins for components, position of bins, and so on—or have a workstation for packaging components needed. Identify jobs and their responsibilities—packager, assembler, disassembler, supervisor. Go into production. Time students at various tasks and observe their work-adjustment skills. Get student reaction. Discuss project applications to the world of work.

SELF-AWARENESS

Characteristics of individuals can be identified in many ways. Inventories have been developed to identify interest, values, reward preferences, temperament, and worker behaviors, to name a few. Also, a variety of aptitude and talent tests are available to assist in the process of defining the work interest and potential of students. (See Chapter 9, "Resources.") Many of these procedures, however, assume that the student is making knowledgeable choices. When developing instruction in self-awareness, use these instruments with caution. Reserve them for use after there has been an opportunity to evaluate ideas expressed by the student. The self-awareness activity presented here is designed to help students generate information about themselves, which in turn makes them aware of their many characteristics.

A "Me Book" is a notebook activity through which students develop self-knowledge. The first task in starting the project is to have students state ways that people are identified—physical data, family, jobs, group membership, and so on. Then have students brainstorm the ways people demonstrate individuality through things they do and by choices they make or would like to make. Tell the students that they will create a book about themselves using the ideas generated. The following page titles are a few of the more than fifty page titles generated by a group of students for their "Me Books." Notice that topics vary greatly and are not only descriptive but also reflective and projective.

This Is My Family	Personal Data
Classes I Enjoy	Jobs I Have at Home
The Way I Like to Dress	Jobs That Interest Me
Foods I Like	Foods I Dislike
If I Had $500 . . .	If I Had $50,000 . . .
Things That Make Me Sad	My Favorite TV Shows
Things I Like to Do Alone	How I Spend My Spare Time
Things I Like to Talk About	Classes I Want to Take
Things I Do Well	I Have Problems with . . .
Sports I Like	Sports I Would Like to Try
People I Think Are Great	If I Could Change the World
I Think a Friend Should . . .	It Pleases Me When . . .

A pocketed notebook folder makes an excellent organizer for the book as it is being developed. The students may be given a few page titles to work on each week or all of the titles may be given to them at one time. Students may also want to add titles of their own in addition to those required. The objective of the project is to get students to express ideas freely about themselves; therefore, the way they choose to present information should not be restricted by a specific format, neatness, or minimum number of entries for a topic. Individuality and elimination of inhibitions must be encouraged. Students involved with the project made lists, wrote paragraphs, drew pictures, and used pictures from magazines, newspapers, and catalogs. They also knew that the only person that they had to share their work with was the teacher. Generally, however, the students wanted classmates to see their work.

The project is an ongoing activity that integrates very well with other self-awareness activities. It helps prepare the students for making appropriate choices concerning vocational development and assists the teacher in evaluating the breadth of experiences and understandings that each student may have.

VOLUNTEER WORKERS CORPS

Teachers and administrative personnel are always in need of assistance. Their needs can themselves provide students with a wide variety of experiences that develop skills needed in various jobs. A Volunteer Workers Corps could be developed that would provide workers for specific tasks. The classroom teacher may be expected to teach the basic skills of tasks through the special class and, after assignments are made, to make frequent checks with cooperating staff to see that tasks are done properly. Some jobs that could be considered are:

Collating materials
Message delivery/attendance report collection
Library Assistant—shelving books, book checkout
Overhead projector cleaning—especially for the math department

Media Assistant—delivery and set-up of media equipment and materials
Production—photocopying, offset press, and so on
Mail Sort

STUDENT BUSINESS

Consider developing a student-managed/operated business. A very successful business was developed by one class that involved the making of caramel corn and cookies. The students sold their products at school ball games and to customers in the community (Schmalle, 1987). Not only did the students learn to prepare the products, but they also were involved with sales, inventory, money skills, and many other related tasks. The reactions and attitudes toward their experiences provided teachers with an opportunity to observe directly student performance, relationships with coworkers, and other jobsmanship skills. A business can provide work activity for students before they go to off-campus positions, to those that are not ready to move into community placement, and to those that may be between positions. Students at upper levels of their programs can also develop leadership skills through supervision and training assignments. The profits can be used to provide social experiences and for special class projects. There are many possibilities that could be considered for a class business, such as:

School Supply Store—sell paper, pencils, pens, and so on
Button Maker—make school logo buttons, or special requests and orders.
Greeting Cards and Stationery—using computer programs, make personalized design according to orders.
Maintenance Crew—provide supervised work teams to clean houses or offices.

WORK EXPERIENCE

Many of the student activities in the vocational component take place outside of the classroom as a form of work activity. Most of these activities are coordinated by work-experience consultants (teacher-coordinator) and not by classroom teachers. Teachers, however, continue to have very important responsibilities to carry out before and after students are placed at the worksite. Acceptance of these responsibilities comes from an understanding of the process and instruments used in coordinating work-experience activity, the types of positions that will be used, and the fact that work experience is a continuation of the school activities.

Services provided by the work-experience consultant include training-station development, student placement, visitations, consultation and coaching of training sponsors, and student coaching and evaluations. Another very critical function of the coordinator is to keep classroom teachers informed about needs for related instruction.

The work of the consultant in selecting and developing appropriate work experience is greatly dependent on information provided by the classroom teacher. Records of instructional activities, for example, can provide information about students' aptitudes, skills, and interests. Also, through ongoing assessment of affective behaviors, the teacher can help define the work-adjustment behaviors of students and determine if these behaviors are appropriate for a selected worksite.

The worker-behavior inventory is provided in Appendix 8.3 as an example of an instrument that can be used to evaluate observable behavior. The rating scale recognizes a continuum of behavior from appropriate (5) to unacceptable (1). It can be used by teachers in special or regular classes and by supervisors of on-campus activities. Having students rated over time in a variety of settings by numerous individuals will distinctly identify problems that may develop and under what types of situations. Intervention strategies can then be initiated by the classroom teacher to eliminate problem behaviors. Information concerning the effectiveness of implemented strategies with individual students is very valuable to the consultant in advising training sponsors about techniques that can be used in working with specific students.

Work experience begins on the school campus. Initially, on-campus experiences are used to determine acceptance of responsibility, dependability, willingness to learn, and basic jobsmanship skills. Work assignments can be concurrent with classroom work involving readiness and self-awareness. As ideas formulate and awareness improves, job families or clusters that are appropriate for the student will become evident and exploratory positions will become more specific. Community-based positions can then progress through three general types of placements.

Work Exploration

This type of position is used to help students more accurately understand a job. It is not designed for skill development and is not a paid position. Job shadows and tryouts are included in this type of placement. Placements may be for as short a time as one entire day or may be as long as six to eight weeks. During the time at the worksite, students should learn about skills and training that would be needed to be employed as a worker in this area. Characteristics of workers, environment, and demands of the job should be identified by the student. Worksite activities are to be paired with classroom activities that help develop knowledge related to the job family.

Training

Students in this type of work activity learn skills and knowledge related to a specific job through a prescribed training program at an actual worksite in the community. Skills are also developed in related vocational classes and in the special class as is needed. These positions can be paid or unpaid. Students may be at the worksite from one to three hours daily. Placement duration can be for a relatively short time (six weeks) during which a student would concentrate on very specific skills. Most training stations, however, are designed for a semester or year during which the complete scope of a job is used in the training plan.

Employment

Students who have demonstrated appropriate work-adjustment skills and skills appropriate to specific jobs can be involved with employment situations. Involvement in specific vocational instruction related to the employment of the student is encouraged, and additional related instruction should be provided in the special class as is needed. These students are paid for their work, and students may be at the worksite for as much as half of their school day for the entire year.

Coordination of Work Activity

All of these positions require that a well-defined process is used to coordinate placements. Cooperative work-experience techniques used by vocational education programs provide a model for this process. Training agreements, training plans, and related instruction are essential components of the system.

The *training agreement* is a document that reflects the philosophy, objectives, and regulations of the program for which it was developed. It becomes a management tool for coordinating the individualized vocational programs of the students participating. It recognizes that instruction relating to career development takes place both within and outside the school. By defining the responsibilities of the training sponsor, student trainee, parents, and teacher/coordinator, the role each will take in the instructional process can be recognized as complementing the others. An example of a work training agreement is found in Appendix 8.4.

The second document used in coordinating work-experience programs is the *training plan*. This document is an outline of the tasks and activities that a student should experience during the time frame of the contract. The plan is used as a guide to direct the training progress of the student. The work-experience coordinator is generally the person who develops the plan with the assistance of the employer (training sponsor). (See Appendix 8.5, "Training Plan Outline for Dietary Aide.") An evaluation instrument documenting training and the degree of independence and acceptability of the student's work is generally part of the training plan (Appendix 8.7). The purpose of the training plan is to insure that training is provided in all aspects of a student's job, that everyone understands the training that should be accomplished, and that training is coordinated with the student's classroom instruction.

The third component in cooperative work-experience programs is *related instruction*. Coordinators are to determine student needs for supportive instruction according to the progress of the student at the worksite. Timely communication is a persistent problem, however, in coordinating vocational programs for special education students. Coordinators may visit the worksite as frequently as once a week, but it is not uncommon for visits to be made as infrequently as every three to four weeks. Special class teachers, however, can alleviate this communication problem by assuming responsibility for collecting information on a daily basis concerning the work activity of students. By using a process such as that used with the Job-Task Reporting System, information about work performed is provided daily by the student. With this system, a simple calendar format is used as the report form, and the enumerated components of a student's training plan serve as code numbers that students use to record involvement with specific work activity each day (Schmalle & Retish, 1989). These reports also become a record of time on the job and attendance. Most importantly, the reports help identify whether or not progress is taking place according to the schedule of the training plan. By giving concerned attention to student reports, teachers can determine if progress is not evident and alert the coordinator to the situation so that appropriate intervention can be initiated. By accepting some of the responsibility of monitoring the on-the-job activity of student workers, communication among the facilitating team members improves, as does the training of students (see Appendix 8.6).

The vocational development of students with special needs requires substantial work experience in realistic settings. It also requires that teachers and support personnel work together so that student development is appropriate and efficient. Keeping informed and having in place procedures for being a contributing member of the facilitating team will help special class teachers effectively assume part of the responsibility for the vocational success of students.

SUMMARY

Vocational preparation cannot be left to chance. Students deserve the opportunity to find their way in the world of work through choices and decisions made as the result of knowledge and skills developed through carefully planned instructional programs and appropriate work experience. Several elements must be considered in developing an effective vocational program. Foremost is the determination of goals and objectives. The adoption of assessment and evaluation instruments and procedures should be part of the process. Strategies, activities, and materials for instruction should be identified as well. It will also be necessary to define policies and procedures so that they can be properly approved. When completed, the program should define a developmental process that incorporates the school and the community in both the instructional and work experience components.

Work experience is a critical component of a student's program. Successful programs are characterized by personnel who work judiciously to provide appropriate work experience that is guided by well-developed training plans, supported by related instruction, monitored by thoughtful evaluation, and regulated by thorough training agreements.

As the components of a program are being developed, the roles of the instructional staff and resource personnel emerge as team members with shared but specific responsibilities. The role of special educators is complex. At times they will be counselors; other times, coordinators or evaluators; but at all times, student advocates.

Special education services and programs are affected greatly by legislation. Recent congressional action gives special educators the legal backing to secure access to vocational programs for students with handicaps as in no other time in history. Teachers should welcome these mandates and make a concerted effort to keep abreast of exemplary ways that regulations are being addressed in other programs.

Having the right to access vocational classes cannot be equated with vocational success or achievement. The benefits of vocational instruction may be minimized for some students with handicaps because of their academic problems. In the next chapter, we will discuss the academic component of special education programs and provide insight into skills needed to improve academic achievement as well as accommodation strategies that can be employed.

STUDY QUESTIONS

1. What is known about special education students in general that can help teachers make programming decisions?
2. Name the four vocational phases and state the primary goal of each phase.
3. What is related instruction? Identify this instruction as a part of each vocational phase.
4. Why is evaluation and reevaluation an integral component of vocational programs?
5. What legislation mandates that all students with handicaps are to be provided vocational education?
6. What is the role of a work-experience coordinator?
7. What is the purpose of a training agreement? Who should be involved in the completion of a training agreement? What responsibilities are delegated to the teacher? Parents?
8. What is a training plan, and how is it developed and used?
9. In what ways can a teacher serve as an advocate for students? Why should teachers be willing to assume this role?
10. How is work performance evaluated? How can the teacher become involved with evaluation when students are at off-campus worksites?

REFERENCES

Brolin, D. E. (1976). *Vocational preparation of retarded citizens*. Columbus: C. E. Merrill.

———— (Ed.). (1978). *Life-centered career education: A competency-based approach*. Reston, VA: Council for Exceptional Children.

————. (1983). Career education: Where do we go from here. *Career Development for Exceptional Individuals, 6*, 3–14.

Bullis, M., & Foss, G. (1986). Guidelines for assessing job-related social skills of mildly handicapped students. *Career Development for Exceptional Individuals, 9*, 89–97.

Burrow, J. (1983). *Improving coordination skills of work experience teacher-coordinator: Work-experience modules*. Des Moines: Iowa Department of Public Instruction.

Clark, G. M., & White, W. J. (1985). Issues in providing career and vocational education to secondary-level mildly handicapped students in rural settings. *Career Development for Exceptional Individuals, 8*, 42–49.

Fardig, D. B., Algozzine, R. F., Schwartz, S. E., Hensel, J. W., & Westling, D. L. (1986). Postsecondary vocational adjustment of rural, mildly handicapped students. *Exceptional Children, 52*(2), 115–121.

Glascoe, F. P. & Levy, S. M. (1985). A multidimensional observational approach to vocational assessment and placement. *Career Development for Exceptional Individuals, 8*, 73–79.

Gugerty, J. J., Tindall, L. W., Heffron, T. J., & Dougherty, B. B. (1988). *Profiles of success: Serving secondary special education students through Carl D. Perkins Vocational Act, 12 exemplary approaches*. Madison: University of Wisconsin. Vocational Studies Center.

Hasazi, S. B., Gordon, L. R., & Roe, C. A. (1985). A statewide follow-up on post high school employment and residential status of students labeled mentally retarded. *Education and Training of the Mentally Retarded, 20*, 222–234.

Ianacone, R. N., & Ianacone, R. A. (Eds.). (1985). *Transition issues and directions*. Reston, VA: The Council for Exceptional Children.

Ianacone, R. N., & Leconte, P. J. (1986). Curriculum-based vocational assessment: A viable response to a school-based service delivery issue. *Career Development for Exceptional Individuals, 9*, 113–120.

Ianacone, R. N., & Stodden, R. D. (Eds.) (1987). *Transition issues and directions*. Reston, VA: Council for Exceptional Children.

Iowa Department of Public Instruction. (1984). *A mental disabilities curriculum framework*. Des Moines: Department of Public Instruction, Special Education Division.

Kolstoe, O. P. (1972). Programs for the mildly retarded: A reply to critics *Exceptional Children, 39*, 51–56.

Langone, J., & Gill, D. H. (1986). Developing effective vocational programs for mentally retarded persons: Cooperative planning between rehabilitation and education. *Journal of Rehabilitation, 52*, 63–67.

Okolo, C. M. (1988). Instructional environments in secondary vocational education programs: Implications for LD adolescents. *Learning Disabilities Quarterly, 11*, 136–148.

Okolo, C. M., & Sitlington, P. (1986). The role of special education in LD adolescents' transition from school to work. *Learning Disability Quarterly, 9*, 292–306.

Phelps, A. L., & Lutz, R. J. (1977). *Career exploration and preparation for the special needs learner*. Boston: Allyn & Bacon.

Robinson, G. A., & Palloway, E. A. (Eds). (1987). *Best practices in mental disabilities*. Des Moines: Iowa Department of Education.

Robinson, G. A., Patton, J. R., Palloway, E. A., & Sargent, L. R. (Eds). (1988). *Best practices in mental disabilities* (Vol. 2). Des Moines: Iowa Department of Education.

Schmalle, B. (1987). Could the corny cookie corner work in your school? Vocational, affective, and cognitive programming for rural special education students. In *Proceedings of the Seventh Annual National Rural Special Education Conference*. Bellingham: American Council on Rural Special Education, Western Washington University.

Schmalle, B., & Retish, P. (1989). Job-task reporting system. *Teaching Exceptional Children, 21*(2), 15–18.

Sitlington, P. (1981). Vocational and special education in career programming for the mildly handicapped adolescent. *Exceptional Children, 47*, 592–598.

Stodden, R. A., & Broder, P. M. (1986). Community-based competitive employment preparation of developmentally disabled persons: A program description and evaluation. *Education and Training of the Mentally Retarded, 21*, 45–53.

U.S. Commission on Civil Rights. (1983). *Accommodating the spectrum of individual's abilities*. Washington, DC.

Wehman, P., Hill, M., Hill, J. W., Brooke, V., Pendleton, P., & Britt, C. (1985). Competitive employment for persons with mental retardation: A follow-up six years later. *Mental Retardation, 23*, 274–281.

Weisenstein, G. R., & Elrod, G. F. (1985). Transitional services for adolescent age individuals with mild mental retardation. In R. N. Ianacone and R. A. Stodden (Eds.), 1987. *Transition issues and directions*. Reston, VA: Council for Exceptional Children, Division of Mental Retardation.

Will, M. C. (1984). Let us pause and reflect but not too long. *Exceptional Children, 51*(1), 11–16.

APPENDIX 8.1. SECONDARY CURRICULUM FRAMEWORK

Career Education: Prevocational

1. Expresses interest in and knowledge of various occupations
2. Lists reasons for working
3. Lists rewards for working
4. Uses and cares for basic hand and power tools
5. Expresses short-range and long-range personal and career goals
6. Names a variety of occupations and qualifications: education, experience, interest, or ability
7. Names local occupational opportunities and job requirements
8. Describes characteristics of successful workers: work habits, attitude, role in work group, etc.
9. Describes minimum wage and company fringe benefits
10. Lists criteria for taking the job: wages, skills, travel, etc.
11. Explains advantages of obtaining advanced job training. Lists postsecondary schools providing job training
12. Lists prerequisites to employment in an area of interest
13. Lists likes and dislikes about a variety of occupations
14. Fills out job application forms, social security forms, union forms, and credit applications
15. Locates and names employment resource agencies
16. Describes the types of and reasons for payroll deductions
17. Demonstrates how to notify an employer when ill or tardy
18. Describes different working conditions and wages
19. Describes pressures, strains, and anxieties on the job and solutions
20. Describes methods to resolve on-the-job work conflicts
21. Participates in career-education placements for job exploration/preparation
22. Lists steps to properly terminate employment
23. Demonstrates job safety.
24. Maintains postschool job placement or training
25. Describes some factors affecting jobs (labor demand, wages, economy, resources, size of community, types of industry, etc.)

Career Education: Work Skills

1. Demonstrates appropriate work behaviors such as: promptness, following directions, regular attendance, accepting authority, accepting responsibility, and getting along with coworkers
2. Works at a competitive pace
3. Accepts criticism of work
4. Works without supervision
5. Initiates new tasks
6. Demonstrates appropriate hygiene and grooming habits for work
7. Demonstrates employment search skills
8. Dresses appropriately for job interviews and work situations
9. Expresses knowledge of union functions, employment benefits, group insurance programs, workmen's compensation, and community service agencies

10. Avoids interfering with fellow workers
11. Exhibits sufficient stamina to hold a full-time job
12. Follows supervisor's directions and completes tasks
13. Completes assigned work tasks
14. Conserves time and materials
15. Uses break times appropriately
16. Meets quality standards for job
17. Drives or obtains transportation to place of work
18. Uses and maintains equipment and tools for work experience or employment

---

Source: Des Moines: State of Iowa, Department of Public Instruction, Special Education Division. (1984). *A Mental Disabilities Curriculum Framework.* The document states that "a framework is an outline of general skills, conpetencies and content expected to be taught . . . , as well as the sequence, scope, and continuity of skills to be taught."

APPENDIX 8.2. VOCATIONAL ANALYSIS

Date: _____

Student: _____   Grade: _____

1. Does the student demonstrate an appropriate attitude toward work? _____
   How? _____
   _____

2. Identify job families/clusters that have been included in the student's program. _____
          Job clusters   Types of Experience
   _____   _____
   _____   _____

3. How has the student demonstrated knowledge of self? _____
   Summarize: _____

4. Identify the strengths and weaknesses of the student's workadjustment skills. _____
   Strengths: _____
   Weaknesses: _____

5. Identify the strengths and weaknesses of the student's personal-social skills. _____
   Strengths: _____
   Weaknesses: _____

6. Identify the vocational choices that have been named by the student. _____
   _____

7. Identify involvement with specific vocational classes. _____
   Course: _____   Result: _____
   _____   _____
   _____   _____
   _____   _____

8. List exploratory site experience and the results. _____

Employer	Job Title	Dates	Results
_____	_____	_____	_____
_____	_____	_____	_____
_____	_____	_____	_____

(continued)

9. List on-the-job training experiences and the results. _____

Employer	Job Title	Dates	Results
_____	_____	_____	_____
_____	_____	_____	_____
_____	_____	_____	_____

10. Identify work experience that has not been a part of the student's school program. _____

11. Has the student had a formal vocational evaluation? _____
    Date? _____ Briefly summarize results? _____
    _____
    _____

Recommendations

Phase Placement: _____
Support Staff Needed: _____
Vocational Classes: _____
_____

Instructional Objectives: _____
_____
_____

APPENDIX 8.3. WORKER BEHAVIOR INVENTORY

Student: **Job Site:**   **Date:**
                                Ratings

Groomed properly						Not groomed properly
A_____	5	4	3	2	1___	
Dressed appropriately						Inappropriate dress
B_____	5	4	3	2	1___	
Requests work assignment						Must be told to get work assignment
C_____	5	4	3	2	1___	
Prepares self for work assignment (wash hands, etc.)						Does not follow work preparation procedures
D_____	5	4	3	2	1___	
Initiates work assignment						Works only when prompted
E_____	5	4	3	2	1___	
Works Independently (attends physically and visually to task)						Idle (ceases physically to work at task)
F_____	5	4	3	2	1___	

Maintains materials
   (locates and gets
   materials for task
   completion)

Fails to get materials as
   needed

G_____5____4____3____2____1_____

Keeps work area in
   order (organizes
   area, discards
   trash, etc.)

Leaves work area messy and
   disorganized

H_____5____4____3____2____1_____

Completes job task in
   an appropriate
   amount of time

Work incomplete (substan-
   tially behind/slow)

I_____5____4____3____2____1_____

Finds work to do
   after main job task
   is completed

Remains idle until directed to
   new task

J_____5____4____3____2____1_____

Works-talks (attends
   physically to task
   while listening and
   talking with others)

Stops working when listening
   or talking with others

K_____5____4____3____2____1_____

Gives help (provides
   assistance to others
   while listening and
   talking with others)

Interrupts and/or interferes
   with coworkers' job tasks

L_____5____4____3____2____1_____

Receives help from
   peers (coworkers
   assist in completion
   of task: advice,
   problem solving)

Will not accept help from
   peers/inappropriate remarks
   or actions when assisted

M_____5____4____3____2____1_____

Receives help from
   supervisors
   appropriately
   (training, advice,
   etc.)

Reacts inappropriately to
   assistance from supervisors

N_____5____4____3____2____1_____

Asks for help
   appropriately (in
   proper manner and
   when necessary)

Fails to request help when
   necessary or seeks help
   when not necessary

O_____5____4____3____2____1_____

Follows safety rules
   and procedures

Disregards safety rules and
   procedures

P_____5____4____3____2____1_____

Record examples of behaviors on back of this form. Make instructional and training
recommendations when appropriate.

APPENDIX 8.4. TRAINING AGREEMENT, NORTH FAYETTE COMMUNITY SCHOOLS, WEST UNION, IOWA 52175

By this agreement _____ will permit
                              Training Agreement

_____ to enter its establishment
                    Student

for the purpose of securing vocational occupational training and on-the-job work experience in

_____.
                    Occupation

We recognize that training on-the-job is a form of vocational education when the experience includes a progressive sequence of duties learned under supervision, factural information, adjustments in thinking and attitudes, and working and meeting other people successfully.

We accept this training agreement as a guide for all cooperating parties by providing the student with opportunities and training in the basic skills of the occupation he/she has chosen and the technical information related to it.

In addition to providing instruction, the employer agrees to pay the student for the work done while in the training program.

The beginning wage will be _____.

The approximate number of hours the student will work per week:
   minimum _____

   maximum _____
Training begins _____, 19__ __ , and extends through _____, 19__ __ .

Responsibilities of the Training Sponsor

1. The sponsor will develop and implement in cooperation with the teacher-coordinator a training plan for the student trainee that contributes to the attainment of the student's career objective.

2. The sponsor will employ and train the student trainee as defined by this agreement.

3. The sponsor will provide supportive supervision to the student learner.

4. The sponsor will consult with the teacher-coordinator in regard to the student's performance on the job and assist the teacher-coordinator in the evaluation of the student's progress during on-site visitations and by written evaluations.

5. The sponsor will keep the teacher-coordinator informed concerning all problems directly related to the student trainee and the job and will not terminate the student without consulting the teacher-coordinator.

6. The sponsor will permit the student trainee necessary time off for school activities.

7. The sponsor will adhere to federal, state, and local regulations regarding child labor laws and other applicable regulations.

Responsibilities of the Student Trainee

1. The student agrees to become informed of the duties and responsibilities connected with the student training station and agrees to discharge those duties to the best of his/her ability.

2. The student trainee agrees to be present and on time each day, both in school and at work. On no occasion is the student allowed to go to the training station on a day that he/she has been absent from school.

3. The student trainee agrees to appear neat, well-groomed, and properly dressed for the job.

4. The student trainee will notify the training sponsor and the teacher-coordinator if he/she is unable to be present.

5. The student will furnish the teacher-coordinator with necessary information about his/her training program and complete promptly all required records and reports.

6. The student trainee will not terminate his/her training station without consulting with the teacher-coordinator.

7. The student trainee understands that his/her work will be evaluated regularly by the training sponsor and the teacher-coordinator, and the student trainee will be required to complete periodic self-evaluations.

Responsibilities of the Student Trainee's Parents/Guardians

1. The parents/guardians grant permission for work-experience program participation by the student and encourage his/her effective performance.

2. The parents/guardians will share with the teacher-coordinator information relating to the successful development and performance of the student.

3. The parents/guardians will participate in conferences necessary for the review and updating of the student's work-experience program.

4. The parents/guardians will purchase required school insurance for the student.

5. The parents/guardians will obtain promptly for the student physicals and/or other needs that are required for employment.

Responsibilities of the Teacher-Coordinator

1. The teacher-coordinator will develop in cooperation with the training sponsor a training plan for the student trainee that contributes to the attainment of the student's career objective.

2. The teacher-coordinator will correlate classroom activities with the training plan and assist the student with job skills training, safety training, and other job concerns.

3. The teacher-coordinator will make periodic visits to the training station to observe the student trainee, to consult with the employer and training supervisor, and to render any needed assistance with training problems of the student trainee.

4. The teacher-coordinator will supply the training sponsor with evaluation forms at regular intervals regarding the evaluation of the student trainee.

5. The teacher-coordinator will assess and grade the student's progress at regular intervals

(continued)

and will grant credit toward graduation according to school policy upon successful completion of the work experience.

6. The teacher-coordinator will contact the employer if the student is absent from school and has not reported.

7. The teacher-coordinator will make a concerted effort to arrange conferences with parents/guardians for the purpose of reviewing and updating their child's work-experience program at times that are convenient to them.

*　　*　　*　　*　　*　　*　　*　　*　　*　　*　　*　　*　　*

Date　_____

_____　　　_____
Student　　　　　　　　Training Sponsor

_____　　　_____
Parent/Guardian　　　　Teacher-Coordinator

Source: Courtesy of the North Fayette Community Schools.

APPENDIX 8.5. TRAINING PLAN OUTLINE FOR DIETARY AIDE

Orientation

1. Visitation to training site
2. Introduction to trainer and care-center director
3. Dress code
4. Personnel policies
5. Job description
6. Health and safety regulations

Dining-room responsibilities

1. Transporting dinnerware from storage areas
2. Setting tables
3. Seating of residents
4. Serving of beverages and meals
5. Reporting, securing, and serving special resident requests

Cleanup and sanitation responsibilities

1. Cleaning tables
2. Applying sanitation procedures to tables following meals
3. Preparing eating utensils and dinnerware for the dishwasher
4. Loading dishwasher
5. Operating dishwasher
6. Unloading dishwasher
7. Delivering of utensils and dinnerware to storage areas

Responsibilities in using kitchen equipment

1. Using the grill
2. Using the blender
3. Using mixers both large and small
4. Using the steam table
5. Using the toaster
6. Using the plate warmer
7. Applying procedures for cleanup and sanitation

Responsibilities in food preparation

1. Using recipes for making juice, milkshakes, and coffee
2. Buttering bread and making toast
3. Making salads
4. Garnishing plates
5. Preparing foods on the grill
6. Following instructions for food that is to be pureed

Responsibilities in dealing with special diets

1. Learning terminology that identifies special dietary needs
2. Setting up residents' trays according to specifications listed for each resident
3. Setting up snack trays to meet dietary restrictions
4. Learning when to provide special eating utensils and/or aids

General responsibilities

1. Learning residents' names
2. Developing an awareness of residents needs for special utensils and eating aids
3. Comprehending individual problems that must be met by a food-service employee
    a. Communication—speech and hearing problems
    b. Special serving considerations, for example, not filling cups full

Expected Outcomes

1. The student-trainee will demonstrate knowledge of resident personnel policies and safety regulations.
2. The student-trainee will show that he or she can accept and follow directions in tasks assigned by his or her trainer.
3. The student-trainee will demonstrate adequate work skills in the various areas that are stated in this plan.
4. The student-trainee will demonstrate appropriate social skills and communication skills in dealing with residents.
5. The student-trainee will be employable as a dietary aide in a retirement-care facility.

Source: Courtesy of the North Fayette Community Schools.

APPENDIX 8.6. DAILY CALENDAR

Month: _February_			Name: _Dan_	
8:30 – 9:30 2, 5, 1, 7 <div align="right">3</div>	No school No lab <div align="right">4</div>	8:30 – 9:15 1, 5 11:00 – 11:15 11 <div align="right">5</div>	8:25 – 9:40 1, 18, 16, 5, 6 <div align="right">6</div>	8:30 – 9:40 5, 9, 16 <div align="right">7</div>
8:20 – 9:15 1, 5, 6, 11 <div align="right">10</div>	8:30 – 9:40 5, 6, 1, 9 11:00 – 11:15 11 <div align="right">11</div>	8:20 – 9:40 8, 9, 11, 6 <div align="right">12</div>	8:20 – 9:40 1, 5, 8, 11 <div align="right">13</div>	8:20 – 9:40 1, 5, 11 <div align="right">14</div>
8:20 – 9:15 1, 5, 6 <div align="right">17</div>	8:20 – 9:15 8, 9, 5 11:00 – 11:15 11 <div align="right">18</div>	8:20 – 9:40 18, 15, 9, 5 11:00 – 11:15 11 <div align="right">19</div>	8:20 – 9:40 1, 5, 8, 11 <div align="right">20</div>	8:20 – 9:40 1, 5, 11 <div align="right">21</div>
8:30 – 9:15 25, 1, 7, 6 <div align="right">24</div>	8:30 – 9:40 5, 6, 18, 9 <div align="right">25</div>	8:25 – 9:40 8, 9, 5, 6 <div align="right">26</div>	8:20 – 9:40 5, 9, 11 <div align="right">27</div>	8:20 – 9:40 8, 9, 5, 6 <div align="right">28</div>

JOB TASKS FOR THE CORNY COOKIE CORNER

1. Candy making
2. Pop corn
3. Measure flour
4. Measure sugar
5. Wash dishes
6. Dry dishes
7. Get/fold towels
8. Mix cookies
9. Shape cookies
10. Recipe measurement (dry ingredients)
11. Clean up
12. Set up
13. Bookkeeping
14. Set up orders
15. Mix bread
16. Knead/shape bread
17. Monitor oven
18. Package corn
19. Make deliveries
20. Go out on scales
21. Clerk games
22. Complete payroll
23. Do banking
24. Inventory
25. Complete shopping

IDENTIFICATION OF INFORMATION RECORDED

Feb. 3: Time at the worksite (8:30–9:30 a.m.)
       Tasks completed—
          #2, Popcorn
          #5, Wash dishes
          #1, Make candy
          #7, Get/fold towels
Feb. 4: Reasons for not working (no school)
Numbers 2 through 25 (code numbers relating to job tasks outlined in training plan)

Source: Courtesy of the North Fayette Community Schools.

APPENDIX 8.7. EVALUATION INSTRUMENT FOR DIETARY AIDE

Cash Register Procedures	Completed	Date of Completion	DEGREE OF INDEPENDENCE Without Assistance	With Assistance		ACCEPTABILITY IN COMPETITIVE EMPLOYMENT Acceptable	Not Acceptable
A. All paper currency faced one way in cash register							
B. Rolls of change not opened before needed							
C. Change making							
1. Manually							
2. Using change maker							
D. Knowledge of food stamp policy							
1. Types of foods eligible							
2. Types of foods ineligible							
E. Knowledge of taxable and nontaxable items							
F. Knowledge of bottling deposits							
G. Identification of food categories							
1. Produce							
2. Meat							
3. Groceries							
4. Dairy							
5. Frozen food							
6. Health and beauty aids							
H. Identification of three different cash registers used at grocery store							
I. Knowledge of stamp-dispenser use							

CHAPTER 9

Resources

If a book such as this is to be of direct assistance to readers it must give other resources to draw on to continue the process of learning and growing in expertise and usefulness as an educator. On the following pages are tools and sources of help that we or professional friends have used; we believe they will reduce the time you have to spend, only to find what others have already discovered.

This chapter includes:

Suggestions for further reading on (1) curriculum and (2) effective teaching
A list of computer-generated resources compiled by Michael Kallam of Fort Hays State University
Publishers of (1) information on curricula and (2) commercial material organizations
Toll-free special needs resources
Regional resource centers
Department of Health and Human Services regional offices for civil rights

These resources are in addition to the vocational assessment instruments and their sources listed at the end of Chapter 3.

Also, one should never overlook the many agencies and corporations that will, if asked, contribute materials and resources to any teacher. In our experience, corporations have provided local and national maps, tools, and other material that was useful for classrooms. Realistic teaching aids to accompany the suggested curriculums in this book will make the transfer of learning for the students much easier. Social security applications, employment forms, bus schedules, and lists of agencies that are a resource are all forms that can assist the learner with a special need outside of the school.

Direct assistance at the local level can be maintained by keeping a folder of employers who have hired graduates and would be willing to hire more workers. Agencies that have a history of assistance that the student should know about must be available so that the student can make that important transition from school to community. We would emphasize that the first year or two after the student leaves school is the most crucial. Therefore, there is a need for the student to know who can be of assistance and how to take advantage of the assistance provided. A support system after school is over is of importance to get many of the ex-students to the point of being successful on their own.

Finally, we should point out that it is deliberate that the resources listed in the following sections are not evaluated by us. We give them so that you can determine by your use if they are worthwhile in your situation. It is our experience that we spend a great deal of time trying to reinvent what others have discovered, instead of developing these existing resources to our own use.

FURTHER READING

Curriculum

Ash, P. (Ed.). (1987, Spring). *Educator's guide to exemplary special education curricula: Results of a national field-based survey.* Indianapolis: Council for Exceptional Children (Indiana Federation).

Burell, L. P., & Talarico, R. L. (1982). *Project prevocational: prevocational curriculum and prevocational assessment battery.* Columbus: Ohio State Department of Education.

Philosophy—explanation: practical; skill—thirty-one goals in six areas (academic, physical, social, work attitude, work behavior, and work performance); battery—measures preparation for thirty vocational programs.

Fiscus, E. D., & Mandell, C. J. (1983). *Developing individualized education programs.* St. Paul: West.

Annual—describes what can be reasonably accomplished in a calendar year;—based on assessment; student demonstrates increased proficiency in multiplication; student complies with regulations; Short term I.E.P. goals: objectives describe specific terminal behaviors—write, isolate, count, list . . . given conditions performance will occur. . . . list criteria 90 percent to 100 percent mastery, particularly when tasks are essential to other learning or expectations.

Garland Independent School District (1986, Spring). *Special education curriculum (computerized IEP catalog).* Garland, TX.

George-Nichols, N. (1982). *Special education—Instructional skills guide for identifiable perceptual or communicative disorders (IPCD) and significant identifiable emotional or behavioral disorders.* Denver: Denver Public School.

1. Patterned after regular grade curriculum; 2. Objectives, task analysis—readiness, math, language arts, and daily learning skills; 3. Evaluation of materials for content, sequencing, and skill.

Haigh, J. A. (1986). *Maryland Life Skills Curricular Framework.* Baltimore: Maryland State Department of Education.

Goals and subgoals in six curricular areas—communication, socialization, daily living skills, vocational, functional.

The Illinois Plan. (n.d.). A Curriculum Guide for Teachers of the Educable Mentally Handicapped. Danville, IL: Interstate Printers and Publishers.

Robinson, G. A., Patton, J. R., Polloway, E. A., & Sargent, L. R. (1988). *Best practices in mental disabilities* (Vol. 2). Des Moines: Iowa Department of Education.
   Readings in curricular areas.

Rusch, F. R., Schutz, R. P., Mithaug, D. E., Stewart, J. E., & Mai, D. K. (1982). *The vocational assessment and curriculum guide*. Seattle: Exceptional Education.
   Produced from study of food service and custodial and maid (hospitality) occupation; Attendance, independence, production, learning, behavior, communication social skills; Supplemented by specific skilled training and analysis.

Sargent, L. R. (1988). *Systematic instruction of social skills (Project SISS)* (2nd ed.). Des Moines: Iowa Department of Education.
   Objective, criteria, teaching sequence, evaluation.

Sheldon, J., Sherman, J. A., Schumaker, J. B., & Hazel, J. S. (1982, May 9). Developing a social skills curriculum for mildly handicapped adolescents and young adults: Some problems and approaches. Paper presented at Minnesota Conference on Programming for the Developmental Needs of Adolescents with Behavioral Disorders, Minneapolis, MN.

Social studies exceptional child education curriculum K-12 (Vol. 1). (1986). Louisville, KY: Jefferson County Public Schools.
   Philosophy, goals; scope: sequence; objectives: activities; locally developed.

Special education curriculum guide. (1986). Sacramento, CA: Riverside County Office of Education, Division of Special Schools Service.

Wehman, P., & McLaughlin, P. J. (1980). *Vocational curriculum for developmentally disabled persons*. Baltimore: University Park Press.
   Goal, objectives with task analysis; For moderately and severely involved.

Effective Teaching

Berliner, A. C., & Rosenshine, B. V. (1987). *Talks to teachers*. New York: Random House.

Chernow, F. B., & Chernow, C. (1981). *Classroom discipline and control 101 practical techniques*. West Nyack, NY: Parker Publishing Co.
   Discipline directed at prevention—routines, physical environment, positive statement of rules. Observer for good things, correct things.

Christensen, D. D. (1986, March 4–8). Curriculum development and instructional planning: A model for developing quality instruction. Paper presented at the Association for Supervision and Curriculum Development, San Francisco, CA.

Dubelle, S. T. (1986). *Effective teaching: Critical skills*. Lancaster, PA: Technomic Publishing Co.
   Beginning acts—preparation of objectives, motive;—reinforce, encourage.

Fisher, C. W., & Berliner, D. C. (1985). *Perspectives on instructional time*. New York: Longman.

Gagne, R. M., & Briggs, L. J. (1988). *Principles of instructional design* (3rd ed.). New York: Holt, Rinehart and Winston.

Gentry, R., & Briggs, S. (1987, April 12). Beefing up teaching strategies in educating the mildly handicapped. Paper presented at the Council for Exceptional Children, Chicago, IL.
    Small-group, hands-on material; clear oral and written communication; provide feedback; remediate weaknesses.

Hall, G. E., & Hord, S. M. (1987). *Change in schools: Facilitate the process.* Albany: State University of New York Press.

Johnson, E. W. (1987). *Teaching school: A book for anyone who is teaching, wants to teach, or knows a teacher* (Rev. ed.). Boston: National Association of Independent Schools.
    Classroom order: discipline, study skills, planning, organizing, evaluation, objectives.

Kindsvatter, R., Wilen, W., & Ishler, M. (1987). *Dynamics of effective teaching.* White Plains, NY: Longman.

Lieberman, A., & Miller, L. (1984). *Teachers, their world, and their work—Implications for school improvements.* Alexandria, VA: Association for Supervision and Curriculum Development.

Mandrell, C. D., & Shank, K. S. (1987). *Teacher effectiveness in special education.* Charleston: Eastern Illinois University.

Mastropieri, M. A., & Scruggs, T. E. (1987). *Effective instruction for special education.* Boston: College Hill Press.
    See chapter on "effective" behaviors and techniques.

Porter, A. C., & Brophy, J. E. (1987). *Good teaching: Insights from the work of the institute for research on teaching.* (Occasional Paper No. 114). East Lansing: Michigan State University Institute for Research on Teaching.
    Information on new practices likely to make teaching more complex. Effort to improve will not make individual mechanistic. Perception that teachers are "rational" and conform to model. Goals to be accomplished exceed the number that can be accomplished with time and energy. Effectiveness in attaining goal—knowledge of subject matter, pedagogy, students, classroom management and instruction skills. Because of autonomy, teachers must focus attention to simplify environment.

Raphael, T. (1986). *The contexts of school-based literacy.* New York: Random House.

Regional Laboratory for Educational Improvement of the NE and Island. (1988). *Teacher instructional effectiveness.* Andover, MA.
    An annotated resource list linking R&D to practice.

Reilly, R. R., & Lewis, E. L. (1983). *Educational psychology: Applications for classroom learning and instruction.* New York: Macmillan.
    Qualities of good teachers; warm, understanding, and friendly; responsible, businesslike, and systematic; stimulating and imaginative. Students—flexible, good discipline, high expectations, consistent, good planning and organization, knowledgeable. Conditions under which teachers may not be able to be changed; resources and support; ability of student. Difficult to measure what a student has learned.

Reyes, D. J., Alter, G. T., & Smith, R. B. (1986). *Applying teacher effectiveness research in the classroom.* DeKalb: Northern Illinois University.
    Bibliography.

Richardson-Koehler, V. (Ed.). (1987). *Educator's handbook: A research perspective.* New York: Longman.

Rosenshine, B., & Stevens, R. (1985). *Handbook of research on teaching.* New York: Macmillan.

Rowan, B., Edelstein, R., & Leal, A. (1984). *Pathways to excellence: How school districts can improve instruction.* San Francisco: Far West Laboratory for Educational Research and Development.
   Process for developing curriculum.

INFORMATION SOURCES FOR HARDWARE AND SOFTWARE FOR TECHNOLOGY AND COMPUTER USERS WITH SPECIAL NEEDS

List compiled by:
Michael Kallam
Fort Hays State University
Department of Special Education
210 Rarick Hall
Hays, KS 67601-4099
913/628-4216   CompuServe: 73717,3057

This list is provided as a practical guide to the changing world of technology and the resources that may be called upon to break down the barriers for the disabled. This list is drawn primarily from not-for-profit and government agencies. It is correct, as far as can be determined, but should be used with the knowledge that this field is undergoing rapid and constant change.

License is granted to reproduce any or all parts of this document with appropriate acknowledgment.

Abledata
    The Catholic University of America
    National Rehabilitation Information Center
    (NARIC)
    4407 Eighth St., N.E.
    Washington DC 20017
    (800) 34 NARIC (voice or TDD) or
    (202) 635-5826

    A computerized database containing
    information about rehabilitative products
    and assistive devices.
ABLENET
    360 Hoover St., N.E.
    Minneapolis, MN 55413
    (612) 331-5958

    A resource center providing technology-
    related training and support services to
    the disabled.
Accent on Information
    PO Box 700
    Bloomington, IN 61701
    (309) 378-2961

    Subscription-supported database of aids
    and information for disabled individuals.
    Publishes *Accent on Living* magazine.

AccessAbility Resource Center
    1056 East 19th Ave.
    Denver, CO 80218-1088
    (303) 861-6633

    An information and resource center
    providing technology based training and
    adaptations for most training and adapta-
    tions for most handicapping conditions.
Access Unlimited-Speech Enterprises
    9039 Katy Freeway
    Suite 414
    Houston, TX 77024
    (713) 461-0006

    An information source and referral center.
Activating Children through Technology
(ACTT)
    Western Illinois University
    27 Horrabin Hall
    Macomb, IL 61455
    (309) 298-1634

    A university-based evaluation and referral
    service that provides training and technol-
    ogy adaptations across most handicapping
    conditions.

Adaptive Computer Technology Center
30 Warren St.
Brighton, MA 02135
(617) 254-3800 x. 616

Provides diagnostic and training-related technology assistance for most sensory-impaired and movement-impaired conditions.

Adaptive Technology Resource Center
523 19th St.
Bemidji, MN 56601
(218) 751-2320

Resource for diagnosis, evaluation, training, and implementation of computer and technology-related solutions for most disabilities.

Advanced Rehabilitation Technology Network (ARTN)
ACS Medicom
25825 Eshelman Ave.
Lomita, CA 90717
(213) 325-3055

Provides information and referrals for technology-related adaptations.

AIDS Action Council
2033 M St., N.W.
Suite 801
Washington, DC 20036
(202) 293-2886

Provides AIDS and HIV-related information, including adaptation that may be necessary for appropriate care.

Alexander Graham Bell Association for the Deaf
3417 Volta Pl., N.W.
Washington, DC 20007
(202) 337-5220

Resource and support services for the hearing impaired.

Aloha Special Technology Access Center (Aloha STAC)
3103 Pualei Circle, #102
Honolulu, HI 96815
(808) 922-0771

A source of information for technology-based solutions to allow access to the disabled.

ALS Association
15300 Venture Blvd.
Suite 315
Sherman Oaks, CA 91403
(818) 990-2151

Provides information, support, and referral information to ALS-related problems and technology-based solutions for these physical and speech-area disabilities.

American Academy for Cerebral Palsy and Developmental Medicine
1910 Byrd Ave.
P.O. Box 11086
Richmond, VA 23230-1086
(804) 355-0147

The national organization for cerebral palsy information and referrals for technology-based solutions.

American Council for the Blind
1010 Vermont Ave., N.W.
Suite 1100
Washington, DC 20005
(202) 393-3666

List of sources for computer technology for the blind.

American Foundation for the Blind Technology Center
15 W. 16th St.
New York, NY 10011
(212) 620-2000

The national organization for many local services for the blind and visually impaired. The Technology Center offers services to enhance accessibility to computers and technology for this group. Additionally, the *Directory of Services for Blind and Visually Impaired Persons in the United States* is available for $39.95 plus $4.50 postage. (Will accept check, money order, Visa, or MasterCard.)

American Printing House for the Blind
Box 6085
Louisville, KY 40206
(502) 895-2405

A major research and referral service that disseminates technology-related material and adaptations for the visually impaired.

American Speech-Language-Hearing Associa-

tion (ASHA)
10801 Rockville Pike
Rockville, MD 20852
(301) 897-5700

A professional scientific association of speech-language pathologists and audiologists focused on developing computer technology to assist the disabled.

Apple Office of Special Education Programs
20525 Mariani Ave.
MS 23-D
Cupertino, CA 95014
(408) 996-1010

Apple Computer's APPLELINK network contains information for disabled users of Apple computers with 1,200+ fully annotated records about specialized software, adaptive peripherals, and support organizations, such as the Apple bulletin board on SpecialNet, and publications. Apple sales representatives can provide users with information on how to connect to APPLELINK.

ARTS Computer Products, Inc.
145 Tremont St.
Suite 407
Boston, MA 02111
(617) 482-8248

Products for vision-impaired computer users.
PC LENS—enlarges and enhances IBM PC screen image.
PC VOICE—verbalizes screen image.

Association for Educational Communications and Technology (AECT)
1126 16th St., N.W.
Washington, DC 20036
(202) 466-4780

A more than sixty-year-old society devoted to the use of technology in instruction and education. Publishes *Tech Trends*, a journal of instructional technology, and operates TechCentral, an electronic network concerned with technology in education.

The Association for Persons with Severe Handicaps (TASH)
7010 Roosevelt Way N.E.

Seattle, WA 98115
(206) 523-8446

Provides information on computer technology to help the severely handicapped.

Association for Rehabilitation Programs in Data Processing (ARPDP)
University of Pennsylvania
Physically Handicapped Training Center
4025 Chestnut St.
Philadelphia, PA 19104

Provides information about nondegree programs operated by several colleges, public and private organizations that train disabled people for employment in computer/data processing fields. Publishes *Viewpoint*, a quarterly newsletter.

Association for the Development of Computer-Based Instructional Systems (ADCIS)
Western Washington University
Miller Hall 409
Bellingham, WA 98225
(206) 676-2860

International organization for professionals using instructional technology. Educators of the Handicapped is one of its special-interest groups.

AT&T National Special Needs Center
2001 Route 46
Suite 310
Parsippany, NJ 07054-1315
(800) 233-1222 (voice)
(800) 833-3232 (TDD)

Specializes in providing equipment to facilitate communication and the quality of life of people with disabilities.

AudioBionics
9817 Valley View Rd.
Eden Prairie, MN 55344
(612) 941-5464 (voice or TDD)

Specializes in products for speech- or hearing-impaired people. Lifestyle Personal Communicator—portable device with voice synthesizer and forty-character LCD that can be connected to a telephone or used as a portable TDD. Includes word processor, clock and calendar, and calculator.

Augmentative Communication Computer Program (ACCP)
St. Elizabeth Medical Center S-1
Speech Pathology Dept.
601 Edwin C. Moses Blvd.
Dayton, OH 45408
(513) 229-6000

A resource and research center that may provide technology-based solutions and referrals for language-centered problems.

Baruch College
Computer Center for the Visually Impaired
17 Lexington Ave.
New York, NY 10010
(212) 725-7644

Baruch College Computer Center for the Visually Impaired publishes a listing of computer equipment: *Computer Equipment and Aids for the Blind and Visually Impaired: A Resource Guide* ($22.50 plus $2.00 postage and handling; a PC/MS-DOS version on disk is scheduled for future publication.)

Blissymbolics Communication International
24 Ferrand Dr.
Don Mills, ON M3C 3N2
Canada
(416) 421-8377

A research center that can provide technology-based solutions and referrals for language-based problems.

Blue Grass Technology Center for People with Disabilities
898 Georgetown St.
Lexington, KY 40505-1392
(606) 233-1483

A research center providing information and referrals for most handicapping conditions.

Carroll Center for the Blind
Computer Access
770 Centre St.
Newton, MA 02158
(617) 969-6200

Private, nonprofit rehabilitation center for the legally blind; includes a computer

division offering training in technological skills, Project CABLE (Computer Access for the Blind in Employment), a federally funded program to provide assessment and training.

Center for Adaptive Technology and Education (CATER)
3340 Severn Ave.
Suite 300
Metairie, LA 70002
(504) 888-8964

CATER provides information, referral and support services, and training for many learning, physical, and/or speech-related disabilities.

Center for Applied Special Technology (CAST)
39 Cross St.
Peabody, MA 01960
(617) 531-8555

CAST is a research center that provides diagnosis and evaluation of most disabilities except for vision. Training in the use of technology-derived adaptations is available.

Center for Computer Assistance to the Disabled (C-CAD)
617 Seventh Ave.
Fort Worth, TX 76104
(817) 870-9082 (voice)
(817) 870-9086 (TDD)

Nonprofit organization facilitates the development of new computer applications to help the disabled and trains the disabled in the use of computers. Publishers of *Direct Link*, a newsletter that supports of concept of independent living through technology.

Center for Information Resources
University of Pennsylvania
4025 Chestnut St.
3rd Floor
Philadelphia, PA 19104-3054
(215) 898-8108

A research-based resource providing evaluation services, support services, and referral information for technology-based solutions for most disabilities.

Center for Learning and Technology
217 Baldy Hall
Buffalo, NY 14260
(716) 636-2110

A research center providing the disabled with solutions through the use of technology.

Center for Special Education Technology
The Council for Exceptional Children
1920 Association Drive
Reston, VA 22091
(800) 345-TECH/TALK
In VA: (703) 860-0710

A taped message service for special educators and parents concerning more than 100 topics about organizations, computers and technology, software, and peripheral devices.

Center for Technology in Human Disabilities
Maryland Rehabilitation Center/Johns Hopkins University
2301 Argonne Dr.
Baltimore, MD 21218
(301) 554-3046

Provides evaluation, diagnosis, support, and information to technology-based adaptations for most disabilities.

Centre for the Handicapped and Technology
P.O. Box 6450
Wellesley St. West
Auckland, New Zealand

Major source of information for disabled persons seeking technology-based solutions, training, support services, and referral information.

Clearinghouse of Information on Microcomputers in Education
CHIME Newsletter
Oklahoma State University
College of Education
108 Gunderson Hall
Stillwater, OK 74078
(405) 624-6254

A bimonthly review of educational software that focuses on information of use to educators, such as grade level, and an evaluation of compatability and ease of operation.

Clearinghouse on the Handicapped
U.S. Department of Education
Office of Special Education and Rehabilitative Services
Switzer Bldg., Room 3132
Washington, DC 20202
(202) 732-1245

This organization provides information on federal funding and legislation for programs serving disabled people. Distributes free copy of *A Pocket Guide to Federal Help for the Handicapped Individual.*

Closing the Gap
P.O. Box 68
Henderson, MN 56044
(612) 248-3294

Publishes *Closing the Gap* newsletter, which provides information on technology for the disabled. Also provides training at its Training and Resource Center and hosts an annual national conference each October.

Committee on Personal Computers and the Handicapped (COPH-2)
P.O. Box 7701
Chicago, IL 60680-7701
(312) 866-8195

Self-aid group for physically impaired, visually and/or hearing impaired, and other severely disabled people. Provides information, technical consultations, and evaluations. Publishes *Link-and-Go* for network members.

CompuServe Information Services
P.O. Box 20212
Columbus, OH 43220
(800) 848-8199 in OH and (614) 457-0802 in Canada

A subscription-supported database with multiple on-line facilities, including special-interest groups related to various areas of exceptionality and technology use. Among them is the Handicapped Users Database (HUD), which offers weekly conferences for participants and an ongoing forum for issues involving the disabled.

Compute Able Network
P.O. Box 1706
Portland, OR 97207
(503) 645-0009

Provides evaluations, systems installations, and training to meet most adaptive technology needs.

Computer Aids Corp.
124 W. Washington
Lower Arcade
Fort Wayne, IN 46802
(219) 422-2424

Products for blind and vision-impaired computer users. SCREEN-TALK—speech synthesizer. BRAILLE-TALK—translates standard text into braille for embossing. WORD-TALK—talking word processing program.

Computer Conversations
2350 N. Fourth St.
Columbus, OH 43202
(614) 263-4324

Products for visually impaired computer user. Enhanced PC Talking Program— software for speech synthesis that is compatible with more than fifty micro- computers.

Computer Users in Speech and Hearing (CUSH)
Ohio University
School of Hearing and Speech Sciences
Lindley Hall
Athens, OH 45701

An organization of speech-language and audiology professionals incorporating computers in work with disabled individ- uals. Publishes *The Journal for Computer Users in Speech and Hearing*.

Connecticut Special Education Network/ Software Evaluation
University of Connecticut
Special Education Technology Lab
U-64, Rm. 227
249 Glenbrook Rd.
Storrs, CT 06268
(203) 486-4031

A research and resource center disseminat- ing technology-related information and

providing training and referrals for most handicapping conditions. Publishes *Consense Bulletin.*

Council for Exceptional Children (CEC)
1920 Association Dr.
Reston, VA 22091
(703) 620-3660

A professional organization of teachers that sponsors the ERIC Clearinghouse on Handicapped and Gifted Children and the Center for Special Education Technology Information Exchange.

Dale Seymore Publications
P.O. Box 10888
Palo Alto, CA 94303

Selected materials for special students including vocational topics and study-skills programs.

DEAFNET
508 Bremer Bldg.
Seventh and Roberts Sts.
St. Paul, MN 55101
(612) 222-6866 or (612) 223-5130 (TDD)

Computerized database and information- dissemination network for the hearing and language impaired.

Delaware Assistive Device Center
University of Delaware
012 Willard Hall
Newark, DE 19716
(302) 451-2084

An information dissemination and referral center for technology-based solutions to disabilities. Training, evaluation, and support services are provided in most disability areas.

Disabled Children's Computer Resource Group
2095 Rose St.
1st Floor East
Berkeley, CA 94709
(415) 841-3224

A resource for secondary students and adults with disabilities. Their goal is "to support families and professionals in providing every child with a disability the opportunity to use computers to maximize his/her potential for independence and integration into the mainstream of society."

The Dole Foundation
1819 H St., N.W.
Suite 850
Washington, DC 20006
(202) 877-1946

The Dole Foundation is a national leader in providing grants to local organizations that promote employment of disabled individuals.

Ed-Line
National School Public Relations Association (NSPRA)
1501 Lee Highway
Arlington, VA 22209
(703) 528-5840

Ed-Line is an electronic news service for educators by the publishers of *Education USA* that is subscription supported through The Source computer network and covers multiple topics.

Education Turnkey Systems, Inc.
256 N. Washington St.
Falls Church, VA 22046

Publisher of *Communication Aids in Special Education* (1983), one of four reports funded by Special Education Programs, U.S. Dept. of Education. The report assesses technologies providing communication aids for the handicapped and includes a listing of organizations that make communications devices.

EDUCOM
777 Alexander Rd.
Princeton, NJ 08540
(609) 520-3340

The EDUCOM Software Initiative is a consortium of more than 500 institutions of higher education. One aspect of this group is Project EASI (Equal Access to Software for Instruction). This project will inform higher education institutions on issues, resources, and legislation involving computer accessibility for campus users with disabilities.

Field Publications
Weekly Reader Secondary Periodicals

4343 Equity Drive
P.O. Box 16626
Columbus, OH 43216

Student newspapers: *Current Events*, *Current Science*, *Read*, and *Know Your World*. These programs capitalize on current issues to promote interest and to develop critical reading, writing, and thinking skills.

4-Sights Network
Greater Detroit Society for the Blind
16625 Grand River Ave.
Detroit, MI 48227
(313) 272-3900

4-Sights offers a variety of ways for communication to take place between individuals: E-mail, on-line communications for conferences, etc.

Handicapped Children's Computer Cooperative Project (HCCCP)
7938 Chestnut St.
Kansas City, MO 64132

A cooperative project offering a variety of resource materials for use in special education. This includes a "Selected Early Childhood Microcomputer Bibliography" and *Microscope*, a newsletter.

Handicapped Education Exchange (HEX)
11523 Charlton Dr.
Silver Spring, MD 20902
(301) 681-7372 (301) 593-7033 (BBS)

A microcomputer-based electronic mail system providing information on technology, devices, aids, organizations, and programs for the handicapped. May be accessed by dialing 301/593-7033.

Higher Education and Adult Training for people with Handicaps (HEATH Resource Center)
National Clearinghouse on Postsecondary Education for Handicapped Individuals
One Dupont Circle
Washington, DC 20036-1193
(800) 544-3284

HEATH operates the National Clearinghouse of Postsecondary Education for Handicapped Individuals, an information exchange about educational support services, policies, procedures, adaptations, and opportunities at postsecondary schools, independent living centers, and other training facilities.

High Tech Learning Center
College of the Redwoods
Eureka, CA 95501
(707) 443-8411 x. 570

A research and resource center providing the disabled with evaluation services, information, and support services.

IBM National Support Center for Persons with Disabilities
4111 Northside Parkway
P.O. Box 2150
Atlanta, GA 30327
(800) IBM-2133

Resource for business, home, and school adaptations of computers and technology. Publishers of *Guide to Resources for Persons with Disabilities*.

International Association for Computing in Education (formerly AEDS)
1230 17th St. N.W.
Washington, DC 20036
(202) 223-0709

A professional organization dedicated to the advancement of technology in education. Publications include *IACE Journal of Computing in Education* and *IACE Newsletter*, both quarterly publications geared toward educators and professionals across a wide spectrum of uses.

International Council for Computers in Education (ICCE)
University of Oregon
1787 Agate St.
Eugene, OR 97403
(503) 686-4414

A professional organization of educators using computers in the classroom. Hosts a special interest group for special educators (SIGSPED), which publishes the quarterly SIG *Bulletin* and nine times a year *The Computing Teacher*.

International Society for Augmentative and Alternative Communication (ISAAC)
Michigan State University

Artificial Language Laboratory
405 Computer Center
East Lansing, MI 48824

An organization concerned with communications difficulties and ways of overcoming those difficulties. Publishers of *Communication Outlook*, a newsletter intended for people who are interested in the application of technology to the needs of those who experience neurological impairments.

Janus Book Publisher, Inc.
2501 Industrial Parkway West
Hayard, CA 94545

Excellent source for vocational topic materials. Also provide selected materials for special needs students in the application of basic skills.

Kurzweil Applied Intelligence
411 Waverly Oaks Rd.
Waltham, MA 02154-9990

Voice-recognition products: Kurzweil Voicesystem and Kurzweil Voiceterminal.

Kurzweil Computer Products
185 Albany St.
Cambridge, MA 02139
(617) 864-7000
(800) 343-0311

Manufacturers of adaptive technology. Manufacturer of the Kurzweil Personal Reader, an intelligent character reading machine that can read printed text aloud in a variety of synthesized voices.

The LD College Writers Project
University of Minnesota-General College
106 Nicholson Hall
216 Pillsbury Drive, S.E.
Minneapolis, MN 55455
(612) 625-8384

A resource to design, test, and disseminate writing curricula that serves the needs of learning-disabled persons using microcomputers.

LINC Resources, Inc.
3857 High St.
Columbus, OH 43214
(614) 263-2123

A professional marketing organization for

special educators. Publishes *Specialware Directory*, a resource guide for special educators, which describes courseware and software for special education. Includes extensive index and indication of whether products are specifically designed for or adapted to special education. LINC houses the Special Education Software Center Database and participates in the Center for Special Education Technology Information Exchange.

Living and Learning Resource Center (LLRC)
601 W. Maple
Lansing, MI 48906
(517) 371-5897

A resource and information center that provides diagnostic evaluations, training, support services, and referrals for technology-based solutions for most disabilities.

Make a Difference Network
Landon State Office Bldg., 10th Floor
900 S.W. Jackson
Topeka, KS 66612
(800) 332-6262

A consortium of the helping professions of the state of Kansas that provide an on-line information service for children and adults with disabilities, their families, and their service providers over a broad range of services and resources.

Maryland Computer Services, Inc.
2010 Rock Spring Rd.
Forest Hill, MD 21050
(301) 879-3366

Specializes in products for blind and visually impaired computer users.
Total Talk PC—talking computer based on Hewlett Packard's microcomputer.

Other products include: Audiodata keyboard, Thiel Braille embosser, optical character readers.

Massachusetts Special Technology Access Center
P.O. Box J
Bedford, MA 01730
(617) 275-2446

Provides training and information and makes referrals for most disability areas in applying technology-based solutions.

McKnight Publishing Company
P.O. Box 2854
Bloomington, IL 61701

Complete occupational and life-skills program—*Entering the World of Work*. Includes text, activity manual, film strips, and tapes.

Microcomputer Demonstration Laboratory/ Family Lending Center
University of South Dakota
School of Medicine
Vermillion, SD 57069
(605) 677-5311

An information-dissemination and resource center for the training of microcomputer applications applied to most disabilities.

Microcomputer Education for Employment of the Disabled (MEED)
711 Victoria Ave. East
Thunder Bay, ON P7C 5X9
Canada
(807) 623-6333

A March of Dimes-sponsored training program for hearing and physically impaired persons.

Microcomputer Software and Information for Teachers
Northwest Regional Educational Laboratory
300 S.W. 6th Ave.
Portland, OR 97204
(503) 248-6800

MicroSift, a federally funded clearinghouse for information on educational technology, publishes a quarterly report comprising product descriptions and reviews.

National Braille Press, Inc.
88 S. Stephen St.
Boston, MA 02115
(617) 266-6160

Information on sources for products for blind and visually impaired computer users. Books available in print, cassette, or braille versions.

The Second Beginner's Guide to Personal

Computers for the Blind and Visually Impaired. (Print copy—$12.95; Braille/cassette editions available.)

Add-ons: The Ultimate Guide to Peripherals for the Blind Computer User. (Print copy—$19.95; Braille/cassette copies—$16.96; $3 extra for UPS shipping; orders must be prepaid.)

National Down's Syndrome Congress
1800 W. Dempster St.
Park Ridge, IL 60068
(800) 232-6372 or (312) 823-7550

Professionals and parents of children with Down's Syndrome provide information on computer technology to help persons with Down's Syndrome.

National Easter Seal Society (NESS)
2023 W. Ogden Ave.
Chicago, IL 60612
(312) 243-8400

Local Easter Seal facilities offer a variety of services to handicapped children such as therapeutic programs in speech-language-hearing and recreational programs. Publishes a newsletter, *Computer-Disability News: The Computer Resource Quarterly for People with Disabilities.*

National Information Center for Handicapped Children and Youth
P.O. Box 1492
Washington, DC 20013
(703) 522-3332

A free information and referral center for the parents and educators of handicapped youth about concerns of younger disabled persons through secondary school.

National Institute for Rehabilitation Engineering
97 Decker Rd.
Butler, NJ 07405
(201) 838-2500

A nonprofit organization providing information and educational software to those who work with the physically handicapped or learning disabled.

National Leadership Coalition on AIDS
1150 17th St., N.W.

Suite 202
Washington, DC 20036
(202) 429-0930

Provides AIDS and HIV information, including adaptation information that may be necessary for appropriate health care.

National Library Service for the Blind and Physically Handicapped
1291 Taylor St., N.W.
Washington, DC 20542
(202) 287-5100

General background information is available through this center in the form of their packet *Computer Applications for Blind and Physically Handicapped Individuals* plus resource lists.

National Organization on Disability (NOD)
2100 Pennsylvania Ave., N.W.
Suite 234
Washington, DC 20037
(202) 293-5960 or (202) 293-5968 (TDD)

Nonprofit organization operates information clearinghouse providing specific information on and referrals to computer technology for the disabled.

National Special Education Association
Apple Computer's Office of Special Education
20525 Mariani Ave.
MS 36-M
Cupertino, CA 95014
(800) 732-3131 x. 275 and (408) 996-1010

Operates demonstration centers across the country and tries to match existing technology with disabilities.

National Special Needs Center
(See AT&T National Special Needs Center.)

National Technical Institute for the Deaf (NTID)
1 Lomb Memorial Dr.
P.O. Box 9887
Rochester, NY 14623
(716) 475-6400

A resource center for hearing impairments.

National Technology Center

(See American Foundation for the Blind Technology Center.)

New Readers Press
Department 90, Box 131
Syracuse, NY 13210

Opportunities for Learning, Inc.
20417 Nordhoff St., Dept. 6
Chatsworth, CA 91311

Selected materials for special students from texts such as *Math for Everyday Living* and *English for Everyday Living* to manipulatives to thinking, study, and motivational programs.

Prentke Romich Company
1022 Heyl Rd.
Wooster, OH 44691
(216) 262-1984

Source of communication systems, computer-access equipment, environmental control systems, and mobility control systems.

Project EASI
(See information under EDUCOM.)

Project LINK
Mainstream, Inc.
1030 15th St., N.W.
Suite 1010
Washington, DC 20005
(202) 898-0202
717 N. Harwood
Suite 890
Dallas, TX 75201
(214) 969-0118

Project LINK seeks to match persons who have various mental and/or physical handicaps with employers who are willing to employ those skills. Currently in operation in Washington, DC, and Dallas, Mainstream also publishes the *Project Link Guidebook: A Manual for Operating an Employment Services Program for Persons with Disabilities*.

Project MATCH
Long Island University
University Plaza
Brooklyn, NY 11201
(718) 834-6000 x. 3695

A computer database link to 300 +

employers actively recruiting qualified persons with disabilities within the NY, NJ, and CT areas. Provides a single point of contact for job information.

Project RETOOL
The Council for Exceptional Children
Teacher Education Division
1920 Association Drive
Reston, VA 22091
(703) 620-3660

Ongoing training in microcomputer use within special education classes for teachers and practitioners.

Quercus Division
Globe Book Company
Simon and Schuster School Group
4343 Equity Drive, Box 2649
Columbus, OH 43216

Comprehensive academic materials for special education. Especially good social studies materials and motivational reading books.

Rehabilitation Engineering Center (REC)
Tufts-New England Medical Center
750 Washington St.
Box 75K-R
Boston, MA 02111

Resource for development and implementation of augmentative communication through the use of commercially available technology.

Rehabilitation Technology Associates
West Virginia Research and Training Center
One Dunbar Plaza, Suite E
Dunbar, WV 25064-3098
(304) 766-7138

A professional group involved in rehabilitation and the use of technology in the performance of this task. Publishes *RTA On Line*, a newsletter.

RESNA-Association for the Advancement of Rehabilitation Technology
1101 Connecticut Ave., N.W.
Suite 700
Washington, DC 20036
(202) 587-1199

Research and design facilities for development of prosthetics and rehabilitation technology devices for the disabled.

Resources in Computer Education (RICE)
Northwest Regional Education Laboratory
101 Southwest Main St., Suite 500
Portland, OR 97204
(800) 547-6339

A fee-based source for microcomputer courseware to fit specific applications and a source for software evaluations.

Scholastic, Inc.
2931 E. McCarty St.
P.O. Box 7501
Jefferson City, MO 65102

Comprehensive materials for special needs students including the *Action Reading System*. This is an effective motivating reading program for remedial secondary students. Components include unit books, short-story anthology, play anthology, cassettes, and spirit masters for extended skill development. There are also numerous paperback libraries available.

The Sloane Report
P.O. Box 561689
Miami, FL 33256
(305) 251-2199

A bimonthly newsletter with developments in the computer industry, funding sources, reports on new products, and so on as they relate to special education.

Special Education Computer Technology On-line Resource Project SECTOR Project
Utah State University
Exceptional Child Center
UMC-68
Logan, UT 84322

An on-line database of resources in special education technology sponsored by the Office of Special Education and Utah State Office of Education. Resource to disseminate information on instructional software and IEP management software. Publications are offered at cost to educators nationwide.

Special Education Software Center
333 Ravenswood Ave.
Building B, Room S312

Menlo Park, CA 94025
(800) 223-2711 (voice)
(800) 435-7639 (BBS)

Funded by the U.S. Dept. of Education, the center is operated with assistance from LINC and CEC. The SRI assists developers of special education programs.

SpecialNet
National Association of State Directors of Special Education
2021 K St., N.W., Suite 315
Washington, DC 20006
(202) 296-1800

Electronic network for special educators providing information and communication for persons concerned with services and programs for handicapped students.

Special Times
Cambridge Development Laboratory, Dept. M
P.O. Box 605
Newton Lower Falls, MA 92162
(800) 637-0047

Publishers of a software catalogue describing software for use with learning-disabled students.

Steck-Vaughn Company
P.O. Box 26015
Austin, TX

Comprehensive materials for all academic areas. Adapted reading levels in social studies and science make their materials very useful as parallel coursework or as a supplement for regular program texts.

TASH (Technical Aids & Systems for the Handicapped, Inc.)
70 Gibson Drive
Unit 12
Markham, ON L3R 4C2
Canada
(416) 475-2212

This organization is affiliated with the Canadian government and the Canadian Rehabilitation Council for the Disabled. Hardware available through this group includes ability switches, environmental controls, mobility and living aids. Computer aids include: keylocks, keyguards, keyboards, disk guides.

TechCentral
1126 16th St., N.W.
Washington, DC 20036
(202) 466-4780

An electronic network operated by the Association for Educational Communications and Technology and oriented toward the use of technology in all facets of education.

Technical Education Research Centers, Inc. (TERC)
1696 Massachusetts Ave.
Cambridge, MA 02138
(617) 547-3890

Provides information about and offers workshops on computer use in special education.

Technology and Media
The Council for Exceptional Children
1920 Association Drive
Reston, VA 22091
(703) 620-3660

Organization for special educators concerned with uses of technology and media with disabled users. Publishes *The Journal of Special Education Technology* and conducts teacher conferences, workshops, and training programs.

Technology for Language and Learning
P.O. Box 327
East Rockaway, NY 11518-0327

Nonprofit organization dedicated to advancing the use of technology and computers with children and adults. Maintains a special education public domain software collection.

Telecommunications Exchange for the Deaf (TEDI)
P.O. Box 508
Great Falls, VA 22066
(703) 759-2993 or (703) 759-2112 (TDD)

A telephone-relay service for the deaf, using computers to link hearing and nonhearing individuals in telephone communications.

Telesensory Office of Special Education and Rehabilitation

455 No. Bernardo Ave.
Mountain View, CA 94043
(415) 960-0920

Resource for information about specialized products for visually impaired users within the educational and business environment.

Trace Research and Development Center (for Communication, Control, and Computer Access for Handicapped Individuals)
University of Wisconsin—Madison
S151 Waisman Center
1500 Highland Ave.
Madison, WI 53705
(608) 262-6966

Provides information on development of nonvocal communication and alternative computer access for severely handicapped individuals.

UCLA Intervention Program for Handicapped Children
1000 Veteran Ave.
Room 23-10
Los Angeles, CA 90024
(213) 825-4821

An information and referral service is provided through this agency for technology-based services to support most disability areas.

Vocational Education Special Needs Exchange
Ohio State University
1960 Kenny Rd.
Columbus, OH 43210-1090
(614) 486-3655

A university connected resource and database to provide information on vocationally related solutions to problems of the disabled through the use of technology.

Western Center for Microcomputers in Special Education
1259 El Camino Real
Suite 275
Menlo Park, CA 94025
(415) 326-6997

Publisher of the quarterly *The Catalyst*, which addresses special education applications of technology.

Young Adult Institute (YAI)
460 W. 34th St.
New York, NY 10001
(212) 563-7474
A nonprofit organization providing

counseling, training, and educational and
residential support services to mentally
retarded or developmentally disabled
children.

Source: Kallam, Michael. (1989). *Information Sources for Hardware and Software for Technology and Computer Users with Special Needs.* Hays, KS: Fort Hays State University.

PUBLISHERS

Currently Available Social Skills Curricula

American Guidance Service
Publishers' Building
Circle Pines, MN 55014

Bennett Publishing Co.
Peoria, IL 61615

Developmental Learning Materials
One DLM Park
P.O. Box 4000
Allen, TX 75002

Ebsco Curriculum Materials
Box 11542
Birmingham, AL 35202

Hubbard
P.O. Box 104
Northbrook, IL 60062

Human Relations Media
175 Tompkins Ave.
Pleasantville, NY 10570

Interpretive Education
Communications Park
Box 3000
Mt. Kisco, NY 10549

Janus Book Publishers
Department E24
2501 Industrial Pky.
Hayward, CA 94545

Media Materials, Inc.
2936 Remington Ave.
Baltimore, MD 21211

Research Press
Box 31773
Champaign, IL 61821

The Ungame Co.
P.O. Box 6382
Anaheim, CA 92806

Commercial Materials (Selected List)

Academic Therapy Publishers
Box 899
1539 4th St.
San Rafael, CA 94901

American Guidance Service
Publishers' Building
Circle Pines, MN 55014

Benefic Press
10300 West Roosevelt Rd.
Westchester, IL 60153

Charles E. Merrill Publishing Co.
1300 Alum Creek Dr.
Columbus, OH 43216

Conover Company Ltd.
Box 155
Omro, WI 54963

Developmental Learning Materials
7440 Natchez Ave.
Niles, IL 60648

Edmark Associates
13249 Northrup Way
Bellevue, WA 98005

Educational Activities
P.O. Box 392
Freeport, NY 11520

Fearon Publishers
6 Davis Dr.
Belmont, CA 94022

Follett Publishing Co.
1010 West Washington Blvd.
Chicago, IL 60607

Frank E. Richards Publishing Co.
324 First St.
Liverpool, NY 13088

Guidance Associates
757 3rd Ave.
New York, NY 10017

The Instructor Publications
P.O. Box 6099
Duluth, MN 55806

Matex Associates
111 Barron Ave.
Johnstown, PA 15906

McKnight and McKnight
Box 854
Bloomington, IL 61701

New Readers Press
Laubach Literacy
Box 121
Syracuse, NY 13210

Scholastic Book Services
904 Sylvan Ave.
Englewood Cliffs, NJ 07632

Steck-Vaughn
Box 2028
Vaughn Building
Austin, TX 78767

Teaching Resources Corp.
100 Boylston St.
Boston, MA 02116

Xerox Corp.
600 Madison Ave.
New York, NY 10022

ORGANIZATIONS

American Personnel and Guidance
Association
1607 New Hampshire Ave., N.W.
Washington, DC 20009

American Vocational Association
2020 N. 14th
Arlington, VA 22201

Association for Children with Learning
Disabilities
5225 Grace St.
Pittsburgh, PA 15236

Bureau of Education for the Handicapped
U.S. Department of Education
400 Maryland Ave., S.W.
Washington, DC 20202

Bureau of Occupational and Adult Education
(Disadvantaged and Handicapped Specialists)
7th and D St., S.W.
Washington, DC 20202

The Clearinghouse on the Handicapped
Office for Handicapped Individuals
Hubert H. Humphrey Bldg., Room 338D
Washington, DC 20201

Council for Exceptional Children
1920 Association Drive
Reston, VA 22091

Division for Career Development
Council for Exceptional Children
1920 Association Drive
Reston, VA 22091

Federation Employment and Guidance
Service
215 Park Ave. South
New York, NY 10003

ICD Rehabilitation and Research Center
(Formerly Institute for the Crippled and
Disabled)
340 East 24th St.
New York, NY 10010

Midwest Curriculum Coordination Center
State Department of Vocational and
Technical Education
1515 West Sixth Ave.
Stillwater, OK 74074

National Association for Retarded Citizens
2709 Ave. East
P.O. Box 6109
Arlington, TX 76011

National Association of Vocational Education
Special Needs Personnel
c/o American Vocational Association
2020 N. 14th St.
Arlington, VA 22201

National Center for Research in Vocational
Education
Ohio State University

1960 Kenny Rd.
Columbus, OH 43210

National Information Center for the
Handicapped
Closer Look
P.O. Box 1492
Washington, DC 20013

National Network for Curriculum
Coordination in Vocational and Technical
Education
East Central Curriculum Management
Center
100 North First St.
Springfield, IL 62777

Midwest Curriculum and Instructional
Materials Center
1515 West 6th Ave.
Stillwater, OK 74074

Northeast Curriculum Center
New Jersey Department of Education
Bureau of Occupational and Career Research
Development
Division of Vocational Education
225 West State St.
Trenton, NJ 08625

Northwestern Curriculum Coordination
Center
Airdustrial Park, Bldg. 17
Olympia, WA 98504

Southeast Curriculum Coordination Center
Mississippi State University
College of Education
Box 5365
Starkville, MS 39762

Western Curriculum Coordination Center
University of Hawaii
College of Education
Wist Hall 216
1776 University Ave.
Honolulu, Hawaii 96822

President's Commission on Employment of
the Handicapped

1111 Twentieth St., N.W.
Washington, DC 20210

Rehabilitation International USA
17 East 45th St.
New York, NY 10017

Rehabilitation Services Administration
330 C St., S.W.
Washington, DC 20201

TOLL-FREE SPECIAL NEEDS RESOURCES

Center for Special Education Technology, Technology Information Exchange	800-345-8324
ERIC Clearinghouse on Adult, Career, and Vocational Education	800-848-4815
Higher Education and the Handicapped (HEATH) Resource Center	800-54-HEATH
Job Accommodation Network	800-526-7234
National Committee for Citizens in Education	800-NETWORK
National Health Information Clearinghouse	800-336-4797
National Information Center for Media	800-421-8711
National Special Needs Center	800-233-1222
	(TDD) 800-833-3232
Orton Dyslexia Society	800-222-3123
Resource Center for the Handicapped	800-22-SHARE
Special Education Software Center	800-327-5892
American Association on Mental Deficiency	800-424-3688
National Organization of Disability	800-248-2253
National Rehabilitation Information Center	800-34-NARIC

REGIONAL RESOURCE CENTERS

States served:

Northwest Regional Resource Center
  University of Oregon
  Clinical Service Building, Third Fl.
  1590 Willamette St.
  Eugene, OR 97401

Alaska, Hawaii, Samoa, Guam, Trust Territory, Washington, Idaho, Oregon, Montana, Wyoming

California Regional Resource Center
  600 South Commonwealth Ave.
  Suite 1304
  University of Southern California
  Los Angeles, CA 90005

California

Southwest Regional Resource Center
  University of Utah
  2363 Foothill Dr., Suite G
  Salt Lake City, UT 84109

Nevada, Utah, Colorado, Arizona, New Mexico, B.I.A., Schools

Midwest Regional Resource Center Drake University 1332-26th St. Des Moines, IA 50311	North Dakota, Oklahoma, South Dakota, Iowa, Nebraska, Kansas, Missouri, Arkansas
Texas Regional Resource Center Texas Education Agency 201 East 11th St. Austin, TX 78701	Texas
Mid-East Regional Resource Center George Washington University 1901 Pennsylvania Ave., N.W. Suite 505 Washington, DC 20006	Maryland, Delaware, West Virginia, North Carolina
Mid-South Resource Center University of Kentucky Research Found. Porter Building, Room 131 Lexington, KY 40506	Kentucky, Tennessee, Virginia
District of Columbia Regional Resource Center Howard University 2935 Upton St., N.W. Washington, DC 20008	District of Columbia
Southwest Regional Resource Center Auburn University at Montgomery Montgomery, AL 36117	Louisiana, Mississippi, Alabama, Georgia, South Carolina, Florida, Puerto Rico, Virgin Islands
Pennsylvania Regional Resource Center Pennsylvania State Department of Education 443 South Gulph Rd. King of Prussia, PA 19406	Pennsylvania
Great Lakes Regional Resource Center Michigan State Department of Education P.O. Box 30008 Lansing, MI 48902	Minnesota, Wisconsin, Michigan, Indiana
Illinois Regional Resource Center Northern Illinois University DeKalb, IL 60115	Illinois
Ohio Regional Resource Center Ohio State Department of Education 933 High St. Worthington, OH 43085	Ohio
Northeast Regional Resource Center New Jersey State Department of Education 168 Bank St. Hightstown, NJ 08520	Maine, Vermont, New Hampshire, Massachusetts, Rhode Island, Connecticut, New Jersey

New York State Regional Resource Center   New York
New York State Education Department
55 Elk St.
Albany, NY 12234

New York City Regional Resource Center   New York City only
City University of New York
33 West 42nd Street
New York, NY 10036

DEPARTMENT OF HEALTH AND HUMAN SERVICES REGIONAL OFFICES FOR CIVIL RIGHTS

Region I

(Connecticut, Maine, Massachusetts, New Hampshire, Rhode Island, Vermont)
140 Federal St., 14th Floor
Boston, MA 02110
(617) 223-6397

Region II

(New Jersey, New York, Puerto Rico, Virgin Islands)
26 Federal Plaza
New York, NY 10007
(212) 264-4633

Region III

(Delaware, District of Columbia, Maryland, Pennsylvania, Virginia, West Virginia)
Gateway Building
3535 Market St.
P.O. Box 13716
Philadelphia, PA 19101
(215) 596-6772

Region IV

(Alabama, Florida, Georgia, Kentucky, Mississippi, North Carolina, South Carolina, Tennessee)
101 Marietta St.
10th Floor
Atlanta, GA 30303
(404) 221-5934

Region V

(Illinois, Indiana, Minnesota, Michigan, Ohio, Wisconsin)
300 South Wacker Drive
Chicago, IL 60606
(312) 353-2521

Region VI

(Arkansas, Louisiana, New Mexico, Oklahoma, Texas)
1200 Main Tower Bldg.
Dallas, TX 75202
(214) 655-3951

Region VII

(Iowa, Kansas, Missouri, Nebraska)
Twelve Grand Bldg.
1150 Grand Ave.
Kansas City, MO 64106
(816) 374-2474

Region VIII

(Colorado, Montana, North Dakota, South Dakota, Utah, Wyoming)
Federal Bldg.
1961 Stout St.
Denver, CO 80294
(303) 837-2025

Region IX

(Arizona, California, Hawaii, Nevada)
100 Van Ness Ave., 14th Floor
San Francisco, CA 94102
(415) 556-8586

Region X

(Alaska, Idaho, Oregon, Washington)
Arcade Plaza Bldg. MS 508
1321 Second Ave.
Seattle, WA 98101
(206) 442-0473

CHAPTER 10

Not Conclusion, but Commencement: Transition to Adulthood

The instructional applications that have been presented in this book are but a few that can be used to prepare students for the mainstream. Appropriate behavior, organization, and study skills are all necessary for adequate academic functioning whether in regular classes or in special classes. Helping students learn how to learn is paying benefits. More and more, students with handicaps are experiencing success in higher education. Colleges and universities are developing support programs so that the potential of these students is given greater promise.

Emphasis on regular class adjustment and related requirements cannot replace the commitment of special education to the development of life-skill needs of students. Decisions concerning the courses students should take require examination of the student's ability to carry on adult life functions. These decisions must be made early in a student's high school program. For some students, parallel courses will have to be substituted for regular courses. Parallel courses concentrate more on needed information than on what may be nice to know. Material used in these courses is selected for the level of functioning that suits the capabilities of the student.

For most of these students, educational intervention efforts should be shifted from a remedial to a more preventive approach by focusing on the demands inherent in postschool environments (Palloway et al., 1988). They claim that to be truly preventative, curricula should reflect considerations down from the goal of successful adjustment rather than up from the elementary curriculum focused on remediating basic skills. To emphasize objectives that focus on the kinds of information that are needed to function adequately as an adult, we have included several curricular categories from Iowa's mental disabilities framework. This framework brings together many of the ideas presented in this book and embodies our philosophical approach: learners with mild handicaps especially need to receive material high in functional use.

This framework was taken from *A Mental Disabilities Curriculum Framework*, State of Iowa Department of Public Instruction, Special Education Division, 1984. The document states that a framework is an outline of general skills, competencies and content expected to be taught . . . , as well as the sequence, scope, and continuity of skills to be taught.

Intermediate (Grades 4–6) **Junior High (Grades 7–9)** **Secondary (Grades 10–12+)**

D. Citizenship/Economics

D. Citizenship/Economics Government, History

1. Names important positions within the community government
2. States reasons for various kinds of laws
3. States consequences of lawbreaking
4. States basic functions of federal, state, and local governments and effect on economy
5. Respects personal and public property
6. States importance of not littering or polluting the environment and conserving natural resources
7. Cites important current events in the community
8. Cites national holidays and their significance
9. States location of national and state capitals and cities and examples of business conducted there
10. Explains why and how we vote
11. States contribution of community workers in production and service occupations
12. Cites examples of different cultures, attitudes, and values within the American society
13. States responsibilities of employers and employees
14. Explains reasons for paying taxes
15. Describes function of community leaders and

1. Describes the purpose of the Constitution
2. Describes basic functions of the three branches of the federal and state governments
3. Describes responsibilities for community citizenship
4. Describes purposes of different kinds of taxes and laws
5. Names citizen and taxpayer responsibilities
6. Secures aid of police and other public safety agencies
7. Exhibits understanding of rights of personal ownership
8. Identifies and secures services needed from public service agencies such as: vocational rehabilitation, welfare, public health, and county mental health agencies
9. Names responsibilities and procedures for elections and voting
10. Describes own rights in the event of difficulty with legal authorities
11. Simulates obtaining services of a lawyer, both privately and through Legal Aid
12. Expresses advantages of participating as a community member
13. Expresses consequences of breaking the law and one's

Intermediate (Grades 4-6)	Junior High (Grades 7–9)	Secondary (Grades 10–12+)
	groups	rights in dealing with law enforcement agencies
	16. States purposes of financial institutions	
	17. States major historical persons and events	14. Names major components of services of local governments
		15. Names services offered through Social Security, Job Service of Iowa, etc.
		16. Describes the selective service system and armed forces
		17. Lists jobs available in governmental agencies for which one is qualified
		18. Describes major historical places, events, and persons
		19. Compares peoples and cultures of other countries to the U.S.
		20. Describes process of supply and demand on workers, business, industry, agriculture, etc.
		21. States effects of technology on work, business, industry, and own lifestyle

E. Communication

1. Responds appropriately to directions
2. Repeats a short verbal message
3. Tells others about own experiences
4. Makes introductions
5. Asks questions and gives responses for directions and help
6. Gives directions

E. Communication

1. Listens courteously
2. Carries out detailed spoken instructions
3. Retells a story
4. Makes telephone calls with or without an operator
5. Describes simple procedures for a meeting
6. Attends to oral

E. Communication

1. Listens courteously
2. Speaks pleasantly and courteously
3. Modulates voice to appropriate levels for the situation
4. Uses appropriate vocational vocabulary
5. Participates in group discussion
6. Carries on acceptable

(continued)

Intermediate (Grades 4–6)	**Junior High (Grades 7–9)**	**Secondary (Grades 10–12+)**
7. Uses telephone; takes and gives phone messages	presentation	social conversation
8. Initiates conversation; carries on a conversation	7. Judges a speech or oral report for facts or opinions	7. Describes a procedure and gives directions
9. Speaks in turn	8. Demonstrates proper telephone etiquette	8. Follows verbal directions.
10. Participates in group discussions appropriately	9. Speaks orally in front of group	9. Describes an event/ story/occupation
11. Identifies initial, final, and medial sounds of spoken words	10. Speaks with complex sentences	10. Asks for directions/ information
12. Listens to poems, stories, and conversations—gives main ideas	11. Gives three-part directions	11. Demonstrates proper use of telephone and telephone etiquette
13. Follows increasingly complex directions	12. Uses acceptable grammar in speaking	12. Tells about personal experiences
14. Identifies absurdities and draws conclusions	13. Uses communication skills in seeking information about jobs	13. Describes different emotions of a speaker
15. Expresses thoughts and shares experiences with others		14. Relates oral communication skills to career choices
16. Uses question form "why?"		15. Uses communication skills in job interviews
17. Uses appropriate voice volume for specific occasions		
18. Uses grammatical structures in speech (articles-conjunctions)		
19. Reports an emergency		
20. Retells a major part of a story		
21. Reads written words aloud		
22. Identifies jobs that require oral communication skills		
	F. Family Living	**F. Family Living**
	1. Describes family member roles and responsibilities	1. Describes the importance of self-reliance and not being overly dependent on others
	2. Shares in family	

Intermediate (Grades 4–6)	Junior High (Grades 7–9)	Secondary (Grades 10–12+)
	responsibilities 3. Protects small children 4. Takes simple phone messages for family members 5. Demonstrates understanding of own position and contribution in the family and community 6. Describes own values in comparing good and poor family relationships 7. Describes changes that occur as family members grow older, work, attend school, etc.	2. Describes basic responsibilities of married individuals toward their spouses 3. Describes the adjustment process in marriage 4. Names methods to plan or control family size 5. Describes good parenting practices 6. Demonstrates child care 7. Recognizes and names childhood illnesses. 8. Describes children's psychological needs for love, acceptance, and support 9. Names behaviors that constitute child abuse and spouse abuse 10. Describes conditions that affect family life, e.g., drug abuse, wages, cooperation, alcoholism 11. Considers marriage and family in choosing career goals 12. Describes community services that relate to marriage and family
	H. Home Management 1. Operates home appliances safely 2. Uses basic hand tools at home/school 3. Cleans rooms and performs other home maintenance tasks: dusts, vacuums, washes, mops, disinfects, etc.	**H. Home Management** 1. Demonstrates appropriate cleaning procedures 2. Uses home and laundromat laundry facilities 3. Maintains clean and orderly working/living area 4. Operates most home appliances

(continued)

Intermediate (Grades 4–6)	Junior High (Grades 7–9)	Secondary (Grades 10–12+)
	4. Follows recipes and prepares simple meals for self and others	5. Prepares and serves simple meals for others
	5. States advantages of quantity/quality buying	6. Shops for groceries
	6. Describes some costs in maintaining a home	7. Plans balanced family meals
	7. Conserves natural resources, e.g., heat, electricity, etc.	8. Stores food to prevent spoilage
	8. States precautions to protect home from weather	9. Explains need to purchase different food types
	9. Mends clothing	10. Describes responsibilities as a good neighbor
	10. Launders, irons, and stores clothing	11. Describes differences between necessary and luxury purchases for the home
	11. Maintains home exterior, interior, and yard	12. Selects appropriate and affordable housing
	12. Stores food properly	13. States how to secure housing
	13. Relates common housekeeping activities to various occupations	14. Explains the purpose and content of leases, rental agreements, mortgages, credit agreements, and household insurance
		15. Describes tenant and landlord responsibilities
		16. Describes advantages of home ownership and renting
		17. Verbalizes prerequisites for home ownership
		18. Describes or simulates timely payment of rent, utility bills, time payments, etc.
		19. Makes minor repairs to building structure and plumbing, electrical, and heating systems
		20. Makes minor repairs and services family vehicle
		21. Maintains home

Intermediate (Grades 4–6)	**Junior High (Grades 7–9)**	**Secondary (Grades 10–12 +)**
		interior, exterior, and yard
		22. Verbalizes methods for economical use of energy
		23. Keeps basic financial records
		24. Considers own interest and abilities in career goals related to home management
	L. Money	**L. Money**
	1. Makes savings account deposits and with-drawals	1. Names and distin-guishes coins and bills accurately
	2. Makes purchases by dozen, carton, case, bulk, per foot, etc.	2. Makes computations with money
	3. Explains purpose of a budget	3. Makes change accurately for up to $100
	4. Makes change for up to $50	4. Uses money or check to make purchases
	5. States services available at banks and other financial agencies	5. Makes bank deposits and withdrawals
	6. Computes sales tax	6. Writes checks accu-rately
	7. Budgets small earnings	7. Maintains balanced checkbook
	8. Correctly uses coin-operated equipment	8. Describes hidden costs such as installation fees, delivery charges
	9. Compares prices when shopping	9. Describes the meaning of interest, principle, installments, service charges, and late penalties
	10. States the meaning of a trade-in	10. Explains the meanings of discounts, sales, special offers, and special purchases
	11. Refuses to purchase unwanted merchandise	11. Designs a budget and sets spending priorities
	12. Writes number words	12. Compares prices when shopping
	13. States credit buying procedures and precautions	
	14. Describes differences between necessary purchases and luxuries	
	15. Compares desired life-	

(continued)

Intermediate (Grades 4–6)	Junior High (Grades 7–9)	Secondary (Grades 10–12+)
	style to various skills, occupations, and wages	13. Computes own wages
	16. Estimates a family budget	14. Fills out forms to report income tax
	17. Figures costs involved in ownership of articles	15. Describes procedures for use of credit
	18. States number of ways money is earned or lost, e.g., interest, investments, jobs, gambling	16. Describes consequences of credit abuse
	19. States responsibilities of workers and family members who handle money	17. Computes interest in finance charges
		18. Uses travelers checks and money orders
		19. Computes cost of transportation by auto, bus, and other means
		20. Evaluates the content of advertising
		21. Describes jobs involving handling of money
		22. Relates job wages and benefits to desired life-style and career goals
		23. Demonstrates shopping through catalogs

N. Personal Living Skills (Junior High)

1. Demonstrates appropriate situational manners
2. Makes introductions
3. Maintains clean appearance and grooming
4. Behaves honestly
5. States own clothing sizes
6. Selects appropriate apparel for situation
7. Describes feelings, interests, abilities, emotions, etc.
8. Describes differences between needs and wants
9. Demonstrates feelings of self-worth

N. Personal Living Skills (Secondary)

1. Behaves honestly
2. Demonstrates good grooming and hygiene skills
3. Practices everyday courtesies
4. Selects, purchases, and maintains own clothes and possessions
5. Cares for personal possessions
6. Names interests and abilities
7. Names personal needs and wants
8. Maintains neat work area
9. Names personal strengths and weak-

Intermediate (Grades 4–6)   **Junior High (Grades 7–9)**   **Secondary (Grades 10–12 +)**

10. Organizes own tasks for completion
11. Interacts with variety of peer groups for work, recreation, and school activities
12. Expresses personal goals
13. Makes personal decisions and states some consequences
14. Describes own characteristics, skills, and values needed for meeting career and vocational goals
15. Accepts traditional and nontraditional roles for own sex

nesses related to school and future jobs
10. Lists realistic personal goals and ways to reach goals
11. Listens to and profits from criticism from adults and peers
12. Evaluates oneself
13. Accepts praise from adults and peers
14. Describes own personal values
15. Makes positive, self-confident statements about oneself
16. Describes own emotions and those of others
17. Protects property of others
18. Tolerates behavior by others
19. Takes responsibility for tasks
20. Follows through on personal commitments
21. Lists important effects of maintaining a positive attitude
22. Looks for alternatives in problem solving
23. Anticipates consequences
24. Recognizes and names satisfactory and unsatisfactory task behaviors
25. Demonstrates systematic steps in decision making and problem solving
26. Selects and names an advocate or helper to assist in dealing with complicated business and legal matters

(continued)

Intermediate (Grades 4–6)	Junior High (Grades 7–9)	Secondary (Grades 10–12+)
		27. Acts assertively when needed
		28. Describes benefits of seeking counseling (if needed)
		29. Interacts with a variety of people

Intermediate (Grades 4–6)	Junior High (Grades 7–9)	Secondary (Grades 10–12+)
	P. Reading	**P. Reading**
	1. Uses reference materials (dictionary, atlas, encyclopedia, etc.)	1. Uses word-attack skills or cues to decode unknown words
	2. Reads to get information and meet needs	2. Reads and demonstrates understanding of survival words
	3. Locates information in newspaper	3. Reads and demonstrates understanding of traffic signs and directions
	4. Verbalizes interest in reading for pleasure and reads books for personal interest	4. Locates words in dictionary and finds word meanings
	5. Uses word-attack skills to decode words	5. Locates names, addresses, and numbers in telephone directories
	6. Comprehends reading materials	6. Locates information in newspapers, magazines, brochures, etc.
	7. Finds items in alphabetized list such as telephone book and dictionary	7. Reads simple food-preparation instructions
	8. Reads for safety and direction	8. Reads and follows simple assembly instructions
	9. Reads vocational sight words	9. Reads essential words on over-the-counter medications/products
	10. Reads menus	10. Uses tables of contents and indexes of books to find information
	11. Reads words on essential vocabulary lists	11. Uses library effectively for informational and leisure reading
	12. Follows written directions	12. Reads and demonstrates understanding of information
	13. Has developed functional ways to cope with reading problems	
	14. Reads common application forms	
	15. Reads about a variety	

Intermediate (Grades 4–6)

R. Science

1. Describes causes and effects of climate, weather conditions, and seasons
2. Describes types and needs of domestic and wild animals
3. Names types and uses of plants and minerals
4. Recognizes and names poisonous substances and plants and can state proper conduct concerning them
5. Describes general characteristics of the earth: natural resources, oceans, landforms, seasonal cycles
6. States reasons for conservation of natural resources and energy resources
7. Describes parts of the universe: planet, moon, sun, stars
8. Describes basic forces in the universe: fire, electricity, gravity, wind, magnetism,

Junior High (Grades 7–9)

of occupations
16. Identifies own interests in reading material
17. Uses library
18. Operates computer programs

R. Science

1. Describes effects of climate and weather conditions on life-styles, cultures, economics, jobs, etc.
2. Compares and classifies living and nonliving things by type, function, role, etc.
3. States several positive and negative aspects of environmental issues such as strip-mining, hunting, dams, and urbanization
4. Demonstrates safe use of common chemicals; states precautions
5. Describes commonly known science objects and events in astronomy, biology, physics, geology, geography, and electronics
6. Describes sources of energy and reasons for conservation of natural resources
7. Identifies and uses simple scientific

Secondary (Grades 10–12+)

pertaining to bills and statements
13. Reads essential information on employment insurance, social security, and human-service forms
14. Names communication industries and resources in regional and local community
15. Reads for leisure

R. Science

1. Describes cause and effect relationships in the environment
2. Describes regular patterns in science and effects of changes
3. Distinguishes fact from opinion in conversations, advertisements, and media
4. States main idea from reading about, listening to, or observing science-related information
5. Uses common metric measures
6. Distinguishes between science, astrology, occult, and mysteries, e.g., UFO, ESP
7. Describes influences of heredity and environment on the growth of living things
8. Describes human reproduction and birth-control options
9. Obtains information from graphs and tables
10. States variety of

(continued)

Intermediate (Grades 4–6)

sound, light, heat
9. Describes aspects of space travel
10. States some cause and effects of change in technology in science, medicine, industry, education, world of work, etc.
11. Operates computer programs
12. States various forms of pollution and ways to improve ecology
13. Describes various types of tools and machines used in science occupations

Junior High (Grades 7–9)

equipment such as the thermometer, scales, weights, measures, telescope
8. Uses concepts of volume, area, and weight in everyday applications
9. Predicts consequences and changes from actions and events
10. States some effects of scientific discoveries on jobs, life-styles, etc.
11. Operates computer programs
12. Uses problem-solving methods in personal decision making

Secondary (Grades 10–12+)

occupations in science and related fields
11. Operates variety of computer programs
12. Explains the purpose of governmental agencies for environmental quality, conservation, consumer protection, research, etc.
13. Describes speed-time-distance relationships
14. Describes major characteristics of geography in Iowa and U.S.

S. Social Skills

1. Demonstrates appropriate behavior in presence of members of the opposite sex
2. Demonstrates tolerance of behavior of classmates
3. Participates and works with others in group activities without disruption
4. Plays games by the rules
5. Behaves appropriately in school environment
6. Resolves conflict in nonaggressive ways
7. Makes and accepts apologies
8. Accepts comments made in jest
9. Describes impact of own behavior on others

S. Social Skills

1. Distinguishes between appropriate and inappropriate behaviors in different social situations
2. Demonstrates acceptable behaviors in boy-girl relationships
3. Discusses importance of responsible relationships with members of the opposite sex
4. Expresses affection in socially condoned ways
5. Expresses anger in socially condoned ways
6. Expresses understanding of purposes of committee or group work
7. Participates in social events

Intermediate (Grades 4–6)	Junior High (Grades 7–9)	Secondary (Grades 10–12+)
	10. Describes careers and occupations that require good social skills	8. Grooms and dresses appropriately for different social situations
		9. Demonstrates proper manners for social situations
		10. Demonstrates proper manners for restaurants, in other people's homes, and in school
		11. Describes characteristics of behavior that gain acceptance
		12. Describes ways to make and keep friends
		13. Accepts supervision
		14. Describes social skills used in finding and keeping a job
		15. Exhibits successful job-interview skills
		16. Exhibits appropriate social skills in resolving job-related and family-related problems

Curricular foci should include maximum participation in regular high school programs but must give attention to transitional needs of students moving into postsecondary settings (Palloway, Patton et al., 1989). There must be a commitment to both current and future needs of students. To insure that this occurs, there are several instructional guidelines that teachers should keep in mind:

1. Make all instruction relevant. Use content that is meaningful. Help students to understand why the information or skill is needed.

2. Do not waste students' time teaching something "new" just to be teaching or because the topic comes up next in the teacher's manual for the text. Pretest students so that what is taught is needed by the student. Match evaluation information with instruction. Spend as much time as is needed to "plan" instruction. Be appropriately prepared.

3. Teach application of strategies while teaching reading, writing, and so on and by using the context and concepts from students' classes. Students who have assignments to complete for a regular class will resent time taken to develop study skills that do not apply to work that must be done.

4. Help students evaluate their work. Point out change and progress. Encourage

students to predict degree of success. Help them recognize the adult standard for completed tasks.

5. Apply behavior expectations of a worksite to the classroom. Use job placement as an incentive for improving attendance, behavior, and achievement.

6. In all subject areas, relate competencies to daily living and the world of work.

7. In all instructional situations, leave students with a sense of accomplishment and success.

As students move into the high school years, a shift in emphasis toward an adult outcomes model must be considered. We cannot assume that the effective transition to postsecondary situations will be satisfactory. The changes taking place in special education are an attempt to address the failures of the past. We must continue these efforts.

Some students will need a more functional emphasis in their programs. Special educators cannot sacrifice the development of daily living competencies for such skills as theme writing and other higher level skills. Instructional time management must consider the final outcomes.

Special educators would like to see dropout rates decrease, and they would like to see employment rates increase for students who have graduated. Such statistics would indicate that special education is addressing the comprehensive needs of students. Meeting the needs of students is a complex process. Whatever the emphasis, whether regular classes or parallel courses, we must not lose sight of what it will take for each student to become a successful adult. Special educators must be ready for change and be willing to work for changes that improve outcomes for students. Success has to be defined by how well students function as adults and as independent individuals. This text is designed to assist you in meeting these goals.

REFERENCE LIST

Palloway, E. A., Patton, J. R., Epstein, M. H., and Smith, T. E. H. (1989). Comprehensive curriculum for students with mild handicaps. *Focus on Exceptional Children*, *21*(8) 1–12.

Palloway, E. A., Smith, J. D., and Patton, J. R. (1988). Learning disabilities: An adult developmental perspective, *Learning Disabilities Quarterly*, *11*, 265–272.

Index